Meanings of
War and Peace

D0932937

NUMBER FIVE
Presidential Rhetoric Series
Martin J. Medhurst, General Editor

MEANINGS OF

War
&
Peace

Francis A. Beer

TEXAS A&M UNIVERSITY PRESS • COLLEGE STATION

The paper used in this book
meets the minimum requirements
of the American National Standard for Permanence
of Paper for Printed Library Materials, z39.48-1984.
Binding materials have been chosen for durability.

Library of Congress Cataloging-in-Publication Data

Beer, Francis A.
    Meanings of war and peace / Francis A. Beer.—1st ed.
      p. cm.—(Presidential rhetoric series ; no. 5)
    Includes bibliographical references and index.
    ISBN 1-58544-123-6 (cloth : alk. paper) —
    ISBN 1-58544-124-4 (pbk. ; alk. paper)
    1. War. 2. Discourse analysis. 3. Language and
languages—Political aspects. 4. World politics—1989–
I. Title. II. Series.
JZ6385.B44 2001
327.1'6'01—dc21   00-012207

To

. . . JEREMY

MARIE

OMAR

DIANA

MURIEL

GENE

ANNE

WILLIAM . . .

CONTENTS

TABLES

PREFACE

"What does it mean?" is one of the most perplexing questions that one can ask about war and peace. What was the meaning of World Wars I and II? What was the meaning of the peace agreements at Versailles and Munich, Yalta and Potsdam? What is the meaning today of the terrorist attacks, the Middle East peace process, the Dayton accords, Indian nuclear testing, *Saving Private Ryan*?

Meanings of War and Peace offers an approach to answering this question. The meaning of war and peace includes three elements. The first is the irreducible facticity of the phenomena themselves, the physical, material objectivity of agents, structures, events, processes. The second includes the ideas, the thoughts, and the feelings of the actors and observers. And the third involves the words that they use to discuss them. Within this frame, the book focuses specifically on the role of language in reflecting and constructing meaning. It analyzes examples of how semantics, rhetorics, and relations with audiences have contributed to the meaning of war and peace, using as examples the Cold War, the Gulf War, and the Somalian intervention.

The book is organized into several major parts. The introduction lays out the motivation and the major themes. It discusses the importance and complexity of the war-peace problem, the centrality of meaning, and the relevance of language. The next part, on semantics, explores the meanings of central terms and concepts in the study of war and peace: war, reason, and validity. This segment develops the idea that meaning varies continuously as a function of multiple contexts, including particularly textual ones. Word strings produce meanings as algebraic strings produce mathematical products. The section on rhetorics suggests how rhetorical structures and stylistic devices convey and create perception and interpretation of war and peace events. Theory, argument, and metaphor are investigated within the context of the congressional debate on the Gulf War. The section on audience carries the rhetorical concern forward, including narrative as an important component of meaning. The focus here is on the interaction between political leaders and followers during the Gulf War, the United States intervention in Somalia, and the Cold War. Political actors speak strategically, shifting their language as they interact with their multiple internal and external audiences. At some point, speakers and audiences merge into one as they jointly identify with powerful collective myths, hegemonic narratives that dominate political space and time. In this moment thought, action, and language are joined in a unified structure of meaning. The conclusion projects ways in which words of war and peace, during the twenty-first century, will convey and create worlds of meaning that reflect and construct our evolving understanding and appreciation of our human identity on a global scale.

ACKNOWLEDGMENTS

In the fall of 1990 I had the good fortune to spend a semester at the Scholar's Workshop in the Rhetoric of Political Argumentation funded by the National Endowment for the Humanities and hosted by the Project on the Rhetoric of Inquiry at the University of Iowa. During that time, I met a number of other scholars developing a school of study focusing on political rhetoric. John Nelson organized and activated the group and continues to lead the field. I developed a long-term collaboration with G. R. Boynton, whose mercurial brilliance, personal integrity, and passion for learning continue to stimulate my own work. Another important collaboration to grow out of my Iowa experience was with Robert Hariman, whose energy, style, and ethics have been a constant joy. Mary Stuckey, a challenging spirit, was also in residence at Iowa at this time. I had the opportunity to interact with distinguished scholars such as Kathleen Farrell, Bruce Gronbeck, Deirdre McCloskey, and Robert Newman. Gradually my circle of acquaintance widened to include associations with Robert Ivie at Indiana University and Christ'l de Landtsheer at the University of Amsterdam. At the University of Colorado I associated and worked with Barry Balleck, Gerard Hauser, Pernilla Neal, and James Collins Ross, and a long collaboration with Alice Healy, Grant Sinclair, and Lyle Bourne has stimulated, enriched, and informed my work. I have also been supported by the friendship and collaboration of Mary Lenn Dixon and Martin Medhurst at Texas A&M University. Finally, my family has lived with this book and its ideas, not just in theory but also in their daily lives, for many years. Their conversation and company have helped to nurture and create it.

All of these people, plus the additional coauthors of chapters found here, have contributed to the development of the themes set forth in this book and to whatever merits it may have—though they are not, of course, responsible for its faults. This book is political and rhetorical. It is also social. These individuals and others are part of this experience, and I gratefully acknowledge the pleasure, sustenance, and joy of their society and collaboration.

Meanings of
War and Peace

Introduction

Dimensions and Interpretations of War and Peace

FRANCIS A. BEER

At the beginning of this new millennium, as we put the twentieth century behind us and begin the twenty-first, we should like to hope that war has finally
become a relic of the past. Humanity has survived its violent pre-history and,
more recently, what one distinguished commentator called "the century of
total war" (Aron 1966). The two world wars and the Cold War are history, the
history of the past century, of the past millennium.

Yet even after the "long peace" embedded inside the Cold War, the fall of
the Berlin wall, and the promise of the immediate post–Cold War period, we
have not reached "the end of history" (Fukuyama 1992; Gaddis 1989). War
continues. In spite of efforts toward the reduction and abolition of war that go
on parallel to its conduct, we seem no closer to general peace today than ever.
During the 1990s there have been approximately a hundred ongoing international and civil wars (Allen 1998, 43–45). Intractable conflicts fester in different
parts of the world. The Middle East remains torn by religious antagonism and
the struggle over the oil wealth under its land. Similar rivalries sweep North
Africa. Farther south, tribal and racial hostilities fracture the political land-
scape from the Sahara to South Africa. In Asia, the Indians and Pakistanis
conduct nuclear tests. Chinese national ambitions pressure Taiwan and transform Tibet. Ethnic rivalries, resource conflicts, and political ideologies in central and Eastern Europe continue the slow-motion disintegration of the former
Austro-Hungarian and Russian empires.

Other important sets of global problems and challenges compete with war
and peace for global attention. One of these is the deterioration of the natural

environment and the challenge of preserving it; another is global poverty and the challenge of turning it into wealth and prosperity; another is global repression and the challenge of human rights. Finally, there is the problem of an anarchic, disconnected, and often violent international society and the challenge of turning it into a global community.

None of these problems is independent of war and peace. There is none that war makes better, nor are there any that peace would make worse. Indeed, progress toward peace implies advances in these other areas as well. War and peace, for these and many other reasons, stand near the top of the list of important issues facing present and future generations. If we can make progress in solving the problems of war and peace, we shall pass on to our children and grandchildren a legacy of a better world and better lives.

War and Peace Behavior: Complexity and Levels of Explanation

War and peace are not only important; they are also complex, containing multiple dimensions and intricate relationships.[1] Scholars in international relations have worked for many years, with some success, to discover, describe, and connect pieces of the puzzle of war and peace.[2] I have been one of these, and this book is a sequel to, a second volume of, an earlier attempt to put the pieces together in a behavioral way (Beer 1981a).

Long-term trends in war and peace have emerged from the research findings. Periods of general peace have become longer and wars have become shorter. Yet war casualties have risen both in absolute numbers and relative to total populations. In the United States, counter to the general trends, periods of peace have become more frequent and shorter as wars have also become more frequent and somewhat longer. War casualties have increased absolutely, though not relative to population (Beer 1983b, 1974).

Theorizing and research about war and peace have particularly focused on behavioral regularities and causal explanation. At the highest level of international relations, the power structure of the international system obviously has an important influence on war and peace. Realism, the dominant theory of international relations, suggests that an essential pattern of international anarchy reflects the deep structure of world politics. The permanent struggle for power among nation-states, according to realists, is an important cause of war and peace. These international systemic effects have appeared to be particularly relevant for most of the twentieth century. During this period, the external dangers posed by other states seem to have overwhelmed most other factors.[3]

The end of the Cold War has lessened some of these international system pressures and other factors have become more visible. These include domestic regime effects, which depend on internal power structures rather than international ones. In the post–Cold War period, the linkage of domestic politics with war and peace has risen in significance. One example of an important effect produced by a domestic regime is expressed by the "democratic peace" hypothesis. The democratic peace hypothesis suggests that international and internal politics are strongly connected. More specifically, it proposes that democratic states have more peaceful relations with each other than they do with non-democratic ones. The United States, England, and France, for example, are less likely to go to war with each other than with China, Iraq, or Libya.[4]

The connections between democracy, on the one hand, and war and peace, on the other, are intricate and subtle. This is particularly true for large, representative republics like the United States. For example, there is some evidence that the domestic electoral cycle may play an important role in facilitating or discouraging the use of military force beyond national boundaries. Research suggests that U.S. presidents are more inclined to initiate international violence during the first two years of the four-year term, when the hazards of the previous election are behind them and the risks of the next one lie on a relatively distant political horizon. As the next election approaches, they tend to be more cautious abroad. Democracies, from this perspective, tend to be most peaceful in the periods preceding elections. (Bueno de Mesquita and Siverson 1997, 1995; Gaubatz 1991; Beer 1984). A military background has also tended to be an asset in the competitive struggle for democratic public office. American presidential candidates with military experience have had better success in getting elected than those without prior military credentials. Once in office, American presidents with greater prior military experience have tended toward more peaceful administrations than leaders with less military background (Beer 1983a).

Individual effects constitute a third set of influences on war and peace. International and domestic power structures contain individuals. That individuals play an important role is simple common sense. Nightly media miniseries show individual world leaders, with distinct personalities, making and defending the decisions that mean life or death for millions of people. Below the leaders in the political hierarchy are the individual followers. Modern democracies, both philosophically and in their policies, focus on individual human rights. Individuals, as political leaders and citizens, enact the rituals and dramas of realism and democracy. Billions of individual minds and bodies are at varying degrees of peace or war with each other. Each individual separately reflects and constructs the microenvironment of international relations. Billions of acting, thinking, speaking components, from this bottom-up perspective, make up a complex living international system (cf. Miller 1978).

War and Peace Cognition: Rationality and Psychology

What individuals do is related to what they think. The preamble to the United Nations Educational, Scientific, and Cultural Organization (UNESCO) constitution puts the strong case for subjectivity in its statement: "That since wars begin in the minds of men, it is in the minds of men that the defences of peace must be constructed" (see also Huxley 1979). How people's minds actually work, however, remains an open question.

We should like to believe that decision makers think rationally, behaving as folk wisdom and a certain common sense suggests, seeking to maximize benefits and reduce costs. We shall leave aside, for one moment, the question whether decision makers are indeed rational in this sense. Even if they are, this kind of reason does not automatically lead to a more peaceful world. The political, economic, social, cultural, psychological, and scientific benefits of peace are obvious and well known. But peace may carry substantial other costs. The European experience in the 1930s teaches that one can pay too high a price in other values for peace. When faced with an aggressive totalitarian leader like Adolf Hitler, for example, democratic leaders concluded that it might be better to fight early to avoid greater damage later on. That was the lesson of Munich in 1938.

The costs of war can also, of course, be staggering—not only for the losers but also for the winners. Wars eat states and people. World Wars I and II helped dissolve the empires of Austria-Hungary, France, Germany, Italy, Japan, and Turkey. The Cold War finished the Soviet Union. War, to use a Washington cliché, puts military men and women in harm's way. Some lose their lives, while others return home with physical and psychological damage that will never heal. The sheer scale of the collective, wholesale destruction of war overwhelms the physical damage caused by most natural disasters—earthquakes, fires, floods, hurricanes, tornadoes—and individual, retail violence—murder, rape, car and airplane accidents.

There is a widespread belief that the potential costs of war have declined. Nothing could be further from the truth. At its most extreme level, war brings mass genocide, omnicide, and extinction. In the face of nuclear spasm and nuclear winter, all past war crimes disappear. There is no answer to Herman Kahn's (1960) famous postnuclear question: "Will the survivors envy the dead?" The Bible warns that the sins of the fathers will return for successive generations. The physical effects of malnutrition and disease, the psychological effects of trauma, and the genetic consequences of chemical weapons and radiation lift this terrible religious prophecy into a present-day secular reality.

In spite of these costs, war can produce benefits. For example, states fight wars to gain control of territory and natural resources. The immediate issues of war are sometimes trivial, as in the 1969 Soccer War between El Salvador and Honduras, but the stakes can be enormous. The American Civil War, World Wars I and II, and the Cold War helped decide the identities and futures of entire societies and civilizations. Some groups within society—for example, what President Eisenhower called the military-industrial complex—profit.

The rational comparison of the costs and benefits is daunting because of the high stakes and the dynamic flow of risk and reward. There is also is no linear metric to align the many dimensions of war and peace. Comprehensive balancing of benefits and costs for different actors, in different issue areas and time frames, is very difficult. Preferences for gains and losses are not symmetrical. Some actors may be attracted by the potential benefits of war; others may prefer not to fight, being less attracted by military options or more averse to risk. Actors react differently to the prospects of gain and loss. The simple avoidance of loss, or unwillingness to walk away from sunk costs, may be powerful incentives to fight. Long- and short-term considerations may also pull in different directions. The immediate, particular, short-term gains of war may overwhelm the general, frequently discounted, long-term benefits of peace. There are, finally, reflexive effects. A cost-benefit discipline may illuminate outcomes that are, in some senses, better. Yet it may also imply additional costs. For example, there can be political or public relations consequences of the analysis itself. More general knowledge of the true costs of war can make public approval more difficult. Political leaders ready to undertake war are unlikely to wish to give such ammunition to their foreign enemies and domestic critics.[5]

Notwithstanding these complexities, the assumption of rational thinking still holds out the powerful promise of better solutions to situations that can lead to war. Thus, peace may be enhanced by manipulating incentives, trying to achieve war's benefits through less costly means. Substituting other actions for military behavior where possible—economic sanctions, for example—has proved useful in avoiding direct force in a number of situations including Iraq, South Africa, and Zimbabwe-Rhodesia (See Baldwin 1985).

Rational choice models have an obvious intuitive appeal. They are clear, spare, and useful; they incorporate a minimalist and pragmatic aesthetic. Rational choice is presumably superior to irrational choice. Nevertheless, whatever the normative appeal, there remain empirical problems. War and peace contain dimensions and are driven by forces that are not completely captured by economic metaphors and models. Contemporary theory and research on human cognition and decision suggest that thought processes are broader and more complex than rational choice may imply. If we wish to understand war and peace better, we must try to comprehend a wider range of what people are really thinking and feeling when they make war and peace. Such an understanding allows us to see conflicts from the many sides that they actually present and to find solutions that might otherwise remain hidden in specific situations.

A substantial library of work also exists on the nonrational political psychology of war and peace.[6] More currently, schema theory offers a new window into cognition and decision about peace and war. Schema theory suggests that the decision process relies on mental models of past experiences (cf. Sylvan and Voss 1998). When activated by appropriate stimuli, these remembered frameworks provide the cognitive organization for interpreting new realities. My own collaborative research program in this area has found a set of cognitive dynamics that affect decisions about war and peace. A set of psychological laboratory experiments, motivated by schema theory, focused on decisions about international cooperation and conflict. Findings included a number of general effects centering on reciprocity and conflict ceilings, peace settlements and continuing conflict, prior agreements and gender, personality and previous knowledge, and conflict escalation and nuclear firebreaks.[7]

Thinking about war and peace, like war and peace itself, is complex. Rational thinking is one dimension of cognition, but even rationality does not guarantee peaceful outcomes. Moreover, some of the schemata activated by war and peace situations may be rational to a greater or lesser degree. Others may not be rational, relying on entirely different templates of perception and reaction. The full script of the Middle East passion play, for example, includes a wide variety of reasoning and psychology.

Patterns of Cognition, Behavior, and Language: Meaning

Schema theory offers an approach not only to the narrow issue of cognition but also to recasting the dimensions of war and peace in a more interpretive frame—as the much broader question of the meaning of war and peace.[8] The meaning of war and peace, in its initial, cognitive guise, is the schema that is activated and dominant as the internal response to specific external stimuli. The cognitive meaning of war and peace is the schema—the idea, the thought— that represents and constructs it.

The question whether ideas or interests are primary motivating factors in world politics is one of the important current debates in international relations, linked to the larger issue of the importance of agents relative to structures (cf. Wendt 1999; Katzenstein, Keohane, and Krasner 1999; Kubalkova, Onuf, and Kowert 1998; Goldstein and Keohane 1993; Onuf 1989; Kratochwil 1989). We are suggesting here that interests are, in an important sense, ideas and that both ideas and interests are schemata—cognitive representations—that help frame the meaning of war and peace.

The cognitive meaning of war and peace includes ideas and interests, and it also comprehends much more. A broader definition of schema and current work in cognitive science imply that cognitive meaning is embedded in larger individual and collective associative networks. Cognitive meaning, to use an imperfect analogy between computers and human cognition, includes the current state and processes of all hardware and software, the structure and processes of the brain and the mind.[9] The cognitive meaning of war and peace thus includes the mental inventory of war/peace descriptions and facts at any particular point in time. It includes all the mental maps or models describing dynamic relations within cognitive war/peace space. It includes, finally, the underlying production functions that produce and refresh mental displays of war and peace (cf. Fauconnier 1997, 1985; Minsky 1994).

Cognitive meaning refers to one dimension of the meaning of war and peace, the mental world of the players and observers. Behavioral meaning on the other hand, focuses on the more material world of agents, actions, interactions, events, structures, institutions, practices, causes, and consequences—more tangible phenomena that cognitive meaning organizes and to which it refers. Just as cognitive meaning denotes patterns in cognitive space, behavioral meaning denotes patterns in the behavioral space of war and peace. Cognitive meaning is concerned with the actors, the internal representations of war and peace. Behavioral meaning orders the external, extrinsic, extensional world of physical phenomena of war and peace that cognitive meaning reflects and constructs (cf. Putnam 1996, xvi).

Behavioral meaning aims at empirically verifiable objective truth. It includes facts about war and peace. For example, World Wars I and II, the Korean and Gulf Wars, the Cold War, and the Long Peace are behaviorally meaningful signifiers because the words supposedly correspond with real-world observables. They describe the world of war and peace, in the famous phrase of the German historian Ranke, as it really is. The "Gworsh War" or "Siddel Peace" are nonsense phrases; they are behaviorally meaningless unless "Gworsh" and "Siddel" have identifiable referents in some possible real or imagined world.

The behavioral meaning of war and peace also includes explanation—that is, ascertainable patterns of regular relations between phenomena as they are described in scientific laws and hypotheses, theories, and models. War and peace may also be behaviorally meaningless in this external sense if observable regularities or relations are missing. War and peace may have no meaningful behavioral pattern if, for example, they are hyper-chaotic or hyper-random, not even displaying regular mathematical forms of nonlinear dynamics or distributed events.

The meaning of war and peace also includes a linguistic component that mediates between cognitive and behavioral meaning. Linguistic meaning as it is used here refers to patterns in linguistic space, words of war and peace. The linguistic meaning of war and peace is in the semantic tradition of lexicography and morphology. This dimension of meaning is logocentric; it is embedded in words and defined by the relations of words with each other. Dictionaries or grammar books are hardly isomorphic with natural language, yet they are simple examples of linguistic meaning—including, as they do, definitions and usage rules for war, peace, and other associated words and phrases. Syntax is also important. The verb *to mean*, in the sense that it is being used here, is generally transitive, taking the form x means y. The noun *meaning* follows the same rules. The meaning of the target x is the source y. Thus, the linguistic meaning of the target x, "war," may be the source y, "organized collective violence between nation-states." A related meaning of the target "peace" can be "absence of such violence." In this case, the target x and the source y are both volatile. At any moment, the same x can refer to a different y; at any moment the same y can attach itself to a different x. "Collective violence between nation-states" can instantiate itself in multiple ways. The "absence of collective violence between nation-states" is even more open. Chapter 2 will show in much more detail semantic examples of the many different meanings of "war"; a similar chapter could have been written on "peace."

Each of these three modes of meaning—cognitive, behavioral, and linguistic—is supported by intellectual partisans who claim ownership of the term *meaning* for themselves and contest the claims of others. In spite of these strong differences, a more general sense of meaning, and of the meaning of war and peace, emerges from the relation of these three dimensions. We need to note that they are neither completely independent nor exhaustive. First, cognitive, behavioral, and linguistic meaning overlap to some extent with each other and with other modes of meaning. Second, if we consider each dimension separately, it combines with each of the others as part of a larger system of meaning. The cognitive linguist Gilles Fauconnier says that we construct meaning as the interaction of thinking, acting, and communicating. "Meaning construction refers to the high-level, complex verbal operations that apply within and across domains when we think, act, or communicate" (Fauconnier 1997, 1). The philosopher Hilary Putnam defines meaning as an interaction between knowledge, the world, and language users. "Knowledge of meaning," he says, "is not something that is possible for a thinker in isolation, . . . it presupposes both interactions with the world and interactions with other language users" (Putnam 1996, xvi; cf. Searle 1998). Finally, according to *The Linguistics Encyclopedia*, "meaning is not an entity or property of an entity; it is a relation between (at least) a speaker, a time, a state of affairs, and an utterance" (Malmkjaer 1991, 339). Meaning in general is associated with words such as form, model, pattern, and frame. It refers to identity, difference, and relationships within a larger ordered context or environment. The meaning of war and peace in this general sense is equivalent to the identification of a location on a three-dimensional topographical map.

The meaning of war and peace at any time can occupy any, some, or all of these cognitive, linguistic, behavioral dimensions. Different modes of meaning attach themselves to multidimensional referents in different manners and degrees. Such meaning can be cognitive, signifying ideas, thoughts, or intentions about war and peace. It is quite appropriate that such meaning may be "something mental" (Hacker 1993). It can be behavioral, signifying observable, physical phenomena in the material world—actions and interactions, structures and processes, instances and events of war and peace. It can also be linguistic, signifying other words.

These modes of meaning blend together. The cognitive meaning of war and peace informs associated actions and words. A broad, multidisciplinary tradition has focused on subjective agents with normative purposes. Intentional meaning has been a particularly important thread in this discourse. From this perspective, goal-oriented intentions give purposive meaning to actions and words (Frankl 1962). Or, more narrowly—in the context of the previous discussion of rationality—thoughts, words, and actions have utilitarian meanings, as they conform to dynamic patterns and flows of costs and benefits (Boulding 1964). War is meaningful, in this sense, to the extent that it is connected to the goals, purposes, and interests of those who fight and die. It is meaningless if it is not. Peace, in contrast, may be meaningless for those whose ends can be achieved only in wartime (Blocker 1974).

Language mediates between thought and action, adding complexity, variety, and power to meaning. Language contributes to one's own thought, structuring internal mental discourse. Actors say what they think about war and peace. Language also has power to shape the way other political actors think and act in war and peace. Actors' words stimulate thoughts in the minds of other decision makers. Language adds forms of behavior and action: verbal behavior and speech action. Further, actors do what they say when they carry out threats or fulfill promises. Allies and enemies react to talk and treaties, or they verbally justify or translate what they do on the battlefield or at the negotiating table.

The meaning of the Cold War or the Gulf War is thus to be found in the related patterns of thought, action, and speech of the participants—groups and individuals—within other larger contexts of similar patterns of war, peace, and general international relations. What did Stalin or Saddam Hussein, Winston Churchill or George Bush, mean? What did the peace of Westphalia or Versailles, World War II or the Gulf War, mean? What does Stephen Spielberg's *Saving Private Ryan* mean? As in an algebraic equation, meaning is the product of the thoughts, words, and behavior of the participants and the observers.

The meaning of war and peace is protean. There are other strands of the meaning of war and peace (for example, artistic meaning, emotional meaning, physical meaning) that we could explore. For the present discussion, emotional meaning is subsumed under cognitive meaning. Following Boynton and Lodge (1993), we assume "hot cognition," where thoughts and emotions are intertwined. Similarly, we place scientific and physical meaning under behavioral meaning, and artistic under linguistic meaning. This is certainly far from doing these topics justice. A fully developed theory of meaning would include a much more extensive discussion of these topics and many more. We have, however, probably gone far enough for the purposes of this book in identifying thought, action, and language as major dimensions of the meaning of war and peace.

The behavioral meaning of war and peace, as suggested above, includes scientific meaning, with different implied scientific functions. The meaning of war and peace can be description, as in the case x means y. In the descriptive case, upon which we have already touched, meaning is an identity, a synonym, clarifying x by substituting a more comprehensible or known y. When one asks for the meaning of "nuclear detonation," one may receive a dictionary definition. Meaning can also be explanation, including causes and consequences. When one asks, "What was the meaning of India's nuclear detonations in May 1998?" one may be inquiring about the reasons that led India's decision makers to undertake them and the likely reactions of other actors and the international system. Responses may include discussions of power status or capabilities of defense and deterrence. If we follow this thread a bit farther, meaning becomes prediction. To speculate about the meaning of these nuclear events also implies an ability to see beyond the immediate situation and into future possible worlds. In this case, one may assess the relationship between nuclear testing, nuclear escalation, and nuclear proliferation. Finally, meaning may become intervention and, possibly, control. To have an opinion about the meaning of the explosions may lead other decision makers to action—Pakistan to its own nuclear tests, other nations to economic sanctions.

The meaning of war and peace is circular and associational: x means y, y means z, z means . . . , and . . . ultimately forms part of the meaning of x. Cognition, language, and behavior ultimately form a closed system. The links of the system do not exist in isolation; they are part of an endless chain of signifiers. As the identities of the elements ultimately return to themselves, they form a network of relations. The connections within this web compose the structure of meaning.

The meaning of war and peace is dynamic and indeterminate (Quine 1992), embedded in an infinite set of forming and dissolving contexts. The meaning of meaning at any specific point in space or time depends on the thoughts, actions, and language that surround it. Meaning's same chameleon nature is also evident in this book. Ultimately, at each point, meaning in the book depends on the connection between the cognition, behavior, and words of the author and the reader.

The meaning of war and peace, as we discuss it here, is the triangulation of thought, language, and action. War and peace have cognitive, linguistic, or behavioral meaning as they are embedded in cognitive, linguistic, or behavioral contexts. This meaning is determined within the state of the associational network that binds the outer and inner worlds, actions and events, minds and feelings, and thoughts and emotions separately and together in specific cases of war and peace. In war and peace, each dimension is important. Without actions, thoughts and words have no meaning. Without words, thoughts and actions have no meaning. Without thoughts, words and actions have no meaning. Individual war-peace phenomena have general meaning as they fit within these larger patterns of thought, language, and action, and the whole patterns, in turn, have meaning as parts of even larger contexts. These are frames within frames, levels within levels. Like a set of Russian dolls, one structure is inside another.

One of the most difficult questions that one can ask about war and peace is: "What does it all mean?" This book offers an approach to answering that question. The meaning of any experience of war or peace is embedded in the cognition, behavior, and language of those associated with it. This is true for war and peace in general and also for particular instances of war and peace. What was the meaning of World War I (Albrecht-Carrié 1965), the meaning of

Munich (Jensen and Wurmser 1990), the meaning of nuclear weapons (Jervis 1989), or the meaning of Operation Desert Storm during the Gulf War (Lambeth 1992)? The answer is that we derive and generate the meaning of each specific instance of war and peace from the interrelationships of thoughts, actions, and words—collectively and individually—of its participants and observers. The meaning of war and peace is about patterns—the existence, activation, emergence, recognition, identification, and naming of general and local shapes, forms, and relations. The most general meaning of war and peace emerges as a larger pattern, together with the particular meanings of the smaller bits and pieces of war and peace.

War and Peace Language: Semantics, Rhetorics, and Audiences

Conventional wisdom in international relations tends to focus on behavioral meaning, the meaning of war and peace that lies in the brute physical phenomena. According to general political and scientific belief, actions speak louder than words. Military force has traditionally been the gold standard of international relations. Mao Tse-tung believed that power grew out of the barrel of a gun. In a famous exchange, Winston Churchill and Joseph Stalin were discussing the attitude of the pope toward an important issue during the Second World War. Stalin dismissed such concern by asking how many divisions the pope had. Today, however, the relevance of the traditional behavioral dimension of meaning has become more questionable as the general effectiveness of military force has become cloudier. The end of the Cold War, combined with the trend toward globalization and democracy, has created increasing resistance to using military force. Democratic voters abhor the black body bags coming home with the lifeless remains of their sons and daughters. Economic interactions have become more important in world politics. Money drives the global economy. When the market speaks, nations listen. When nations do not listen, currencies collapse and investment capital flees. Economics do not replace military forces, of course. They supplement them in areas where armed intervention is ineffective or costly.

As traditional approaches to international relations have overvalued behavioral meaning, they have devalued the linguistic meaning of war and peace. Attention to language, from a traditional perspective, is believed to trivialize war and peace. When men and women are fighting and dying, talk seems beside the point. Nevertheless, despite the weight of military force and material resources, the interplay of abstract symbols is a highly significant part of world politics. Words, images, and numbers are less tangible than armies or dollars, yet they are the currency of contemporary communication, mediating between thought and action. In spite of their devaluation, words matter for international relations and for peace and war. Verbal behavior and speech acts have cash value. At some point, the thoughts and actions of war and peace are translated into words.

One school of thought suggests that military and economic actions are their own languages, performative forms of rhetoric (Beer and Hariman 1998; McCloskey 1998). At the same time, other forms of symbolic action are also significant. Language is one of these, one of the most important—and probably most neglected—dimensions of war and peace. Language contributes to more general meaning to the extent that it is connected with thought and action. Talk is not always "just" talk or "cheap" talk, a waste of time, or a deceitful camouflage for forceful strategy; it is an important currency of global intercourse. The pen may or may not be mightier than the sword in particular situations, but words do have power. Verbal communication is a significant aspect of peace and war. Words are one of the most elaborate and complex technologies that humankind has developed. Words stimulate and activate the schemata of our minds, and words are often the way in which we respond to the outside world. Words create the theory of international relations and its related concepts and data; words combine strategically in different political styles and rhetorical devices; words are an important form of international action, taking different shapes in different issue areas; words are essential signs and symbols in an emerging international virtual reality. Words reflect thought and action, and also mold it.

This book focuses on the role of language in the international system and specifically on how language reflects and constructs the meaning of war and peace. With this concern, it builds upon a significant body of prior work at the intersection of rhetoric and foreign policy. Such work has analyzed in detail the language of foreign policy decision (Botsdorff 1994; Medhurst 1994; Campbell 1992; Hinds and Windt 1991; Campbell and Jamieson 1990; and Medhurst, Ivie, Wander, and Scott 1990). It has examined how actors employ different rhetorical styles (Hariman 1995). It has shown how political actors deploy language strategically in many foreign policy issue areas, for example, imperialism (Doty 1996), the environment (Litfin 1994), and gender (Peterson 1992). In a related vein, there is also relevant work on the relationship between language and international culture (Shapiro 1997), and discourse and political violence (Apter 1997, 1994). The meaning of war and peace is embedded within verbal context. War and peace mean, at least partly, what people say they mean.

From this point, the book proceeds in several directions. The first section, "Semantics," centers rather narrowly on microlanguage—the linguistic meanings of particular words that are important for our understanding of war and peace. This section contains chapters that explore some examples of how language shapes meaning through verbal forms and associations—the permutations and combinations—of words. It concentrates on bits and pieces of language, particular words embedded in specific contexts and used for focused purposes. It examines the way in which verbal context shifts the meanings of central terms and concepts, together with the facts and actions that follow from them. This section also draws from the discussion in this introduction by adding some linguistic pieces to the complex puzzle of war and peace. It graphically illustrates one of the central insights of complexity theory: how minute actions can produce complex consequences. In this case, small speech actions produce large changes in the meanings of war and peace.

Chapter 1, "Words of War: Terms, Concepts, Levels of Discourse," explores the meaning of war from a linguistic perspective. The meaning of the word *war*, a central term in international relations discourse, is defined as a variable whose value shifts as a function of other variables. Some of these variables may be behavioral, involving political actions and events; some may be psychological; and some are linguistic. In this formulation, strings of words function like strings of mathematical symbols. Just as each mathematical operator changes the value of the final product, each word juxtaposed with war changes its meaning.

A metaphor of continuous variation helps to explain not only the verbal meaning of war but also that of other related terms and concepts, for example, reason. Reason is a central word in the discourse of war and peace, consistent with a culture that places a high value on rationality, science, and technology. Chapter 2, "Words of Reason: Rationality and Rhetoric," takes the continuous model of meaning developed in the prior chapter and applies it in another domain. It examines the use of the word *reason* as a powerful rhetorical device in both scientific and public debate. Reason is central to modern political discourse because of its historical and cultural importance and because of the contemporary dominance of a rational model of cognition. The concept of reason therefore justifies closer scrutiny of the word itself. As in the previous analysis of war, the meaning of the word *reason* is constructed as a variable. Standing by itself, reason seems relatively shapeless and empty. Dictionary definitions are circular, although some subtle nuances derive from the network of reason's root words. Much of the variance in the meaning is determined by other words that surround it, with a significant portion of reason's meaning being defined by its context. The meaning of reason thus continuously varies. From this perspective, it becomes clear how reason functions as an important rhetorical trope in political discourse. Its plasticity and flexibility help the word *reason* to stimulate and evoke variable mental images and responses in different settings and situations—all the more important, since these go largely unnoticed. The concept of reason of state—national interest defined in terms of power—is used as an example. It shows reason's rhetorical power and privilege, its normative dimension, its persuasiveness and consequences. Seen in this light, a weak version of reason of state is preferable to a strong one. Pluralistic reason opens new paths for democratic thought and political action in a world of multiple others who share different forms of reasoning about war and peace.

Chapter 3, "Validities: Scientific and Political Realities," focuses on the meaning of another central legitimating word in the lexicon of political science. Validity is a word that connects scientific theory and research with politics and policy. Questions of validity are central to our understanding of war and peace, with particular importance for the extensional, denotational semantics of behavioral meaning—the external world to which the words supposedly refer. This chapter is thus concerned not only with semantics, but also with the validity of validity. It suggests that validity is constrained by uncontrolled and uncontrollable variance in sampling, context, text, and analysis. It concludes that our knowledge of war and peace necessarily includes both scientific and political dimensions, implying serious anomalies. These inconsistencies may be partly dissolved by a semantic strategy of decomposition into multiple, parallel, switchable validities.

This microscopic discussion of semantics now leads into a broader, macroscopic discussion of political rhetoric. Moving away from the discrete lexicology and morphology of individual words, in the "Rhetorics" section we take a broader view of how political participants interact through virtually continuous streams of words. In this process, their persuasive political discourse reflects and constructs the meaning of war and peace. Chapter 4, "Postrealism, Just War, and the New World Order," takes as its starting point earlier work on postrealism and the rhetorical turn in international relations (Beer and Hariman 1996). It begins by recapitulating and reengaging the argument developed there. The standard theory of international relations goes by the name of realism, or *realpolitik*, and represents itself as positive theory and objective science. As noted previously, realism emphasizes the effects of the international system structure on war and peace. In particular, realism describes a world system of nation-states aggressively pursuing national interests defined in terms of power, ruthlessly using all available means, including war, to achieve survival and dominance.

Realist theory flowered in the context of the two world wars and the Cold War of the twentieth century. The end of the Cold War and the collapse of the Soviet Union have, however, provided a radically changed international environment. Changes in international behavior and cognition have encouraged a new interpretation, a new meaning, of realist theory. In light of this new international context, postrealist theory incorporates realist theory and also goes beyond realism to construct world politics persuasively in other ways. Chapter 4 presents an outline of postrealist reasoning. Postrealism changes the subject from validity to construction, from objects to subjects, from the nation-state to other actors, including international theorists.

Postrealism begins by noting that realism is also a powerful rhetoric that helps to construct the very international world that it purports to describe. Realism is speech action: As realism describes, explains, and predicts international relations, it also verbally shapes and controls the world that it observes. As leaders form and implement national policy and action, they also, like famous singers performing well-known operas, play their parts in the latest realist performance. Thus, U.S. and Russian leaders George W. Bush and Vladimir Putin play their parts in an enduring post–Cold War rivalry. In doing so, they and their audience help give international relations a certain meaning, in this case a realist meaning centering around strategic geopolitics.

Postrealism suggests that realist theory of international relations constructs a simple, taut narrative of world politics. Realist science parsimoniously describes a system in which the main characters are nation-states, motivated by their own interests, locked in a permanent structure of deadly combat. Postrealism proposes a more complex theory for a more complex system. It suggests a metanarrative that reframes realist theory as one rhetoric, powerful in its own right, among multiple contending rhetorics. Postrealism emphasizes the increasing importance of characters other than nation-states, driven by motivations other than power, combining in cooperative as well as conflictual ways. Postrealism suggests the benefits of a three-level formulation of strategic policy, blending self-interest, interactions with others, and ethics and morality. This formulation encourages the creation of coalitions that simultaneously advance national and international interests defined and shaped through discourse.

Chapter 4 uses this postrealist model to examine the U.S. congressional Gulf War debate. That debate serves as a prime example of rhetorical behavior related to war and peace; more important, it is also a rhetorical template of the national mind. Congressional representatives do not always express what they think, but they probably do articulate what they believe is in the minds of their constituents. At the same time, congressional rhetoric is a form of political behavior that helps to construct individual and group meanings at all levels of the national and international political systems.

The chapter further describes complex policy arguments, deploying non-linear series of claims and counterclaims developed in the text of the debates. The political use of the just-war argument in the Gulf War debate shows how national interests are articulated through the political rhetoric of the democratic process to shape and justify foreign policy. This political rhetorical process reflects and constructs the institutions and structures of a normative international regime, the new world order, and helps give them and the war a set of particular meanings.

The forms of international rhetoric go beyond the narrative of general theory and the structure of particular policy argument. Rhetoric also reflects and constructs the meaning of war and peace through metaphor. Chapter 5, "Body, Mind, and Soul in the Gulf War Debate," introduces metaphorical reasoning with a particular focus on the metaphor of the body as it is represented in the mind. This chapter suggests that realist reasoning is supplemented and supported by metaphorical reasoning in which the metaphor of the body is particularly important. The prior physical reality of the human body, the existential condition of human embodiment, presents a physically grounded form of deep structure that is prior to and underlies much of our action and thought in the world. Concepts like center and periphery, blockage and containment, balance and compulsion, and contact and collection may be important keys in interpreting and decoding all dimensions and implications of international debate. At the very least, the rhetorical evidence suggests that there are multiple dimensions of consciousness, cognition, and decision in war and peace situations. Bodily *topoi* are very much part of the meaning of war and peace.

Chapter 6, "Women's Words: Gender and Rhetoric in the Gulf War Debate," continues along the same path. It focuses on gender-based rhetorical differences of congressmen and congresswomen with particular reference to the Gulf War debate, showing how gender and rhetoric work together to reflect and construct meaning. Gender differences are analyzed along four rhetorical dimensions. Two of these are the familiar international ideas of realism and idealism. The other two come from metaphorical and feminist reasoning; these are images of the body and maternalism. The strongest gender difference that emerges from the Gulf War debate is that women are more likely than men to rely rhetorically on a maternal dimension. Maternal rhetoric is also associated with a more dovish foreign policy position.

The next section, "Audiences," continues the rhetorical theme and also goes beyond it. It examines the way that language transmits and creates meaning pragmatically through the dynamic interaction of speakers and audiences. Chapter 7, "Talking About Dying: Rhetorical Phases of the Somalian Intervention," continues the prior focus on the body. This chapter shows how members of Congress strategically recognize and use the fundamental conditions of living and dying to modulate the meanings of the domestic audience. Congressional rhetoric joins itself to the political task at hand, rhetorically reflecting and shaping public opinion through different phases of war and peace. Thus, as the United States intervened militarily in Somalia, the U.S. House Foreign Affairs and Senate Foreign Relations Committees held hearings. Four of these are analyzed. During the hearings, representatives and senators spoke of dying, and this language varied through four phases of the policy cycle: (1) mobilizing attention and support, (2) self-congratulation, (3) critical reflection, and (4) policy making. The chapter suggests that speaking about dying changes dramatically as Congress, the administration, and the nation move through the foreign policy cycle.

Chapter 8, "Beer and Quiche in the Fast Lane: Signaler's Dilemma, Democratic Debate, and the Gulf War," also continues an earlier theme, this time of rational cognition and decision. A rational choice model is here applied to the foreign policy elite's rhetorical problem of simultaneously communicating with multiple audiences. The chapter uses ideas derived from game theory to take another cut at the rhetoric of the congressional Gulf War debate. Beginning with the idea of a signaler's dilemma, it focuses on the tension between domestic and international audiences and multiple associated meanings of war and peace rhetoric. Domestically, the Gulf War debate signaled the willingness of democratic leaders to follow established traditions and procedures; this willingness was important in mobilizing public support. Internationally, however, the debate may have had another meaning, signaling weakness. From this beginning, the signaling game, in the specific form of the "beer and quiche" model, is developed and applied to international communication between a democratic state and an opponent in a war and peace situation. In the game formalization, democratic states are configured along two dimensions: they may be weak or strong, and they may debate or not debate. Opponents may fight or withdraw. The model implies that the debate may have weakened U.S. efforts at deterrence and strengthened Iraq's resolve to remain in Kuwait: Saddam Hussein may have perceived this discussion as a sign of American irresolution and division. His perception of the debate as a sign of U.S. weakness possibly contributed to his decision to fight. The debate may, therefore, have contributed to the onset of war. At the same time, our analysis also suggests that Saddam Hussein may have perceived U.S. weakness independently of the debate. Based on the assumptions and applications of the model, the chapter concludes that democracies can avoid signaler's dilemma by either military or political successes: winning wars following domestic debates or converting their international opponents to democratic procedures.

Chapter 9 returns to the theme of rhetorical form. The prior discussion of metaphor focused on the way in which the rhetoric of the body incorporated meaning. Now, a consideration of narrative extends this stylistic theme. "Between Maastricht and Sarajevo: European Identities, Narratives, Myths" revisits the reason of the body, this time in a larger narrative structure that guides the audience into a political identity associated with a community of belief. It reinterprets the Cold War as a hegemonic myth and European identity in the light of that myth. The skeletons of the Cold War myth, and of Europe's Cold War identity, hang on the bodily *topoi* previously discussed. The end of the Cold War has weakened the authority of the myth and lessened the political power of the Cold War Europe identity. In a more pluralistic, multivocal environment, there are competing narratives, and European identity is increasingly open to revisionist interpretations and previously repressed rivals. A legitimate heir of Cold War Europe is Europe-Maastricht, an integrative identity that beckons into the future with a Europtimistic vision. Based on instrumental rationality and development, it promises peace and prosperity. It is, however, challenged by Europe-Sarajevo, a disintegrative identity that emphasizes deeper historical ethnic and cultural roots and threatens the dominant political and economic construction of Europe that has occurred during the last half-century. Where rhetoric and audience appeared relatively independent in our earlier analyses, here they merge to create meaning jointly, in the form of collective identity and myth.

Language and the Meaning of War and Peace

The concluding chapter, "Language and the Meaning of War and Peace," argues that war and peace are part of the global struggle for meaning where the human project, in the poet Rilke's terms, may be less about finding the answer than living the question. Language plays a crucial role in this struggle, mediating between thought and action in the emergence and recognition of patterns in international relations. Understanding how language works with cognition and behavior to convey and produce meaning gives us insights into dimensions of war and peace that would otherwise remain obscure. Appreciating the importance of language and meaning in world politics can help us to make sense of the world of war and peace as it exists, and to create a more thoughtful and articulated, peaceful, and meaningful world for ourselves and those who follow.

A book on the meaning of war and peace might be an interpretation of Leo Tolstoy's great literary masterpiece. Tolstoy's epic is a work of a different kind and scale, set within a different time and place, yet it deals with many of the same themes that concern us here. A Russian understanding of the Napoleonic wars is conveyed through the masterful use of language, depicting the thoughts and words, actions and interactions of the novel's characters. They too struggle against meaninglessness as they seek coherence. They seek to recognize patterns in their lives and to maintain connections between past, present, and future; themselves and others; instrumental power and core values; the objective outer world and a subjective inner life. As an old international political order dissolves and a new one—a New World Order—appears, we, as they, continue to try to understand the meaning, to find the map, of war and peace. We do this not through the pages of a classic historical novel, but in the unfolding, hyper-complex space and time of global politics in the twenty-first century.

PART I

Semantics

The great linguist Ferdinand de Saussure, who was twenty-one when he began his formal work, undertook "to cross the most unexplored regions of Indo-European linguistics." He provided the following justification: "If we have nevertheless ventured to go there, convinced in advance that our inexperience will go astray many times in the labyrinth, it is because, for anyone engaged in these studies, attacking such a question is not temerity, as has often been said, but a necessity. It is the first school through which one must pass, for it is not a matter of transcendental speculations but of the quest for elementary data, without which everything wavers, everything is arbitrariness and incertitude" (quoted in Benveniste 1971, 30).

Such an attitude is commendable for a language scholar who specializes in the study for its own sake. But why should questions of language interest those who seek to understand war and peace? Language is the very bedrock of political knowledge and intersubjectivity, the true currency of political communication. We express ourselves and understand each other in political communities through symbolic interaction, primarily through the written and spoken word. Words are critical in creating and defining our common existence; to be silent is to disappear and socially to die. Yet in spite of its political importance, language remains virtually invisible and inaccessible to many. We attend to the message, not the medium; we notice what we say, not how we say it. Language appears transparent and inconsequential. We take it for granted, as though it were trivial or unimportant. It is neither.

Modern work suggests a possible linguistic turn in political studies, analogous to that of philosophy and other social sciences.[1] This seems natural, since a sophisticated political science must reflexively take account of the language in which it expresses itself. To explore language, however, opens the ground beneath our feet. We use words to describe and explain words. As we try to touch and grasp them, however, words that seem real in themselves, or that appear to represent things that are real in themselves, shatter and evaporate. How can we use the words to study themselves? Reexperiencing the insights of Heisenberg and Gödel, we find it difficult simultaneously to use the apparatus and examine it. If we study the words under a microscope, how can we retain their macroscopic common sense meaning? How can we use the microscope to study the microscope? Nevertheless, we can and do use language reflexively to analyze language. We do this by seeing language in two senses at once. We use language, in the traditional way, as a medium of analysis; at the same time, language itself becomes the proper object of analysis. In so doing we begin what Quine (1960, 270) called the "semantic ascent" in the study and practice of politics.

Beginning with this general emphasis on language, we move forward to consider three particular words that are fundamental to contemporary world politics and our knowledge of them: war, reason, and validity. The chapter titled "Words of War" begins our consideration of the way important terms and concepts assume meaning. Such meaning, it argues, is not as standard belief would have it: fixed, stable, and hierarchically ordered. It comes only partly from a constant identity or meaning core. Much of a term's meaning arises from cognitive, behavioral, and textual context. As the context changes continuously, so does the meaning. This chapter on words of war illustrates both the continuous variations in the meaning of a central concept and also the instability of the empirical facts themselves as they follow and depend on it.

The next chapter, "Words of Reason," takes the argument of the previous chapter as its foundation and applies it to a different subject. According to this argument, meaning is embedded in specific contexts and shifts continuously. As a simple demonstration of this contextual effect, the chapter on reason repeats a selection of textual blocks from the earlier chapter on war. In their new setting, old words blend almost imperceptibly into new contexts and, as they do so, take on new tonalities. Moving forward, the chapter presents examples of reason's role and importance as a central *topos* and trope in war and peace discourse. It argues that political actors use the weight and variability of reason as part of an arsenal of persuasive policy argument. Audiences well understand the importance of reason, but less well its complexity. Accepting one meaning of reason in the early part of an argument, audiences are rhetorically turned and led to conclusions that depend on quite different meanings later on. As the conceptual ground shifts imperceptibly beneath their feet, they fall into the ensuing policy traps that the speaker has prepared for them. The chapter concludes by making a case for recognition of a pluralist reason and acceptance of a weaker conception of reason of state.

This section on semantics concludes with a chapter on validity. Following reason, validity is the second conceptual pillar of logical empiricism, the epistemology that underlies the contemporary science of war and peace. Yet, like reason, the meaning of validity varies with context. This variability exists with regard to validity's conceptual identity and for the theories and data that follow from it. As the meanings of core terms and concepts—war, reason, and validity—shift, so do the facts and truth-values that follow from them. The meaning of truth, like other meanings, is embedded within specific cognitive, verbal, and behavioral contexts that reflect and create patterns and textures of possible worlds of meaning.

I

Words of War

Terms, Concepts, Levels of Discourse

FRANCIS A. BEER

Terms and concepts are taken for granted in the course of scientific work. They appear as transparent windows onto reality, as mirrors of nature (Rorty 1979, 1982). We assume that terms and concepts have face validity. This approach has the pragmatic virtue of common sense, since it allows us to get on with the job at hand. From a more analytical standpoint, however, the unexamined term is not worth using. We cannot understand the products of our discourse if we do not understand the terms of the discourse itself. In this chapter my aim is to help to develop a clearer and more complex understanding of the meaning of political concepts, terms, and levels of discourse. I use *war* as a special focus and illustrative example.

Meanings as Variables: Two Approaches

Terms and concepts refer to semantic variables that can take multiple meanings. A traditional view constructs these variables in a hierarchical way, as nominal structured pattern variables with clearly defined boundaries and identities. An alternative formulation, developed here, considers terms and concepts as continuous variables.

NOMINAL VARIABLES — DISCRETE STRUCTURED PATTERNS

An array of terms and concepts includes other terms and concepts. Viewed in this light, terms and concepts are higher-order metavariables. They exist not only in their own right, but they also take other terms and concepts as referents.

One accepted definition of war (see Beer 1981a), for example, comprehends the following operational measures:

War_1
a. Legal international entities (states)
b. Formal declaration of war on other legal international entities (states)
c. Direct battle deaths > 1000

The War_{1abc} criteria define a possible world. Simple application of the criteria allows the construction of a historical database and the provision of answers to important political questions. Assuming the criteria of War_{1abc}, how much war has there been? What have been the major causes and consequences of war? How much war is there likely to be in the future? How can war best be reduced or fought more effectively?[1]

War_1 thus includes a complex of variables that can be operationalized. War_1 is, at the same time, itself a variable. The specification of War_1 includes some events, but it excludes others. War_1 does not include, for example, the following experiences, believed by many to be wars:

- *Civil wars*, for example the American War between the States, fall outside the operational definition.
- *Colonial struggles* for independence, no matter how long or bloody, also fail to exist under this definition. It would probably surprise the Algerians to realize that their long conflict with the French was not a war.
- *Diffuse, extended conflicts*, for example in the Middle East, also fail to qualify except for brief periods.

War_1 does not make these events disappear, but it makes them disappear as wars. It constructs a world of wars where such events simply become invisible, even though they might be visible in alternative possible worlds of War_{-1}.

A classificatory approach, similar to the Linnaean system used in biology or the table of elements in chemistry, solves this problem by the development of additional categories structured in hierarchical levels: multiple families, genera, and species nested within each other. War, as illustrated in table 1.1, includes the set $War_{1...n}$, each element of which includes its own subset of indicators that, in turn, arrange the elements of data.

TABLE I.I. WAR WORLDS

Indicators and Data

War$_1$
    Indicators
        Data

War$_2$
    Indicators
        Data

War$_n$
    Indicators
        Data

The different forms of war run the changes on their subordinate conditions. War$_2$, for example, might relax condition (a) but involve conditions (b) and (c) above, that is, include formally declared violence by entities other than states with direct battle deaths > 1000. War$_3$ might relax both conditions (a) and (b) but retain condition (c), thus including non-state violence not formally declared with direct battle deaths > 1000. War$_4$ might relax the third and final constraint (c) in the original definition, direct battle deaths > 1000. Wars involve indirect as well as direct casualties. The great wars of history have involved deaths by malnutrition and disease. These are not considered central in current scientific formulations. Yet these were precisely the factors that finally defeated Napoleon's invasion of Russia. They are essential aspects of modern atomic, bacteriological, and chemical warfare.

The three constraints show only the tip of the iceberg. As analysis proceeds, there are more serious problems. For example, there are no time constraints. This seems appropriate in the case of contemporary protracted conflicts like that in the Middle East. Some wars go on for a long time, and they should be included in a scientific analysis. At the same time, however, the war criteria as formulated do not require closure—ever. The Balkan War would fit under this category, possibly extending backward in history a millennium. An inclusive and sophisticated terminological field should, therefore, allow for multiple alternative temporal cut points.

The conceptual ground here is clearly treacherous. The arrangement of terms and concepts in a hierarchy of levels puts the analyst between a rock

---

and a hard place. On one hand, such a hierarchical ordering is necessary if we are simply to get on with the research job. We must decide what we mean by a war, specify it is clearly as we can, and finally bring the project to closure by measuring the phenomenon and relating it to other phenomena. In order to do this, we need hierarchical ordering and stable structure. Yet the order and the structure inevitably exclude many of the phenomena that we, or others, might appropriately believe ought to be considered. In order to include those, we broaden the typology. At this very moment, however, the clarity and stability earlier achieved begin to dissolve. Instead there is an explosion of terms, concepts, and data—a potential infinity of political realities.

Imagine the unlikely circumstance that we temporarily restrain our collective creativity and elaborate only the set $War_1 \ldots War_9$. We should now have not only nine combinations of war concepts and terms but also have nine different historical war databases. This expanded set is scientifically appropriate since it adds precision and clarity to the meaning of war. But it can also lead to confusion for our colleagues, the general public, and us. $War_1 \ldots War_9$ may be clearer, but war in general is more confused. The entire set of war—as opposed to the subsets—now refers only to the commonalities across all of the subsets. We are back where we started before we specified the subset of concepts and terms. This exercise in operationalization, like the mythical worm Ourobouros, finally ends by eating its own tail.

INTERVAL VARIABLES — CONTINUOUS CHANGE

These definitional difficulties become apparent as knowledge becomes more developed. At this later stage of evolution it is appropriate to elaborate a more complex understanding of the meanings of concepts and terms. This task is already well under way. Collier and Levitsky (1997) and Collier and Mahon (1993) discuss the contributions and problems of traditional taxonomic hierarchy and offer imaginative new formulations of "family resemblances" and "radial categories" to deal with conceptual "traveling" and "stretching." At this point, however, it seems to me that we are approaching in the conceptual domain the position in which we found ourselves at $War_{1 \ldots 9}$. The proliferation of concepts and terms ($CT_{1 \ldots 9}$) promises to create a new metavocabulary that can similarly overwhelm its referents.

As the subsets of concepts and terms—and of metaconcepts and metaterms—multiply, it may make some sense to think of them, or at least parts of them, as continuous rather than discrete. The meaning of a term like *war* is now shaped in the form of a metaphor that is less skeletal and more fluid.

In such a formulation, meaning (M) is partly determined by a constant. This constant is the core meaning, here given the symbol (0). Another major determinant of meaning is context (X). Context, in turn, includes cognitive (C), behavioral (B), and textual (T) dimensions. We have considered these dimensions earlier in our discussion of meaning. Cognition stands for an array of psychological states and processes. Behavior involves dimensions of human interaction usually associated with the social sciences. For example, political authority, economic incentives, social interaction, cultural interpretation, or body language all have influences on word meaning. Text includes the effects of anterior meaning shifters (A), nominal referents (N), microtext (I), and macrotext, including textual narrative or story (S).[2]

$$M = 0 * X$$
$$X = C * B * T$$
$$T = A * N * I * S$$

This formulation is consistent with preexisting general theory formulated by contextual linguists and general semanticists. Thus, Ruhl (1989, vii) "argue[s] that words [themselves] contribute much less to meaning than usually supposed; the apparent lexical meaning of a word includes in large part a contribution of contextual factors, both linguistic and extralinguistic" (cf. Quine 1960).

How does war look in this formulation? The constant (0) describes the basic meaning, distinguishing war from nonwar. It focuses on war as a broad covering term that includes all usages of the word—scientific and popular; actual and potential; past, present, and future. This is a wide enough tent to include all who might wish to enter. The other major determinant of meaning, context, modulates the kind of war being discussed at the moment.

Textual Modifiers

Text is an important element of context, including in turn four components: anterior meaning shifters, nominal referents, microtext, and macrotextual narrative.

ANTERIOR MEANING SHIFTERS

Much variance in meaning comes from juxtapositions, connections, and oppositions in specific practical contexts of discourse. Other words and nonverbal cues surrounding war serve as pointers to meaning, closing and stabilizing the intent of the speaker/writer and the understanding of the hearer/reader.

Among these other words are anterior meaning shifters, words that come immediately before war and modify it.[3] Anterior meaning shifters are like adjectives, but they are symbolically broader and richer. In the case of concrete nouns like *tree*, most of the meaning remains stable when other words are placed before it. Whatever tree may mean to any given individual, a brown tree and a green tree appear probably similar in most attributes, except for their color. This lexical stability is much less true for an abstract noun like war. When modified by preceding words, anterior meaning shifters, the sense of war can shift radically and dramatically.

Table 1.2 presents a very partial list of examples showing how war can be combined with anterior meaning shifters. War itself is the central term in each phrase. It sets whatever may be the outer boundaries of meaning; within these boundaries, the meaning of war is free to vary with its textual environment. The meaning of each of the phrases in table 1.2 is determined and directed primarily by its anterior meaning shifter, which combines with war to produce a specific, individual rhetorical effect. For example, a speaker referring to scientific war has something very different in mind than one who talks of political war.

The anterior meaning shifters index different families of meaning, helping us to switch between and enter into different possible worlds. Each phrase means something different to the special discourse community that serves as its primary audience. Together, the words form multiple clusters of meaning with war at their core. The common term *war* is the mathematical origin of the graph of meaning. Each anterior meaning shifter defines a separate dimension of this graph. We can think of war traveling along different axes in each dimension, depending on its combination with other words. Multiple associated words project war into multidimensional space (see Lakoff 1987).

NOMINAL REFERENTS

The anterior meaning shifters are much closer to the beginning than to the end of the war story.

War is defined in the history of its use in different communities. The meanings of war and other words vary across space—the external worlds of communities and the internal worlds of individuals. Meanings also vary across time, as crossword puzzles of different eras will attest. Munich meant something very different in 1935 than it did in 1940. Hiroshima meant something very different in 1940 than it did in 1950.

War's meaning can be more explicitly indexed in a given space-time context through spatio-temporal referents. The spatio-temporal matrix indexes war at multiple levels of decomposition, down to the level of individuals and perhaps

TABLE 1.2. WAR

Some Anterior Meaning Shifters

Academic War	Higher War	Phony War
Agonistic War	Holy War	Political War
Ancient War	Horizontal War	Postmodern War
Antiwar	Hyperwar	Professional War
Atavistic War	Hypermodern War	Practical War
Border War	Ideological War	Primitive War
Brutal War	Imaginary War	Procedural War
Bureaucratic War	Imperfect War	Propaganda War
Civil War	Imperial War	Proxy War
Clean War	Imperialistic War	Prudent War
Cold War	Impersonal War	Pure War
Colonial War	Imprudent War	Rational War
Communications War	Information War	Reasonable War
Computer War	Intentional War	Regional War
Constitutional War	Interstate War	Rhetorical War
Conventional War	Invalid War	Ritual War
Culture War	Issue War	Sacred War
Cyberwar	Judicial War	Scientific War
Deep War	Judicious War	Sectoral War
Democratic War	Just War	Semantic War
Darwinian War	Legal War	Shooting War
Defensive War	Legislative War	Soccer War
Democratic War	Light War	Space War
Diplomatic War	Limited War	Speaking War
Dirty War	Linguistic War	Splendid War
Drug War	Linkage War	Sports War
Dysfunctional War	Logical War	Structural War
Economic War	Logistic War	Suicidal War
Electronic War	Low-Intensity War	Superficial War
Environmental War	Major War	Systematic War
Evolutionary War	Mathematical War	Techno War
Executive War	Mercenary War	Technological War
Exponential War	Military War	Television War
Extended War	Modern War	Territorial War
Formal War	Monetary War	Thick War
Functional War	Moral War	Total War
Gang War	National War	Trade War
Gender War	Nationalistic War	Undemocratic War
General War	Natural War	Unjust War
Genocidal War	Neocortical War	Unlimited War
Geometrical War	Net War	Urban War
Guerrilla War	Nuclear War	Valid War
Heavy War	Offensive War	Vertical War
High-Intensity War	Perfect War	Video War
High-Modern War	Personal War	Virtual War
High-Tech War	Permanent War	World War

even moment by moment. Different meanings of political war and scientific war emerge, depending on who is involved and when. War can be described as

scientific war (United States, 1994).

This is hardly identical with

scientific war (France, 1812).

The meaning of war can be further defined in combination with proper names of canonical individuals. Examples of meaning specificity through nominal referents include

scientific war (Clausewitz)
scientific war (Singer).

The nominal referents index very different meanings and subtexts. What is meant in the first case is the systematic prosecution of war using general principles; in the second, the systematic study of war using quantitative measures and techniques. There are general similarities between the two, but also substantial differences. One does not necessarily imply the other.

MICROTEXT: WORDS AND PUNCTUATION

Up to this point, we have focused on the meaning of the word *war* by concentrating on the word itself. War also derives meaning from the massive cluster of associated phenomena. Small differences within a body of text, microtext, may create significant differences in what we understand in the context of a particular war, or of war in general. Some of these are obvious and within the bounds of normal discourse. Others are subtler. Compare six items concerning nuclear weapons:

1. President Bush drop[ped] nuclear weapons on the USSR.
2. President Bush [(said) that he drop(ped)] nuclear weapons on the USSR.
3. President Bush [(said) that he (would)] drop nuclear weapons on the USSR.
4. President Bush [(said) that he (might)] drop nuclear weapons on the USSR.

5. President Bush [(hinted) that he (might)] drop nuclear weapons on the USSR.
6. President Bush [! D]rop nuclear weapons on the USSR.

These six items seem successively weaker in the warlike messages that they convey. Yet the lexical differences are not very large. Item 1 differs from items 2–5 primarily through the later addition of a spacer consisting of the words "... that he ..." (see Fauconnier 1985). Items 2, 3, 4, and 5 basically vary from each other in only one word. Item 3 adds *would*. Item 4 changes *would* to *might*. Item 5 changes *said* to *hinted*. Item 6 is lexically the closest to, yet semantically the farthest from, Item 1. It differs only in an exclamation mark, a space, and a capital letter. Yet semantically it is perhaps the most different. It suggests a voice in the wilderness, calling on the president to perform an unnatural act. The patterns of ink, letters, and spaces are statistically very close, yet minute microtextual variance produces recognizable, disproportionate, quantum-type effects on meaning.

MACROTEXT — NARRATIVE

The meaning of war further depends on the larger body of macrotext, usually structured as the narrative or story that surrounds and frames it. Poets recorded the experience of war in earlier times. The *Odyssey*, the *Iliad*, and the *Chanson de Roland* are epics that have come down to us through history. The poetic form persisted through the nineteenth century, as in Stephen Crane's *Red Badge of Courage* and Alfred Lord Tennyson's *Charge of the Light Brigade*. In modern times, war has been recorded through diverse narrative forms, including biographies, novels, and journalism.

Narrative is important not just as a dimension of popular understanding but also in scientific research. To some extent, scientific analytic narrative replaces words with numbers. This creates an entirely different phenomenological reality, replacing the stories of novelists with those of accountants and bookkeepers, mathematicians and engineers. Most scientists would protest that they are engaged in a fundamentally different enterprise. At the same time, narrative remains an important component of scientific discourse, both as the framework for explicating numbers and technical symbols and also as a rich, though deeply repressed, subject for further research (Latour 1987).

An Experimental Example

A psychological laboratory experiment (Beer, Healy, Sinclair, and Bourne 1987) designed to investigate the individual dynamics of international conflict and cooperation illustrates interactions of text, action, and cognition. In this experiment, subjects were provided with a scenario modeled on the Falklands/ Malvinas crisis and one of two vignettes recalling either the trench slaughter of World War I or Allied weakness at Munich before World War II. A control group received no priming vignette. The subjects were then asked to choose from an inventory of possible cooperative-conflictual foreign policy acts in five sequential rounds. Both war vignettes produced more subsequent conflictual foreign policy act choices for subjects with dominant (i.e., aggressive) personality attributes and more cooperative choices for subjects with submissive personality attributes.

A second, follow-up study adapted and replicated the first experiment a year later in South Korea (Park 1988). One hundred South Korean college women were given English- and Korean-language versions of the original materials. The replication established the cross-cultural and cross-gender stability of the earlier U.S. results. In each case, the textual narrative or story in which war was embedded helped determine meaning and action for the subjects.

At the same time, the two studies suggest that text alone does not fully determine meaning. For example, textual understandings of experimenters and subjects may be incongruous. Subjects may see the same materials as being different. At the beginning of each experiment described above, all subjects read the same initial scenario, which the authors had modeled on the Falklands/ Malvinas crisis. Twenty-seven of the sixty subjects in the American experiment identified it as the experimenters intended. The results for these subjects were different than for those who did not recognize the situation. The vignettes only tended to activate underlying personality dispositions for those who did not recognize it. Priming of personality did not occur for those who clearly saw a representation of the Falklands/Malvinas crisis. For the group that did recognize the real-world referent of the experiment, there was little difference between high- and low-dominance groups in the cooperative-conflictual mix of actions that they finally chose. In the South Korean replication, thirty-two of the one hundred subjects also recognized the situation. As in the first case, such recognition suppressed personality effects for subjects who recognized the action scenario.

The striking difference between the two experiments lies in the fact that South Koreans who recognized the situation recalled a different case than

Americans. Instead of the Falklands/Malvinas, they believed that the experiment represented the situation of Tokdo, a small group of islands between Japan and Korea. South Korean recognition thus produced effects on other experimental variables similar to those of the original American experiment, but the cognitive referents were completely different. The same text, the scenario, stimulated the same response, recognition. But in different contexts, the same response had very different meanings—the Falklands/Malvinas or Tokdo. These meanings were revealed only through subsequent questions asking whether subjects recognized the scenario and what they recognized.

Subjects may also understand different materials as being the same. The experimenters had developed the two original World War I and World War II vignettes to prime the subjects about the costs of war and the costs of not going to war. Each vignette was supposed to convey a dramatically different message. The Korean adaptation added two new vignettes—the costs of the Korean War and the mistake of the Acheson line—to duplicate this distinction in a more familiar Korean context. In neither experiment did subjects seem to discriminate between the two types of messages. In both cases, students reacted to the priming vignettes in virtually identical ways. The main priming cue, the principal message that they seemed to receive, was war. The flavor, directionality, and difference of the war experience—the costs of action and inaction—did not significantly affect subjects. The message that the experimenters had intended to send was not received as the experimenters had intended to send it. Different texts stimulated similar responses; the two vignettes apparently primed equivalent psychological schemata. From this perspective, the alternative versions might be considered to be nondiscriminant and collapsed theoretically to one vignette.

From these results, it is evident that intended face meanings of different texts do not translate directly into cognitive schemata. Separate groups perceive texts in different ways. Authors and readers, Americans and South Koreans, understood both the introductory scenarios and the priming vignettes quite differently. The exact causes of these differential perceptions are not clear. For example, it is easy to believe that cultural factors determined whether individuals recognized the initial scenario as the Falklands/Malvinas or Tokdo. Nevertheless, two South Korean researchers adapted the original experiment for the South Korean context, and they did not make this connection. Furthermore, it is not immediately evident how two such apparently different vignettes could stimulate similar responses or what other kinds of vignettes might prime different schemata and give different results. The full dynamics of subtextuality, intertextuality, and supertextuality in our understanding of war remain to be explored.

The Utility of Continuous Meaning in Multiple Dimensions

Seeing the meaning of terms and concepts in a continuous way that is partly dependent on text has a number of significant implications. First, it points to an important aspect of scientific research, the arbitrary construction of the world through the specification of terms and concepts, and of the data that flow from them. It sensitizes scientific researchers to the complexity and openness of the world that the terms and concepts aspire to comprehend. Second, it points in new directions for research on meaning. Third, it suggests a multidimensional semantic space in which terms and concepts play continuously and simultaneously through multiple levels of discourse.

Terms and concepts construct the world in a variety of arbitrary ways. One of these involves the hierarchical structuring of reality into abstract forms or patterns that are matched against experience. Observations, and the conclusions drawn from them, are very much dependent on the addition or relaxation of general constraints.

Terms and concepts are used to construct data. In the case of war, a dedicated group of scholars has collected and refined an extensive body of data on wars over a long period of time. The data, are, however, very different from the phenomena from which they are derived. As was suggested earlier, time constraints are important dimensions of terms and concepts. Relaxation of conventional time constraints blurs identity-boundary issues. Wars that are usually defined separately need not be conceived as independent of each other. World Wars I and II are usually treated as separate wars, but many analysts have suggested that they were actually two separate segments of the same war. In the same way, wars are not independent of other phenomena to which they may be related. For example, crises may be defined in the framework of subsequent wars. If the war had not occurred, what preceded it might not have been defined as a crisis. The error may be compounded if we wish to examine the extent to which crises predict wars. Peace and war may also be conjointly defined and related with similar problems.

Wars do not necessarily have crisp dates on which they neatly begin and end. The same definitional problems surround war initiation and war termination. Dates of entry and exit are, to some extent, arbitrary markers of ill-defined points in the process; belligerents often slide slowly into and out of war (Beer and Mayer 1986).

The identity and stability of war actors are not stable. National names—Austria, China, France, Germany, Italy, Japan, Russia, Turkey, and United States—have meant very different things across time and space, even phonologically and orthographically. Under the names, little has remained absolutely constant.

Casualty statistics are fraught with dangers. The most defensible numbers are direct battle casualties, but the Vietnam experience clearly taught the distortion of body counts. Contemporary data archives may contain multiple estimates of battle casualties, but these estimates are not necessarily independent. A study of the genealogy of the data may trace their derivation back to the same earlier questionable source (Beer 1974). If direct battle casualties are problematic, indirect casualties are almost impossible. Famine and disease rival weapons, and in many cases supersede them, as causes of war-related death. Nevertheless, their relationship to war is not necessarily clear or stable, and the statistics are even more ephemeral. Even where there is general consensus on the statistics, statistical homogenization creates illusions of comparability. The same casualties may have very different meanings depending on different actors in different situations. The Korean and Vietnam conflicts had roughly the same casualty levels, but they were very different wars.

There is a mutual dependence between terms and concepts, on one hand, and data, on the other. Terms and concepts shape the data, which in turn help form our understanding of the meaning of terms and concepts. Structured terms, concepts, and data are cognitively congruent but imply a solidity that dissolves in real-world experience. A more continuous formulation of terms, concepts, and data allows a more fluid and dynamic view of experience. Continuous construction inhibits the reification of any one formulation of data and helps to liberate us from the powerful myth of absolute meaning.

A structured view of stable terms and concepts is part of the heritage of social science, won through the hard labor of primitive fact accumulation. A new metaphor of shifting terms and concepts—dynamic, continuous, partly dependent on text—supplements this legacy, putting it in a new and different intertextual light (see Der Derian and Shapiro 1989). Recognition of continuous variation in terms and concepts suggests, for example, an important linkage with work in artificial intelligence focusing on the technology of pattern recognition.[4] Continuous variation in surrounding text drives discontinuous structured pattern variables—the meanings of terms and concepts and their empirical referents: A constantly changing textual environment helps determine which meanings of terms and concepts are in play.

Psychological laboratory experiments define an additional direction for research on the continuous meaning of war. As was suggested earlier, such experiments have shown that priming with different textual narratives induces subjects to undertake different cooperative-conflictual behavior. Subjects understand wars, and texts about wars, in ways different from each other and from the experimenter. In this perspective, war moves from an objective to a subjective phenomenon. The exploration of the subjective understandings of war, and variations in that understanding, become rich fields for further exploration of reactions to terms and concepts (cf. Beer and Balleck 1994; Beer, Ringer, Healy, Sinclair and Bourne 1992).

Rhetorical analysis also promises advances in our understanding of the meaning of war. The congressional debates on the 1991 Persian Gulf War provide striking evidence of the importance of rhetoric as part of war behavior. Strategic discourse rationalized and justified the behavior of political elites. It was, moreover, an important precondition to hostilities. The speaking war preceded the shooting war. Work on continuous variation in meaning promises to illuminate behavior and strategy in the use of terms and concepts (cf. Beer and Balleck 1996; Beer and Hariman 1996; Bostdorff 1994; Nelson, Megill, and McCloskey 1987).

Multiplicity: Dimensions, Pluralisms, and Possibilities

An orientation toward terms and concepts as continuous variables partly dependent on text provides a different focus. It illuminates the subjective dimension of the objective world and encourages an objective view of the subjective world. Terms and concepts are decentered, disoriented from their familiar traditions and contexts.[5] They are separated from the myth of denotative meaning and the correspondence theory of reality; they begin to reapproach the world of dreams. Terms and concepts become more problematic, strange, alien. At the same time, terms and concepts become more applicable to new concerns and problems. They are connected at multiple levels, through different databases and meanings, to multiple new and different theoretical and practical uses.

In this formulation, terms and concepts do not have fixed fundamental meanings. They are, instead, part of the community of signs, embedded in multiple levels of discourse. Text is hypertext, and discussants shift easily between and within these levels. As they shift, the meanings of specific terms and concepts shift with them. Boundaries and identities form and dissolve, appear, disappear, and reappear in a world of pluralistic possibility. In this world, we evolve toward a more sophisticated, complex, and flexible understanding of the meaning of war—and peace.

2

Words of Reason

Rationality and Rhetoric

FRANCIS A. BEER

Much has been written about reason, but most of it has focused on the idea, the cognitive meaning of reason as a concept (e.g. Macintyre 1999; Feyerabend 1987; Hollis 1987; Simon 1983; Weizenbaum 1976; Habermas 1970; Foucault 1961).[1] There has been less analysis of the linguistic meaning of the word itself (see Toulmin 1986, 1958; Wavell 1986). To focus on the word implies a relatively specialized and technical interest—lexicography, semantics, rhetoric—and narrows the audience. Yet reason-the-word evokes and defines reason-the-concept. If we wish to understand the idea of reason, and its contemporary significance, we must, like the Gospel According to John, begin with the word.

A political focus on reason is self-evident. Reason-the-concept is a politically important *topos*. Reason is a part of great communities of government and discourse, dating from the time of historical civilizations, drawing on diverse springs of political philosophy and political usage. It is not too strong to state that reason is the foundation of modern politics and political science. As descendants of the Enlightenment and heirs of the utilitarians, we have inherited a well-developed model of rational decision. We construct ourselves politically as reasoning and reasonable men and women.

In political science at the end of the twentieth century, rational choice emerged as a dominant paradigm describing, explaining, and predicting political agency and action. Theorists such as Buchanan, Downs, Riker, and Tullock helped to found the political science empire of rational choice, and other scholars have followed them in different areas of political science (see

D. C. Mueller 1989). In my own field of study, international relations, an ancient tradition of "reason of state" preceded these developments. Reason of state is a discourse with the most hegemonic ambitions, the most privileged of meanings. Reason of state has long informed the traditional realist theory of international relations, exemplified by a wide range of theorists: Lao Tzu, Mencius, Thucydides, Machiavelli, Hobbes, Richelieu, Ranke, Meinecke, Friedrich von Ghent, Clausewitz, and many others (cf. Held 1989; Waltz 1979; Schnur 1975; Friedrich 1957). In a recent formulation, reason clearly means rational choice: "key (foreign policy) leaders are *expected utility maximizers* who estimate the welfare that will devolve on their state in the course of . . . disputes . . . [and] also . . . estimate the *utility* expected by their opponent in the dispute" (Bueno de Mesquita and Lalman 1986).

Reason and rationality figure prominently not only in formal political theory, but also practically in concrete political debate (cf. Beer and Boynton 1996; Boynton 1990; Raz 1990; Bratman 1987). Hearings on Cambodia conducted by a U.S. Senate subcommittee in 1990, for example, show former senator and secretary of state Edmund S. Muskie attempting to frame foreign policy as a rational, logical enterprise:

> Mr. MUSKIE. Well, I have difficulty in understanding the *rationale.* I think until the August meetings in Paris, my impression was that we considered Sihanouk an important part of any solution.
>
> And I do not think I would quarrel with that, at the time, or have any disagreement with it. That would seem to have required an agreement between Hun Sen and Sihanouk, that hopefully Sihanouk might be able to persuade the Khmer Rouge to agree to. It seemed sort of logical and *rational,* on the basis of what we have been for before (U.S. Senate 1990; emphasis added).

The following quotation from the U.S. congressional debate on military intervention in the Persian Gulf in 1991 also shows practical reason at work, although in a slightly different way:

> Mr. Jeff Bingaman (D-New Mexico). . . . Let me cite four *reasons* that I oppose the use of force at this time. First I believe that economic sanctions need more time to work. . . .
>
> A second *reason* that we should not resort to force at this time is that just as we need more time to see if sanctions will work, we also need more time to pursue a diplomatic resolution of the crisis. . . .

A third *reason* for us to stop short of a declaration of war at this time is the enormous loss of life that may well result if war begins.

The fourth *reason* that a declaration of war would be premature at this time is the potential cost of early military action to the stability of that region and to the U.S. role in that region. (U.S. Congress 1991; emphasis added).

The use of reason appears straightforward. Bingaman's reasons respond to the *why* question. Why does he oppose the use of force at this time? The answer is formed in terms of *because:* because of the following *reasons* ($R_{1...4}$). Interestingly, the reasons are framed in terms of the utilitarian benefit-cost calculus. The first two involve the economic and diplomatic benefits of delay. The second two suggest the military and political costs of premature action.

Meanings and Identities of Reason

The importance of reason-the-concept in the theory and practice of politics thus leads us to a closer examination of reason-the-word. The meaning of reason-the-word as defined by current political science and political practice appears simple, clear, and settled. The examples given above offer strong evidence of this. Yet if we look further, reason's definition becomes more complex and problematic. We think we know reason when we see it, using our common sense, our natural reason; but when we try to grasp it, reason dissolves like a cloud. As we shall see, reason has multiple dictionary definitions that are highly circular. Furthermore, reason has a variety of subtle alternative meanings that depend on different contexts. Reason ultimately is largely rhetorical and political, defined by individual speakers, with specific aims, for different audiences, in the context of overlapping political communities.

CIRCULARITY

The dictionary is an obvious place to begin the search for meaning, although it certainly does not reflect all the nuances of natural language. Dictionary definitions are privileged by tradition. In the dictionary stand formal, mainstream, conventional, "context-free, speaker-free, non-referential meanings, . . . what linguists call 'lexical meanings'" (Wavell 1986, 29–30; see also Robinson 1954).

Most words have a number of possible formal definitions. These definitions look separate but are actually interconnected. They are conjoint, intersecting, overlapping. Each word in the dictionary is defined in terms of the other words in the dictionary. Ultimately, all the words are defined in terms of each other. The definitions are circular; the area of the circle is measured by lexical space, the number of words in the dictionary.

Definitions may, nonetheless, vary in the visibility and directness of their circularity. Reason would probably score high on such a circularity measure; it is defined by a small subset of words identified largely in terms of themselves. This circularity is obscured in comprehensive compilations, like the *Oxford English Dictionary,* that provide many examples of usage, where reason is embedded in multiple contexts, many of which are obsolete or archaic. It emerges more clearly, however, in collections that are shorter and devoted primarily to functional modern use.

Such a source makes it clear that the words rational, rationalism, rationalist, and logic are commonly defined primarily in terms of themselves or reason. Reason, in turn, includes thirteen separate meanings, identified in table 2.1 by labels referring to their syntactic status: reason-as-noun (RN), reason-as-transitive-verb (RTV), and reason-as-intransitive-verb (RIV). Reason is most clearly circular in two of these definitions, RTV3 and RTV4, where reason is defined in terms of itself. Four definitions—RN6, RIV1, RIV2, and RTV1—define reason in terms of logic. The definitional circularity becomes even clearer as we press on. RN1 involves explanation and justification, which reduce to support with "reasons." RN2 includes cause and motive, which can again be translated back to "reasons." RN1 and RN2 were the meanings of political reason that Bingaman used in his speech on delaying military intervention in the Persian Gulf, quoted above. Reason, in this guise, asks the *why* question. Why are we doing or should we do *x?* It answers with reasons: *y* contains the reasons we are doing or should do *x*.

Action/Decision/Policy	because	Reasons$_{1 \ldots n}$
What	because	Why
x	because	*y*

The whole set of meanings under RN3 has a logical, or reasoning, component. Muskie referred to these in his remarks on U.S. policy toward Cambodia. RN4 and RN5 refer to a mind that is "sound" or "normal," in other words, capable of reasoning. The definitions under RN6 and RN7 refer to steps, components, or mechanics of reasoning.

In the dictionary, reason is significantly tautological, defined largely in terms of itself. Reason is also reflexive in usage. We can, or we believe we can, reason about reason. We are thus in a situation similar to that of the blind man pre-

TABLE 2.1. REASON

Definitions, Short List

Reason as Noun (RN1 . . . 7)

    RN1: an explanation or justification of an act, idea, etc.

    RN2: a cause; a motive.

    RN3: the ability to think, form judgments, draw conclusions, etc.

    RN4: sound thought or judgment; good sense.

    RN5: normal mental powers; a sound mind; sanity.

    RN6: in logic, one of the premises of an argument, especially the minor.

    RN7: ratio; relation between quantities; proportion.

Reason as Intransitive Verb (RIV1, 2)

    RIV1: to think coherently and logically; to draw inferences and conclusions from facts known or assumed.

    RIV2: to argue or talk in a logical way.

Reason as Transitive Verb (RTV1 . . . 4)

    RTV1: to analyze; to think logically about; to think out systematically.

    RTV2: to argue; to discuss.

    RTV3: to support, justify, etc. with reasons.

    RTV4: to persuade or bring by reasoning.

Source: McKechnie (1979, 1502).

---

sented for the first time with an orange that he has never seen. If we did not already have an idea in our minds of what the orange looked like, the verbal definitions would be of little help in describing its color. As Toulmin says, "the 'reasons' which could logically be given in support of any statement formed a finite chain. In every case, a point was reached beyond which it was no longer possible to give 'reasons' of the kind given until then; and eventually there came a stage beyond which it seemed that no 'reason' of any kind could be given" (1986, 202).

Reason initially seemed clear in its relationship to modern politics and political science. Nevertheless, the use of reason to analyze reason reveals multiple circular definitions that fragment and obscure reason's apparently simple common sense meaning.

Polysemy, the existence of multiple meanings for the same word, is hardly news to linguists and rhetoricians. As John Nelson (1987, 418) has noted in another context, every discourse includes major "variance in the meaning of key terms." The more important the concept or word, the greater may be such variance. Words, densely packed with meanings, accreted and combined over centuries, are sent down to us as part of our present heritage. When we receive the words, however, they do not come with a set of instructions. There is no comprehensive inventory of meanings, no directory of ways to use them.

Coming from the dictionary, we know only a bit more than we did before we went there. From this source, it appears that reason's core is simultaneously poly- and amorphous, variable and shapeless. This core, however, helps to provide strength and flexibility. Without a narrow sense of its own to limit its users, reason easily adapts to the shape and color of its surrounding symbolic environment. A good part of reason's meaning is specified extrinsically, through contextual binding and blending (Ruhl 1989). Reason has multiple possible meanings depending on other words whose company it keeps. In combination with other words, reason can assume a dazzling variety: indeterminate by itself, pluralistic in combination. This dynamic becomes clearer when we examine in more detail reason's implicit roots, anterior meaning shifters, and nominal referents.

Implicit Roots. Deeper levels of meaning, finer shadings and nuances, ultimately reside outside the domain of the dictionary. Some of reason's context is implicit and invisible in the form of past origins and associations. Historical roots are a good example of this. Table 2.1 suggests that there are two major historical roots of the complex of words associated with reason: the Latin *ratio* and the Greek *logos*. Ratio—the root of rational, rationalism, and rationalist—is defined in a relatively narrowly numerical sense of reckoning. Ratio evokes arithmetic and algebra, calculation and computing, bookkeeping and accounting, business and economics. Compare this with logos, the root of logic. It is literally translated as speech, but has much broader and deeper connotations. Arendt (1971, 144) reminds us that logos "for the Greeks (was) not just speech but the gift of reasoned argument that distinguished them from barbarians" (cf. Desjardins 1990). Today, logos evokes rich harmonics from history, theology, philosophy, and religion.

These intrinsic historical roots are not available in equal degree to all discussants, yet they form an invisible context that can shape meanings and understandings for those attuned to them. These implicit roots sometimes slide or blend into reason, as in the following passage, which moves in subtle metaphor from the arithmetic of ratio to the words of logos:

(1) When a man Reasoneth, hee does nothing else but conceive a summe totall, from Addition of parcels; or conceive a Remainder, from Substraction of one summe from another:

(2) which (if it be done by Words,) is conceiving of the consequence of the names of all the parts, to the name of the whole; or from the names of the whole and one part, to the name of the other part. (Hobbes 1986, 110; cf. Johnston 1986)

As Wittgenstein tells us about language, the decisive move in the conjuring trick has been accomplished with very few of us the wiser.

In the same way, sophisticated modern discussants may use contemporary branches of reason to evoke or elide very subtle differences. To say that a person is rational is not quite the same as saying that a person is logical, and a person exercising rational choice can be distinguished from a rationalist or a person who thinks logically.

Anterior Meaning Shifters. As we observed in chapter 1, much variance in word meaning comes not from nuances in the historical and customary usage, but rather from juxtapositions, connections, and oppositions in specific practical contexts of discourse. Other words and nonverbal cues surrounding reason serve as pointers to meaning, closing and stabilizing the intent of the speaker/writer and the understanding of the hearer/reader. Among these other words are anterior meaning shifters, words that come before reason-the-word and modify it.

The partial list of examples in table 2.2 shows how reason can be combined with anterior meaning shifters.

Nominal Referents. Anterior meaning shifters, as we saw earlier, are closer to the beginning than to the end of reason's story. Reason is further defined in the history of its use in different times and places. Reason's meaning can be more explicitly described in a given context through spatio-temporal referents. Different meanings of political reason and scientific reason emerge depending on who is involved and when. Reason, as used in the theoretical and practical examples at the beginning of this chapter, can be described as

TABLE 2.2. REASON

Some Anterior Meaning Shifters

Adductive Reason	Inductive Reason
Authoritative Reason	Instrumental Reason
Behavioral Reason	Intrinsic Reason
Bounded Reason	Judicial Reason
Bureaucratic Reason	Legal Reason
Case-Based Reason	Legislative Reason
Celestial Reason	Logical Reason
Commonsense Reason	Mathematical Reason
Computational Reason	Military Reason
Constructive Reason	Model-Based Reason
Contractual Reason	Moral Reason
Critical Reason	Natural Reason
Deconstructive Reason	Nonmonotonic Reason
Deductive Reason	Pluralistic Reason
Democratic Reason	Passionate Reason
Dependent Reason	Political Reason
Dialectical Reason	Practical Reason
Diplomatic Reason	Procedural Reason
Discursive Reason	Pure Reason
Divine Reason	Ritual Reason
Executive Reason	Rule-Based Reason
Formal Reason	Scientific Reason
Geometrical Reason	Situational Reason
Hermeneutic Reason	Sophomoric Reason
Hierarchical Reason	Structural Reason
Higher Reason	Substantive Reason
Independent Reason	Sufficient Reason

scientific reason (United States, Political Science, 1990)

political reason (U.S. Congress, 1990)

These are hardly identical with

scientific reason (Mexico, 1640)

political reason (Athenian Senate, 540 B.C.)

Reason can, moreover, be defined in combination with proper names of canonical individuals. The names of the individuals listed below come from academic communities. They serve as another shorthand to locate reason extrinsically, in the invisible college. Reason, so circumscribed, still calls forth alternative ontological worlds, for example: divine reason, Saint Augustine; sufficient reason, Aquinas; instrumental reason, Machiavelli or Bentham; pure reason, Descartes; moral reason, Kant; formal reason, Frege and Russell; geometrical reason, Euclid; scientific reason, Newton and Einstein; logical reason, Boole; dialectical reason, Socrates, Hegel, and Marx; behavioral reason, Skinner; ritual reason Lévi-Strauss; structural reason, Parsons and Chomsky; bounded reason, Simon; deconstructive reason, Nietzsche, Foucault, and Derrida. On one hand, these referents seem self-evident. On the other hand, they make a difference. We can clearly change reason's identity by varying associations. The celestial reason of Copernicus, the geometric reason of Riemann, the scientific reason of Lakatos, Kuhn, or Feyerabend differ from the brands offered by their cousins.

Textual Narrative. Reason's meaning is further refined when it is embedded in more extensive textual context, when reason is set in a discursive, narrative form. If space here permitted, reason could appear as a character in short stories further directing situational understandings of what reason means in a specific situation, reason's specific identity.

Political Reason and Strategic Rhetoric

The argument presented here has drawn a good deal of strength from the tradition of scientific reason. It began by presenting some examples of the phenomenon to be discussed: reason. It defined the meaning of reason as the dependent variable, searching for operationalization in authoritative literature, in this case the dictionary. The next step was to specify key variables that would determine variance in meaning. Narrowing further, it isolated textual context as a critical independent variable. Key components of textual context were anterior meaning shifters, nominal referents, and textual narrative. As in the case of war, the result could be shaped in the form of an equation. The meaning of reason-the-word, the dependent variable in this equation, is partly determined by its core meaning, a constant term, and context, an independent variable term. Context includes cognitive, behavioral, and textual dimensions, which in turn include the effects of anterior meaning shifters, nominal referents, and textual narrative or story. The meaning of reason in use varies continuously. It can, however, be constructed as a context-switched item (see also Lehrer and Kittay 1992).

What does this argument imply for political science and politics? The answer lies in the political uses to which a word such as reason may be put. In spite of the close connection between reason and politics, and increasing convergence on rational choice as the model for political decision and political science, the meaning of reason is neither clear nor stable. Reason is a strategically critical political rhetorical trope. It can take on many different turns and colorations, meaning different things to different speakers and audiences at different times and places. I should not wish to go so far as Toulmin and suggest, as he does for philosophical ethics, that reason "as used politically—looks very like pure persuasion" (1986, 199). Nevertheless, in its various guises, reason can be a powerful influence, playing upon and shaping thoughts and sentiments (see Brown 1987). In a nutshell, political actors and political scientists use reason-the-word rhetorically, as an important part of political discourse. Political subjects define and use reason strategically in a political context. A famous example is Pres. Lyndon Johnson's famous standing invitation to his colleagues that they come and reason together.

The political rhetoric of reason builds upon the multiple meanings of reason, which gives the rhetoric an extraordinary power and versatility. We have seen that it is possible to consider reason as an objective sign, but it is not a sign with a single signification. Reason is a variable sign that contains virtually infinite sets of possible values, possible worlds (Korzybski 1980). Reason has no single, necessary, simple, determinate meaning. Reason draws from different traditions. The various possible meanings of reason entail very different presuppositions, assumptions, implications, and consequences. We may think of these as subtexts of reason that help define the richness and complexity of political life. They imply connotative networks with deep historical and cultural roots, distinct possible and probable worlds in which reason is contextually embedded. At any given moment, the meaning of reason is open, indeterminate. Reason is polymorphous, taking many possible shapes, varying across space and time, between communities and individuals, a pointer referring to other realities and then falling back again upon and into itself. Reason is joined with other words and cues creating interlocking networks of virtually infinite sets. The infinity of possible verbal meanings leaves us with pluralistic variability, a combinatorial explosion of language, speech, and discourse.

Reason also points to variable subjective realities. Political communities share a common global discourse, which coordinates these subjective realities. Yet local, individual, physio-mental states differ across subjects. The values of reason are identical with neither the individual mental states nor canonical representations of them; the states are not transparent through words. As contemporary cognitive psychology and literary theory remind us, writers or speakers may use different words to refer to similar subjective states or the same words to denote dissimilar ones.

Reason-the-word thus refers simultaneously both to the virtually infinite objective possibilities of a common, collectively constructed concept and to the infinite subjective realities that it can evoke. Reason-the-word is a verbal stimulus that produces multidimensional behavioral responses. Reason is also a response to external stimuli. This response occurs in verbal form. It also occurs in terms of the behavior to which the word ostensibly alludes.

In a more intentional, Heideggerian sense, reason-the-word is a multivalued tool or a resource at hand for use in the practical tasks of daily political life. Reason thus construed is part of the politics of technology. Actors use reason rhetorically, as potters use a shaping tool, to mold material, to create a certain shape, to progress toward their public and private ends. Political actors move each other in various ways, including the symbolic politics of oral and written conversations, arguments, debates, publicity, publication, and propaganda. We join reason with other resources at hand for our political purposes, narrowing and defining reason in the specific context of our actual discourse. We instantiate, limit, and constrain reason—give reason specific meaning—in the particular political context in which we use it. We deploy and manipulate reason to create a collective political world, or to call forth different worlds, out of a plethora of possible worlds. We use reason politically to shape ourselves and each other. Our shaping moves us from the amorphous, vertiginous world of infinite political possibilities and options through probabilistic judgment to a more clearly delineated, actualized, real political world. The discourse of reason, as it appears here and now, helps to construct this specific political world. As we create this world, we draw on the multiple dimensions of reason. In spite of its infinite possibilities, at any given point of space/time, reason is finite. Reason is instantiated, given specific content, by other words and cues that surround it in particular situations and contexts. Reason is concretely bound by particular actors in a specific discourse that sets limits on possibility, that constrains, that forces an amorphous reality into a specific, defined shape. Reason, as it is actually used, excludes most possible political worlds and points to specific probable political worlds that are definable, describable, in terms of other objective referents.

Political reason thus both includes and excludes the chaos of infinite possibility, the abyss of shapelessness and meaninglessness. It provides us with and helps us escape from fluctuation between possible worlds, from oscillation and instability into equilibrium. We use reason-the-word, consciously or unconsciously, to achieve normative results. Our political usage creates a relatively determinate order out of amorphous/polymorphous indeterminacy. From anarchy we create an actualized, real world—a world in which reason offers a complex manifold of comprehension. We give reason meaning in particular situations and contexts, and we use reason to create and shape our collective and individual worlds. Nevertheless, reason retains the full resonance of its many possible disparate chords. Invisible and inaudible, the hidden portions of iceberg reason—the denied, repressed reasons—silently wait.

The multiple meanings and identities, associations and connections, of reason give reason its power and strength. Different reasons stimulate different psychological schemata or nodes, connecting who we are with what we want. The manifest power of reason is measured by the reactions and consequences it produces. The latent power of reason is measured by the reactions and consequences that it could produce.

The rational rhetor carries the possible meanings of reason as part of his or her strategic discursive arsenal. Persuading others to accept reason, he or she induces them to accept a worldview—a world of meaning. This worldview is legitimated by use of the general symbolic and cathectic aura of reason-as-a-whole. But it is actualized as a very limited worldview of reason-in-part, restricted to the specific meaning settled for reason in the particular context.

Reason of State

Reason of state, mentioned at the beginning of this chapter, provides an example of the way in which reason is used as strategic rhetoric. The contemporary form taken by reason of state is the realist theory of international relations. Realism assumes that national interest, defined in terms of power, is the precious metal that backs the hard currency of international relations. Statesmen play the game of nations, roll the iron dice of war or make strategic peace based on the comparative calculation of benefits and costs to the national interest. Embedded in realism is contemporary strategic doctrine, developed and expounded in the early years of the atomic era and the Cold War by theorists like Bernard Brodie, Lawrence Freedman, Herman Kahn, Thomas Schelling, Glenn Snyder, William Kaufmann, and Albert Wohlstetter.

STRONG REASON OF STATE

The argument of reason of state is simple and noncontroversial, perhaps only because the history of international relations has so accustomed us to it. Critical rhetorical analysis might code the following axioms or propositions as moves that construct the privilege of reason of state. Reason, thus interpreted, shifts imperceptibly from *is* to *ought*.

The first and second steps include a core premise and an easy identity:

1. Reason is determinate.
2. Reason is reasonable.

These steps simultaneously make and hide the critical move from the empirical to the normative.

The third and fourth premises are identities that make the normative move explicit:

3. Reason is good.
4. Being reasonable is good.

The next steps involve the simple substitution of argument for reason in steps 2 and 3:

5. The argument is reasonable.
6. The argument is good.

In this process we have taken three apparently value-free terms—reason, reasonable, and argument—and have endowed them with explicit normative characteristics. The logic is simple, yet it is ordinarily obscured. We usually think of reason and argument as empirical, not normative. Yet they must have a substantial normative component or the game would not be worth playing.

The crucial normative machinery is now in place. The next moves, privileging policies resulting from reason of state, naturally follow. Among other things, these moves justify war in general and specific wars of various kinds. Reason imperceptibly leads us both to support those wars and actively to participate in their planning, justification, and prosecution. The good of reason includes the good of its potential policy consequences. Thus,

7. Reason sometimes means war.

The consequent shares the empirical and normative characteristics of the cause:

8. War is sometimes reasonable.
9. War is sometimes necessary or good.

These few moves take us from the abstract analysis of political argument through high foreign policy into and beyond the most critical issues of modern human existence. This is so because

10. War includes nuclear war.
11. Nuclear war is sometimes reasonable.
12. Nuclear war is sometimes necessary or good.

The rhetoric of reason has subtly shaped, defined, and developed our cognitive orientation. We may have come to accept activities that on other bases we might simply have rejected out of hand, for example, the bombings of Hiroshima and Nagasaki in 1945 and the Indian government's nuclear testing in 1998. We have done so on the basis of reason.

WEAK REASON OF STATE

Scientific reason suggests that the meaning of reason itself is largely indeterminate. Critical reason shows that this indeterminacy can be used for major rhetorical effect. Reason emerges from this analysis as lighter, less compelling, less persuasive. The hold of authoritative reason weakens. The view of instrumental reason, that human beings and nation-states are necessarily selfish and brutal, now appears as one view—but only one view—of political reason and of political reality. Such a view may be the result of scientific reason with appropriate nominal and spatio-temporal subscripts. Nevertheless, the heaping of reason upon reason is not sufficient to endow the argument with exclusive privilege or incontrovertible plausibility. The maze goes to its end, but it is not necessary to run it.

We fashion ourselves by the ideas that we accept. To take a particular meaning of reason uncritically and exclusively is to construct a world on that basis—to construct ourselves in that world, actually to become that form of reason. We begin to make a slightly different world with the alternative proposition that

1. Reason is indeterminate.

In this gentler case,

2. Reason may or may not be reasonable.

3. Reason may or may not be good.
4. Being reasonable may or may not be good.

Reason may now be evaluated by a number of criteria, including normative criteria in a specific context. Thus,

5. The argument may or may not be reasonable.
6. The argument may or may not be good.

A less powerful reason permits less compelling outcomes. We loosen the rhetorical bonds joining reason and war, or reason with any other specific policy. Reason in this form does not necessarily change attitudes or drive policy. A more indeterminate reason yields a more indeterminate politics:

7. Reason may or may not mean war.

We judge reason in part by the consequences to which it would drive us:

8. War may or may not be reasonable.
9. War may or may not be necessary or even good.
10. War includes nuclear war.
11. Nuclear war may or may not be reasonable.
12. Nuclear war may or may not be necessary or good.

This second formulation is softer, more problematic. It lays the political world open to greater doubt; it discourages the political actor from certainty. Less certainty means less arrogance, the greater caution and prudence suggested by bounded reason. Where the political stakes are very high, the sacrifice of potential incremental benefits may be a lesser evil than incurring catastrophic costs.

Pluralistic Reason

A kinder, gentler reason is like a bouquet of flowers. The ribbon that ties the bouquet together says "reason." Yet each flower, each kind of reason, has its own identity and fragrance. We perceive the bouquet through our senses. We "see reason," we "feel reasonable," we may even smell or taste "sweet reason." Beyond our senses, the symbolic meanings of the bouquet itself, and of the flowers within it, are mainly in the multiple contexts where they are a part of human relations.

What is the meaning of the bouquet of pluralistic reason in the contexts of politics and political science? First, authoritative reason is power. The power of reason is power over nature and power over human beings. Reason implies command, control, and compliance. Ultimately, the authority of reason is believed to be backed by the force of law: natural law, scientific law, political law. In this context of power, force, and law, pluralistic reason implies greater flexibility and recognition of variety. There may be many kinds and branches of reason-in-part that may be applied differently to individual cases. A more sophisticated reason recognizes the modesty and limits of bounded reason. At the same time, it combines many different bounded reasons to produce a more complex, differentiated, articulated, and powerful concept of reason-as-a-whole.

Second, pluralistic reason is meaningful in a secular, democratic context. The monotheistic "God Reason" is dethroned. Pluralistic reason is foremost contested reason, always open to challenge by other claims. There is no final meaning. Pluralistic reason implies competition between multiple alternative assumptions and arguments, reasons and rationalizations. The form and substance of reason remain fully negotiable. Pluralistic reason is always open to persuasion.

Third, pluralistic reason fits very well in a rapidly changing, multicultural, contemporary system of international politics. Recognizing variety may have an instrumental benefit. To return once more to international relations, Nye (1990) has suggested that soft, virtual, normative power may be stronger than hard, physical, military power in today's world. Soft power, moreover, may be particularly appropriate for a state like the United States with its long democratic tradition. The many possible varieties of reason may actually correspond empirically with mind-sets of different transnational, national, and subnational communities (cf. Shafer and Pearl 1990; Stich 1990; Haas 1990; Bruner 1986). Different cognitive styles may be appropriate for different communities and individuals with different traditions, means, and goals. Pluralistic reason recognizes the empirical and normative force of such global cultural diversity.

There may be situations where strong reason of state is appropriate to different polities as a means of responding to perceived radical evil. Yet a pluralistic conception of reason allows the recognition of alternative ways of thinking. It has the great virtue of protecting dissent at home and abroad, of encouraging diplomatic discourse. Democratic systems are based on the idea that the benefits of dissent and discourse usually outweigh their costs.

It is not always popular to widen the community of discourse. Pluralistic reason is not always convenient. It implies possible threats to political identity, security, motivation, and action. Pluralistic reason can include those dispossessed by conformist thinking, the return of the conventionally unreasonable. Conventional reason is defined not only by what it is, but also by what it is not. In classical times, reason was opposed to traditional Greek and Roman religious beliefs. Similarly, during the medieval period, reason was a reaction to religious dogmatism. Reason has also traditionally stood in opposition to emotion: the rigor of logos contrasted with the feeling of pathos. Conventional reason constructs a particular kind of person, defined not only by what he or she is but also by what he or she is not. He or she is, in particular, not guided primarily by either faith or emotion. Acceptable reasons, answers to the *why* question, are not supposed to include intuition or "trust me."

The choice between the rational and the irrational may appear to be clear. Yet there are circumstances where the apparently irrational has a rational interpretation, awaiting only the proper construction. Furthermore, the long historical belief in reason itself has relied heavily on the passion for truth and the faith in human potential. Finally, emotional styles may be forms of reason that also deserve attention and make a contribution. As Pascal told us long ago and Jane Mansbridge (1990) suggests today, the heart has its reasons that reason does not know.

Pluralistic reason finally makes possible a higher transcendental move. The German philosopher Karl Jaspers suggests the power that realist reason can have in defining our political reality: "Reason is . . . said to show in politics as political realism. We have the nature of average human qualities; we have men, with their impulses, their aggressiveness, fear, and cowardice, their love of adventure, their need for security, their untruthfulness; we have the necessities of the sociological situation. To act successfully, we must know the realities and reckon with them. Reason, we are told, is nothing but realism" (Jaspers 1958, 249).

Yet realist reason is only one story among many. Reason can, as we have seen, mean more than one thing. We may accept the rhetoric of one kind of reason as realism, or we may use a different rhetoric of better, higher uses for reason: "Reason lies in the apperception of our environment, in constructive work, in earning for time and posterity, in peaceful competition, in the vision of beauty, in the contemplation of truth, in the fulfillment of one's destiny" (Jaspers 1958, 218–19).

Are there alternatives to reason? Probably not now, but there are always alternative reasons. Only by exploring and understanding these can we hope to understand what reason has meant, means, and might ultimately come to mean in itself. Such exploration is also essential for understanding the meaning of war and peace.

3

Validities

Scientific and Political Realities

FRANCIS A. BEER

Postmodern, postpositivist discourse has focused on "the movement from confidence to skepticism about standard foundations, methods, and rational criteria of evaluation" (Bernstein 1985, 3).[1] Two topics are central to this conversation. The first of these is reason, which we have just considered. This is the logical term of logical positivism. The second topic is the positive or empirical term—validity.

Our understanding of war and peace depends importantly on the meaning of these two terms. As we have seen in the case of reason, this meaning is unstable, and the instability can be used strategically, in rhetorically powerful ways, to affect the formulation of war and peace policies. As we shall now observe, similar indeterminacies affect validity, the bedrock of what we take to be fundamental empirical truths about war and peace.

Validity is the fulcrum on which positivist method rests, the connection between the work of political science and the world of politics. Validity sums up the ambitions of positive political science for faithful correspondence with reality. Validity is also critically important for philosophical concern with truth conditions and a representational theory of meaning.

Professional political science and other social and applied sciences have long been concerned with validity. Textbooks on method contain a section discussing validity; specialized books and journal articles in many countries and disciplines center on it. Validity is divided into multiple different categories or types denoted by the same kind of anterior meaning shifters that we have considered in other chapters—for example, internal validity, external validity, ecological validity, population validity, situation validity, construct validity, measurement validity, variable validity, outcome validity, conclusion validity, cultural validity, and interpretive validity. Professional consideration is given to factors "jeopardizing" validity, "threats" to validity, sources of "bias," or factors that "confound" or "contaminate" experimental and nonexperimental research (cf. Leichsenring 1985; Andrews 1984; Calder and Phillips 1983; Calder, Phillips, and Tybout 1982; Mook 1983; Cook and Campbell 1979; Carmines and Zeller 1979).

Experimental Validity

Problems of validity are perhaps clearest in experimental research. It is hardly news that there is a striking gap between a sample of experimental subjects and the universe of real political actors. The well known "college sophomore problem" centers on heteromorphism between the undergraduate subjects that are often the subjects of experiments and the non-undergraduate world that they supposedly represent (Greenberg 1987; Gordon, Slade, and Schmitt 1987, 1986; Sears 1986). The unrepresentative sample is, however, only one of many difficulties. As those who work in the laboratory, including me, are well aware, other experimental flaws are equally serious and more complex. These include contextual, textual, and analytical effects.

CONTEXT

The context of any experiment is vastly different from the context of life as it is usually lived (cf. Rosnow and Georgoudi 1986). In many psychological experiments, this disparity may appear to be of marginal relevance. For example, rapid eye movements in reading tasks may seem to be relatively unaffected by their surroundings. Nevertheless, even this trivial stability is less clear than we might expect. Research suggests that general stress may adversely affect eye functioning. The experimental subject does not appear at the laboratory wrapped in cellophane. He or she exists in a specific space/time context, which is the frame for a particular mental and physical state. The larger political context may be particularly relevant for political research. For example, English-language versions of questionnaires administered abroad have the potential to activate anti-American attitudes. These attitudes vary in different countries and according to current political conditions.

The subject also exists within the controlled discourse of the immediate testing context. The simple act of observation—as the Hawthorne experiments and Heisenberg's uncertainty principle have suggested—may change the observed and create a qualitatively different situation. Observation changes the configuration of reality, although in ways that may not be immediately visible if we are not looking for these particular effects or do not yet have the instruments with which to measure them. Observation may take different forms depending on the proximity, evidence, and interaction of the observer. Participant observation and hidden observation mark the opposite poles of these observational dimensions. Subjects may react to observation in different and unexpected ways. Furthermore, subjects may be sensitive not only to the present but also to the past and future. Prior testing experiences are stored in memory. Information about future testing changes subject expectations and perhaps strategies.

Research on subject reactivity suggests that the experimental environment contains crucial semiotic cues that may activate predispositions. There are administration effects resulting from interaction with the tester. Subjects respond to verbal and behavioral hints, the language and voice modulation of instruction, and responses to questions. Body language—a laugh or a frown, for example—can change the meaning of instructions. Subjects generally try to give the researcher what they think he or she wants. Depending on the experiment, even such apparently irrelevant attributes as the age, gender, ethnicity, or even clothing of the experimenter provide pointers to attitudes and possible desirable responses. The temperature or lighting of the room may subtly influence subjects' orientation to the experimental materials (Harris and Lahey 1982; Haynes and Horn 1982).

The mode of the experiment may also be an important variable. Paper and pencil tests may give different results than computer modes (Lee, Moreno, and Sympson 1986). The equivalence between such instruments and others such as video simulations and various internal and external physiological monitors involved in lie detector technology—measuring temperature, brain waves, heart rate, galvanic skin response, hormones—is unclear. Time and place may also include important variables. A long interview may induce fatigue or boredom (Herzog and Bachman 1981). The season or time of day may affect attention and orientation.

CORE TEXT

Many experiments, particularly psychological ones, rely on textual material. Experimental text may be divided into core and peripheral text. The core text consists of those written questions or items on which subjects are asked to focus their immediate attention and to which subjects are asked to respond. The meaning of such text is stable, but only to a degree.

Much experimental procedure is based on an objectivist theory of language in which words of the text are supposed to have definite, determinate meanings. This theory corresponds with the common sense notion that words are independent and transparent. Words have meanings that are reliably denoted in terms of a correspondent reality. Words are the building blocks of questionnaire items. The items also have face validity, explicit meanings that are self-contained, invariant across experimenters and subjects.

This view is strongly influenced by direct experience with other speakers, use of dictionaries and thesauruses, and, in some cases, language training. If the words do not have an essential foundation of meaning, they are, nevertheless, stabilized through convention and in ordinary usage so that intersubjective communication occurs. This stability permits conformity between the intention of the user and the understanding of the receiver (see Ruhl 1989).

An objectivist theory of language is consistent with the notion that small variations in words of text can produce significant differences in meaning. As we have seen, some of these differences are obvious and within the bounds of normal discourse; others are more subtle.

The indeterminacy of text goes beyond the amount of care and attention paid by researchers and subjects. As the dictionary suggests, many words have more than one possible meaning. The reader of the text must decode the text, at least to the extent of decoding the word on the page into the appropriate possible meaning. Yet not all dictionary meanings may be equally accessible to all the actors, especially in a society of multicultural diversity. Furthermore, in an experimental situation, extended oral discourse is not possible to negotiate specific, determinate meaning at each step of the way.

The dictionary partly reflects the meanings of words, but it cannot provide a fully determinate solution. As we have suggested previously, dictionaries are circular. Each word is defined in terms of other words; and the other words, in turn, are defined in terms of each other. At the end of the equation, all words are defined in terms of all other words; the words define themselves in a closed system.

When we look outside the words, we are again caught in a tautology. External reality cannot provide completely determinate meanings for words. Words are defined by nonverbal aspects of reality. Yet words are also a part of reality and help to create other parts. Reality is as the words describe it if, and only if, we accept the words as accurately describing that reality.

Words are defined by nonverbal life experiences and associated naming. Some aspects of these experiences are collectively shared. Words are, at least in part, the result of our common history and customs. They carry with them a heavy freight of collective historical usage and association. Yet they are experienced, to some extent, individually. The experiences are stored and connected within the individual's partly private lexicon. They are interpreted in the idiosyncratic context of the individual's personal biography and circumstance, intention and perception.

The typographical configuration of the text itself—letters, words, spaces, punctuation, sentences, paragraphs, pages—exerts independent semantic priming effects on subjects. Syntax can also be important. Work in survey research has shown that open or closed questions, affirmative or negative expression, can activate preexisting response sets in subjects or elicit nonattitudes (Schuman and Scott 1987; Brody 1986; Schuman, Ludwig, and Krosnick 1986; Norpoth and Lodge 1985; Bishop, Oldendick, and Tuchfarber 1984; Taylor 1983). A panoply of related effects—consistency, framing, proximity—suggests that this is just the tip of the iceberg (Fleishman 1988; Jackson and Jacobs 1983; Schuman and Ludwig 1983; Kahneman, Slovic, and Tversky 1982; Sudman and Bradburn 1974).

As Edelman (1988b, 1336 and 1988a) suggests, "belief in the objectivity of a form of language is a lethal pitfall for researchers." A more sophisticated interpretation of meaning—derived from the work of writers like Wittgenstein, Saussure, Foucault, and Derrida—suggests that each word is a node within a complex, interrelated network of signifiers and signifieds.[2] Words appear to exist discretely, following in serial sequences, separated from each other on the page by blank spaces. But language is deep. Words are multidimensional—densely interconnected in linguistic systems, embedded in culture, laden with assumptions, evoking complexes of feelings.

Modern theory in such diverse areas as literary criticism, semantics, and artificial intelligence clearly suggests that text is at least partly indeterminate. Items are specific types of stimuli that produce responses. If other factors remain constant, the responses generally may fall within bounds defined by a common culture and usage of the experimenter and the subjects. This gives the impression of stable meanings and understandings, but the impression can be very misleading (cf. Herring 1987; Lakoff 1987; Norris 1987; Small, Cottrell, Tanenhaus 1988; Scheffler 1979; Neisser 1976; Fodor 1975).

PERIPHERAL TEXT

Peripheral text surrounds the core text. Although it may contain important material, instructions, or explanations, for example, it is not the focus of direct, immediate subject attention and response. As we have already seen, the surrounding context partly determines the meaning of text, and part of the surrounding context is textual. Questionnaire items are psychological stimuli. The priming effects of peripheral text act upon the core text that the subject is supposed to be processing. Some of the priming effects are anticipated and even included in the experiment, but others may be unintentional and unknowable.

Survey research has been particularly sensitive to the effect of order on meaning (Abramson, Silver, and Anderson 1987; Bishop, Oldendick, and Tuchfarber 1982; Sigelman 1981; Bradham and Mason, 1964). Serial order effects can occur within items—the sequence of words—or between items, questions, or responses. Different chains of items or events may suggest different stories. Responses may also vary with items that are asked but not answered—"don't know," "no opinion," "not sure"—or items that are not asked (Duncan and Stenbeck 1988). If the experiment involves several rounds of activity, successive turns create different contexts that also impinge on the responses in different ways. The effects of textual order have been used as a powerful literary device, for example, in surprise endings of stories.

ANALYSIS

We have discussed experimental context and text as influences on validity. A third major set of uncontrolled factors occurs in analysis: theoretical setting, identification of key variables, measurement, and mathematical and statistical manipulation.

A paradigm, a body of scientific literature and theory, sets the frame, the supertext, for each experiment. Experimenters locate their research in a larger tradition. This helps them to nest their small scientific story within a larger plot and justifies their choices of questions and variables. We have already seen how alternative item order can alter the narrative that subjects perceive. In a similar way, alternative theoretical story lines can reinterpret experimental data. For example, the psychological experiments described earlier were conducted and interpreted from the perspective of schema and personality theory, exploring the way in which scenario and vignettes activated underlying cognitive representations and personal predispositions. The same data, however, can also be interpreted from a rational choice outlook. Different personalities might be coded, in rational choice theory, as substitute sets of preferences. From this vantage point the experimental results give us a surprise ending. Standard rational choice theory assumes stable preferences. Yet in this set of experiments, preferences did not remain stable. They were buffeted by multiple stimuli, switched on by the priming vignettes or switched off by scenario recognition.

Just as different variables can be measured by the same data, the same variables may be assessed through different means. Alternative sets of items may produce apparently similar effects; different scales may profess to measure the same underlying dimension. For example, different personality inventories may be cross-validated to give generally similar results in many settings, but they are not completely interchangeable (Morey, Blashfield, Webb, and Jewell 1988; West 1986. Cf. Krosnick and Alwin 1988).

Standard methods create a world whose assumptions and attributes have varying applicability in different concrete cases: independence, normality, homogeneity, continuity, linearity, homoscedasticity, stationarity, and unrelated error. Some statistical methods give differential weight to factors such as size of the sample. There are also indeterminacies of mathematical formulation and application—multiple alternative choices for cross sections of time and space; variable transformation; model identification, specification, and estimation— that shape final results.

Variations in text, context, and analysis influence the validity of experimental research findings. This is well known and usually downplayed under standard assumptions that the results hold if all other things are equal. Yet it is also well recognized that all other things are rarely equal. In this light, the validity of scientific findings becomes more problematic. The pattern of scientific truth, our knowledge of the reality of war and peace, is less certain and stable, more fluid and indeterminate.

Nonexperimental Validity

Problems similar to those of experimental research appear in nonexperimental research as well. Symmetries are clearest in forms of research that use similar question-and-answer methods: participant observation, unstructured or semistructured oral history in-depth interviews, standardized testing, or survey research.

SURVEY RESEARCH

Survey research resembles to experimental research, but it is usually identified as being closer to the real world. Schuman and Presser (1981, 313) suggest that "psychological theory has developed largely through a kind of controlled laboratory experimentation that is usually far removed from the encounters with ordinary people that characterize surveys." Survey methods usually include sophisticated techniques of sample selection—multiple stages, stratification, or clustering, for example—attempting to represent specific larger populations, to replicate their attributes in microcosm. The results of survey research are then generalized to these populations, assuming common underlying attributes and dynamics. No matter how clever and complex the sampling procedure, however, there exist inevitable residual differences between the sample and other populations. These differences include developmental, social, economic, cultural, or political dimensions. Advances in sampling technique allow us to eliminate and narrow some of these differences. In spite of such progress, it is impossible to say a priori what effect the remaining differences may have on the results. Though we may assume them away as irrelevant, trivial, or insignificant, we cannot specify their values in advance. As in the case of experimental research, these disparities open all generalizations across samples and populations to initial question.

Survey research, except for its concern with sampling, is similar to experimental research. As the analysis above suggests in several places, survey research contains the same instabilities. In spite of attempts at technical fixes—buffers between particularly important items or split-ballot questionnaires, for example—there are multiple uncontrolled and uncontrollable contextual, textual, and analytical variables. As practitioners of these techniques are well aware, all question-and-answer methods are subject to distortions of attention, perception, articulation, and memory. Neither experimental nor survey techniques are well suited to evoke or capture the dynamics of real-time group discussion and decision or the stress and emotion of serious personal or public situations (cf. Lodge, McGraw, and Stroh 1989; Gerstein, Luce, Smelser and Sperlich 1988; Schuman and Scott 1987; Schuman 1986; Turner and Martin 1984).

CONTENT ANALYSIS

Another set of procedures, including much of this book, does not elicit words but takes them as given—for example, analysis of documents like those produced by branches and agencies of government and individual authors. The most systematic form of this work is content analysis. The sampling, contextual, textual, and analytical problems discussed previously are present here as well. A representative sample of the documents may be taken as the basis for research, but the documents themselves hardly mirror all dimensions of the behavior that they may purport to report or reflect. They are produced by specific authors in particular settings for specific purposes.

One genre of content analysis—events data analysis—involves collecting, coding, and analyzing political events from press sources. Researchers begin with samples of newspapers that, in turn, provide samples of events. The events are created through multiple filters: actors, reporters, and coders. The chain grows longer when the reporters talk with other observers, witnesses or commentators, or if their own work is heavily edited before publication (cf. van Dijk

1984; Pollock 1981; Boorstin 1975). The actors, reporters, and coders are not independent as they communicate and consult with peers or superiors. Definitions of some events or variables depend on definitions of other events or variables. Furthermore, the actors, reporters, and coders come from particular national, cultural, and linguistic backgrounds and training that mold their perspectives.

Early content analytic method placed great emphasis on intercoder reliability—the replication of results as a guarantor of validity. Growing experience and sophistication has made it clear, however, that such reliability is a function of background variables such as those just discussed, as well as coding categories, rules, and error checking. The final events data are thus hardly a reflection of an "actual" event. Like other data, they are artifacts manufactured by standardized means and not a natural product.

AGGREGATE DATA

Aggregate data allow us to watch what people do rather than what they say. Aggregate research has different aims and uses different methods, but it implies similar problems. Instead of sampling individuals, aggregate data analysis may rely on samples of larger social units. Like events data, they are not simply facts, but, more importantly, artifacts whose creation is more deeply hidden. Aggregate data go through several stages in the production process, and each of these stages involves omission and inclusion. For example, income inequality is an important statistic, particularly in the study of economic development. At the very lowest level, there is an equivalency problem centering on the relation of the basic unit, money, to the activity actually being undertaken, for example, growing fruit. This problem is similar to the contextual and textual problems discussed above. The monetary unit translates and transforms this activity from a qualitative to a quantitative phenomenon, takes it from the world of individual experience, processes it, and enters it into the homogenized ledgers of social exchange. Through this process, growing fruit becomes an activity comparable to, and, therefore like, all other activities— flying airplanes, ski racing, or murder for hire, for example. This numerical transformation does more than simply condense or lose information. It translates and exchanges one experience into another. It strips away uniqueness or variance in production and consumption; it leaves behind specificity of time and place. The peasant caring for his date trees by hand in Cyprus of 1910 is the same as the American agribusinessman harvesting wheat by combine in 1990. Conversion in the other direction—from money into experience—is hardly easier. Even leaving aside questions involving exchange rates and purchasing power, the same commodities are not evenly available at different times and in different places. Nor do they have the same social and individual meanings. Louis XIV could not have modern plumbing at the palace of Versailles. Apparently similar activities of two different people—a Cambridge philosophy professor and a Tunisian businessman driving a red Ferrari—may have very different social and individual meanings.

Once the conversion of activity to money is accepted, new problems arise. One of these is similar to the sampling problem discussed above. It centers on the accuracy of income reporting, the extent to which the income reported faithfully represents the income received. The peasant growing dates will not report as income the increase in value of his land nor what he, his family, or his friends eat themselves. What he sells privately or at market will almost certainly suffer severe attrition before it enters the formal government bookkeeping system. At upper income levels, there will also be underreporting of income. Land earnings will be hidden behind a curtain of silent appreciation. Individual earnings can similarly be redirected and sheltered behind the corporate veil. Foreign earnings may be protected by bank secrecy, and earnings from bribery, kickbacks, and other improper or illegal activities are of course outside the normal reporting matrix. The government must then further process the numbers reported, taking into account its own interests. Internal and external practices and pressures may mold the outcome. Nations generate statistics using disparate accounting methods. Different countries have different laws, with different penalties, for income reporting. Bureaucracies vary in sophistication and resources. Cultural norms for collection and payment differ. The regimes of socialist countries hold power on the basis of claims to foster equality. Developing countries must justify various forms of assistance to international agencies and donor countries. These data, like the others, are artifacts subject to abstraction, distortions, and omissions.

Noneconomic data have the same problems. As we noted earlier, there is a substantial record of the war experience, beginning with narrative and evolving into statistics, which has replaced words with numbers. This has created an entirely different phenomenological reality, replacing the worlds of writers with those of accountants and bookkeepers, mathematicians and engineers. These war data can be misleading even within their own terms of reference. Like economic data, they are very different from the phenomena from which they are derived.

As we saw previously, the identities of the wars and their participants are basic to this type of analysis, yet the boundaries are fuzzier than the innocent might suspect. Wars are more like clouds than tables; they do not have preexisting sharp edges that give them clear boundaries. Wars can be defined according to different criteria—participants, length, casualties, formal declarations—and the criteria determine where we stick the label *war* and where we do not. Not until we accept a particular definition with its underlying presuppositions and assumptions do wars become commensurable. Wars, moreover, are not independent of each other, and this interdependence further blurs identity-boundary issues.

ANALYSIS

We have already considered some dimensions of analytic indeterminacy in the prior discussion of experiments. Other aspects occur in nonexperimental research. For example, Lewis Richardson and some of his followers have described wars and domestic violence as basically random occurrences whose distribution in time and space conform to stochastic statistics like the Poisson distribution. Later advances created hybrid, Poisson-regression models (King 1989). Yet it seems paradoxical, even bizarre, that supposedly random events should conform to a deterministic formula or model. Moreover, if they do conform, why should it be to one formula rather than another? Subsequent researchers have indeed applied other different formulas to random events, for example, binomial or Weibull distributions. Superordinate randomness could easily apply not only to the events, but also to their distributions.

The evolution of modern applied mathematics into areas like complexity theory suggests that there are virtually infinite degrees of freedom—turning on possible distributions and equations, lines and curves—to which data may conform, creating illusions of shape and movement (cf. Arrow 1988, 280-281). The formulas, in turn, can be tested against data divided by an innumerable number of possible cut points or disaggregations in time and space. Goodness of fit is difficult to compare across models beginning from different premises and taking different forms. Some types of models exist in a kind of free zone where problems of empirical fit are, to some extent, finessed. For example, formal models of rational choice that rely on individual expected utilities or more complex interactions of the mathematical theory of games can be extended to the logic of interdependent political decision. Such political applications of game theory are often developed using very relaxed testing criteria. In some cases, the extensions are largely metaphorical (Beer 1986). Such models proceed as if their assumptions are true; they are properly limited to possible worlds with pervasive symmetries between the theoretical and political worlds.

One answer to the indeterminacy dilemma is reliability through replication. A strong form of replication is multimethod research design, for example, the "comparison and calibration of results obtained by longitudinal surveys, randomized field experiments, laboratory studies, one-time surveys, and administrative records" (Gerstein, Luce, Smelser, and Sperlich 1988, 174; cf. Arlin 1982). In spite of its intuitive appeal, replication is not the final solution to the problems we have uncovered through dissection. It will not lead us to universal commensurability. Reliability supports validity, but the two are not identical. The claim to validity is presumed to be stronger if results are relatively robust and insensitive, if findings are reproducible or converge across research designs, samples, contexts, and designs. When we ask, "What if we change x . . . ?" the answer comes back the same: still "then y." For example, validity claims were enhanced in the experiments on war cues cited above, when the results from the South Korean study, with a dramatically different sample from another culture, virtually duplicated the American outcomes. Nevertheless, simple repetition falls into the trap of naive verification. It applies an algebraic, additive solution to a geometric, combinatorial problem. Replications in different contexts do not measure all the unmeasured or unmeasurable variables; they do not unravel the tangled skein of multiple causality; they do not stabilize analytic indeterminacy. Even if all of these problems were solved and one could be absolutely certain that some hypothetical finding were absolutely invariant in all forms across all contexts, the invariance would apply only to the past. We should have succeeded at retrodiction, but we should be as far as ever from prediction. We should know the worlds of Christmas past and present, but from this we still could not surely foretell the worlds of Christmas yet to come.

Scientists have long dreamed of a demon that would simulate the mind of God. This demon would know all phenomena of the world and their minute, interrelated causes. A modern version of this demon would have to know the same things for a multitude of possible alternative, parallel, simultaneous worlds, both subjective and objective, differing in an infinity of ways at all points in space and moments of time. It also would have to know their rules of activation and valence, transformation and transition, privilege and power—all at the same time (cf. Casti 1989; Wolf 1988; Lewis 1973). In spite of evolutionary progress, science and political science are closer to the beginning than the end of this road.

Variability in context, text, and analysis limit the general validity—the context-invariant meaning—of experimental findings. Nonexperimental research—including survey research, content analysis, and aggregate data—implies the same validity constraints. Contextual, textual, and analytical influences act as internal and external meaning shifters. They subtly change patterns of meaning within research on war and peace, and they create differential connections between that research and the outer world of war and peace to which it refers. This double effect, internal and external, reflects and shapes the scope and limits of the knowledge and meaning of war and peace.

Scientific and Political Validity

This chapter began with a conventional view of validity as found in political and other social and applied sciences. This view in its ideal form suggests that political science can be a window onto political behavior in the wider community. The more valid the theory, method, and research, the more accurate the view. This perspective assumes applicability. It supposes that concepts correspond with—that theory and research accurately map—reality, although in simple, spare, minimalist form. Following an idealized positivist example of natural science, and in the footsteps of such behavioral pioneers as Charles E. Merriam, the value-free "pure science" of politics ultimately aims to provide objective "certain knowledge" through "rigorous scientific method" and the professional "power of prediction and control" (Ross 1991, 391–400).

This view may be abbreviated as V_{ss}, to designate scientific validity that is strong. Very few sophisticated contemporary political scientists would probably subscribe today to this doctrine in its strongest form. We know that there are always validity problems. In most cases, we have very little idea of the proportion or direction of variance introduced by a multitude of unmeasured or unmeasurable variables. Samples are not isomorphic with larger populations. Research contexts are different from the situations of political life. Text is not a completely transparent medium that conveys intended and perceived meanings of researchers and subjects. Language and numbers, statistics and general abstract models, are too parsimonious to carry the rich particularities of specific political situations. Multiple, uncontrolled degrees of freedom lead to a combinatorial explosion of samples, texts, contexts, and modes of analysis, an array of infinite dimensions and possibilities. The expected is never exactly the observed. Political science has long passed the age of innocence. It cannot maintain the strongest scientific form of validity because the problems that have emerged are too serious and too numerous to be totally ignored. Defects of experimental and nonexperimental methods cast serious doubt on validity as an absolutely attainable operational scientific criterion, and on the realistic possibilities for comprehensive validation research (Sussmann and Robertson 1986).

Standard political science adapts according to "the maxim of minimum mutilation," which enjoins us to "disturb overall science as little as possible"

(Quine 1987, 142). Political science has thus evolved a weaker, more complex form of scientific validity, V_{sw}. This weak form of scientific validity nevertheless rests upon the same foundation as the strong form. Political science still aspires to the fidelity of truth. Validity is commonly used in the scientific lexicon as a synonym for verity. Cook and Campbell define validity as "the best approach to the truth or falsity" (1979, 37). Valid research supposedly describes real behavior in the political world. More complexly, Campbell rejects "pragmatism, utilitarian nominalism, utilitarian subjectivism, utilitarian conventionalism, or instrumentalism" in favor of "hypothetical critical realism" (1987, 85). Nothing is perfect. Absolute truth is unattainable. We use a pragmatic standard of evidence; we do the best we can to carry the burden of proof. Bias and its cousins mar the view. We settle for the satisfactory; we satisfice. We act as if our results were true beyond reasonable doubt or within the balance of subjective probabilities, but our confidence level is less than 100 percent. We try to push back the limits (Singer 1988; cf. Fienberg 1989, 191–205).

Validity remains problematic even in this weaker form because it still rests upon the blending of validity and verity. In their classical sense, validity and verity are far from synonymous; they connote quite different ideas. Verity derives from the Latin *veritas,* meaning truth. Validity comes from the Latin *validus,* meaning powerful or strong. Validity, from its origins, thus appears as a political word and a political concept. We may designate this view of validity, political validity, as V_p. The political harmonics of validity are clear both from its genealogy and also from usages in other contexts. Thomas Hobbes informs us that "the validity of covenants begins not but with the constitution of a civil power sufficient to compel men to keep them" (1958, 120). The validity of the written word itself originally derived from the power of the medieval ecclesiastical or secular authority that heard oral speech and wrote it into formal symbols (Illich and Sanders 1988). Today, hearings still lead to writings that provide the validity of law. The U.S. Senate, through the powers granted to it by the Constitution, holds hearings that validate an international treaty. A court, acting under civil law, hears a case and validates a will. The etymology of validity helps to distinguish and distance it from verity. Historical context helps to ground, to instantiate validity with a specifically political content. Validity, from this angle, is not just about the political world but is also a part of it. Our assessment of validity, then, depends not only on the fidelity of the view but also on its power as derived from the power of the viewer.

The claim to validity, as Foucault reminded us, thus reflects the political power and authority of the broader community. The authority of political science derives from the political authority that is its context, the solidification of secular authority and science after the medieval collapse of the church. The currency of political science is backed by the gold of the polity that supports that political science and directs its aims and methods (see Mukerji 1990; Brown 1984; Jagtenberg 1983; Blume 1974). The coin of validity is stamped with the approved seal of expert judgment by the scientific elect. Validity is conventional, based on trial and error, the collective guess, the best bet, the informed hunch of the scientific community, the incomplete sciences of Sherlock Holmes and Herbert Simon (see Eco and Sebeok 1988). Political and scientific laws support validity. Seen in this light, validity is the name we give to the negotiated product of what is satisfactory to scientists and their supporters.

V_p also suggests that validity reflects a narrower politics with a face that turns inward toward political science. Judgments of validity are based on accepted professional standards. In this guise, validity is at least partly a mask for scientific politics, a rhetorical trope, evoking widely shared ideologies and orienting actors in the politics of political science. Scientific politics, like the church Latin of the Middle Ages, flows in a formal pattern of discourse. Its main direction is from the center out, from the top down. This is quite different from the discourse of natural language, a world of subjects that are fully human in all directions, as follows: "Language is . . . the possibility of subjectivity because it always contains the linguistic forms appropriate to the expression of subjectivity, and discourse provokes the emergence of subjectivity because it consists of discrete instances. In some way language puts forth 'empty' forms which each speaker, in the exercise of discourse, appropriates to himself and which he relates to his 'person,' at the same time defining himself as I and a partner as you. The instance of discourse is thus constitutive of all the coordinates that define the subject" (Benveniste 1971, 236–37).

Political science discourse replaces this natural intersubjective equality with its own graded political structure. V_p implies that validity points toward and helps to define the center of scientific power, the mainstream, the politically correct. The members of the core network, the minimum winning coalition, control, in variable degree, the levers of professional inclusion. They back up their judgments and preferences with the prestige of major institutional affiliations, the resources of granting agencies, and access to central professional associations, presses, and journals. Elite consensus thus helps define reality. Validity indexes political position, economic reward, and social status. Those at the periphery suffer validity anxiety (Freund, Kruglanski, and Shpitzajzen 1985). The psychology of invalidity centers on the fear of exclusion and abandonment, of being left outside the magic circle of privilege and survival. There are penalties for nonconformity or dissent. Valid research may or may not be closer to being true, but it is closer to being accepted as true (cf. Hallett 1988).

Validity in this light also assumes a hierarchical researcher-subject structure. The political scientist constructs the agenda and the terms of the interaction; he or she extracts and shapes the data; he or she forges the results, through advanced technology, into new and significant analytical products. The subject has an I-Thou relationship with the scientist. Like the obedient child of an earlier time, the subject speaks only when spoken to, and is otherwise invisible and mute, a black box or a black hole.

In spite of validity's inward dimension, political science is not self-contained within the political science community. It draws power resources from the entire polity and must finally increase the power resources available to that polity. Political science can easily justify itself by its real virtues. It sees, hears, and reads a common political experience and writes it into a new collective political language. It defines, codifies, combines, and processes phenomena in different ways that reform our thinking and generate alternative conclusions. At the same time, it is counterproductive to pretend to what can never be achieved. Excessive claims on validity are losing propositions. Political science cannot support them scientifically or politically. They draw on surplus political capital and oversell the endeavor. They advertise more than political science can deliver, raise expectations that it cannot possibly fulfill. Such large promissory notes overextend the whole enterprise; the scientific reserves are too skimpy to pay the political bill (cf. Glenn 1989).

Validity thus has a Janus face.[3] Scientific validity, V_s, looks outward for an objective, real, true world. Political validity, V_p, looks inward to those who define the view onto that outside world. This Janus-faced quality is a characteristic of natural as well as social and political science. Latour suggests that there are "two sides, one lively, the other severe, of a two-faced Janus. 'Science in the making' on . . . [one] side, 'all made science' or 'ready made science' on the other" (1987, 4, 23). The external view is observation from a distance in which the subject of scientific inquiry is placed in a black box, "away from its conditions of production." The internal view is closer to the scientific process. It opens the black box to show the way in which human beings socially construct scientific knowledge.[4]

This bidirectional context implies anomalies that go beyond the simple innocence of Type I and Type II errors of commission and omission. There are also tautologies. V_p implies an underlying circularity in the definition of truth and reality. The observers are simultaneously a part of reality and shapers of what is accepted as true about it. The political reality that we observe is not valid in its own right. Truth is what the leaders of the scientific community say is true and what the leaders of the wider political community are willing to accept as true. The politics that create and shape our political reality also establish criteria for what we accept as scientifically valid. It is as our science describes it if and only if the scientific and general communities accept the results as fitting within the political lexicon, as accurately describing the reality, as valid.

There are further unresolved inconsistencies. Both political and scientific versions of validity suggest that political scientists are concrete human teleological agents, makers of the glass and observers through it. Thus, under both V_{ss} and V_{sw}, political scientists independently create research tools, test hypotheses, and weigh evidence. We use free will to make decisions and choices, to control our domain. Our ends determine our means. Sometimes we also see our subjects in this light, in a standardized, testable image of political participation, educational achievement, and psychological normality. Yet, paradoxically, the scientific view often sees others quite differently—as objects of our science. They are nodes in a matrix of abstract variables, caught in a determinate, repetitive, general political science where cause and effect, stimulus and response, cues and priming, coexist in an organization of stable predictions. Past political behavior of these objects often determines their future political behavior; their means determine their ends. Our own codification of that past behavior supposedly allows us, or will allow us, to predict scientifically the future behavior of political automata.

It is more pleasant to look at others in this glass, to see them in our image rather than to see ourselves in theirs. As the authors of the story, we assume that we are freer than the characters we create and observe. We are outside the system of abstract, impersonal variables and not fully reducible. Our science is not behavior of the same kind, subject to similar constraint and observation. We tend to believe that we are not fully programmed, that our past scientific behavior does not necessarily determine our future science, that we as scientists cannot predict our prospective scientific behavior and our scientific reactions to that eventual scientific behavior. We may guess from clues; we are not primed by cues. This position is dramatically inconsistent. If our science means anything, it must apply to us as well as them, inside as well as out. Political science must be simultaneously the science of external politics and a definition of our own situation.

The complexity of validity and its implications for science and knowledge are critical components of the meaning of war and peace. The constraints of scientific validity suggest fundamental, irreducible limits on a purely scientific, behavioral understanding of war and peace. The influence of political validity, in turn suggests that war and peace are to some extent within an *Alice in Wonderland* world. In this world, the words and the acts may both mean, to some extent, what the actors want them to mean.

Multiple Validities

A first step toward more complex understanding is gradually to recognize and articulate existing paradoxes, using them to begin to define a lattice of linked definitions of validity, as we have previously attempted for war and reason (cf. Flathman 1987). This may be conceived either as an extension of analytic and scientific method or as a part of a strategy that Cook (1985) has labeled "postpositivist critical multiplism." We see computers simultaneously through different lenses: as hardware and software, display and cognition, components and systems, machines and humans. The patterns of light on the video terminal screen have many alternative meanings, all of which are valid in different ways. Understanding of validity anomalies may be advanced by similar decomposition. Multiple validities portray different realities and reflect differently on each other. Alternative frames of reference reveal different possible meanings and inconsistencies.

COMBINATIONS

The family of validities includes scientific and political validity in both strong and weak forms. These forms may be joined as general attitudes in varying combinations in different communities and individuals. For example, in the United States, political science might include weak versions of both scientific and political validity, V_{sw}/V_{pw}. This implies some degree of belief in scientific method as the basis for the study of politics, the independence of evidence, and the possibility of uninvolved prediction. At the same time, there is recognition that we cannot attain absolute truth, an appreciation of the subjective, artifactual dimension of our knowledge and the dynamics of symbolic interaction. Other combinations—V_{ss}/V_{pw}, V_{sw}/V_{ps}—give heavier weight to one component and lighter weight to the other. A particularly interesting combination is V_{ss}/V_{ps}, where belief in both major forms of validity is held equally strongly. The dynamics of cognitive consistency suggest that this is probably quite rare, if it exists at all. Nevertheless, it is logically possible for science, as for a court of law, to assert that judgment can be simultaneously strongly true and strongly political.

Our assessment of specific validities does not necessarily remain stable over space and time, even within the same individual. As we read and write, observe and create, we differentially validate diverse aspects of our environment. Sometimes we draw attention to the process; Dr. Johnson replies to Bishop Berkeley's subjectivism by kicking a stone; Hume depresses himself with extreme scientific skepticism, then reassures himself by eating a good dinner. At other times we unobtrusively shift validation and meaning for rhetorical effect in the game of language. Explicitly or implicitly we assign relatively strong scientific validity to some theory, research, or experiences, weaker scientific or political validity to others. Some specific findings of psychological laboratory experiments and survey research, for example, may be used to call into question the general results of those and other lines of research.

As we saw in the earlier discussion of textual and contextual variance, possible underlying definitions and interpretations wobble almost imperceptibly in the dense seas of words and circumstances that surround them. Countless configurations of validity exist with other language and social forms. We can easily lose ourselves in the possible combinations. The simplest case is probably plain bivariate nesting—the scientific validity of political validity, the political validity of scientific validity. In a more formal vein, we might think of a possible modal person with a belief structure V_{sw}/V_{pw}. This person might have views on persons with other belief patterns, which we might specify in the form ([modal person's] view of [other persons'] views): ($[V_{sw}/V_{pw}]$ $[V_{ss}/V_{ps}, V_{ss}/V_{pw}, V_{sw}/V_{ps}, V_{sw}/V_{pw}]$). The partial expansion in even this very limited case only begins to suggest the complexity of possible combinations as we approach the limits of ordinary language and understanding.

Linguistic modifiers and specific subjects of discourse are contexts that geometrically expand permutations of meanings. Some modifiers produce compounds—population validity, ecological validity, construct validity—that may make more sense in a V_s framework. They imply a perspective that is more scientific, mechanistic, and deterministic. Other word combinations—cultural validity, situational validity, interpretive validity—imply a V_p interpretation, one that is more political, intentional, and voluntaristic. The full factorial expansion of the formal possibilities of each modifier, however, would reveal a wealth of plausible combinations.

We have considered how alternative metamodels may marry mechanistic and teleological forms of validity in different possible proportions and circumstances. Higher-order models might, moreover, systematically relate research subjects and objects, observers and actors alike, specifying their degrees of freedom and determination in different contexts and interpretations as well as the dynamics of their interaction. This task is complicated by the fact that validity constantly changes shape as we search for a workable synthesis and integration at a higher level of abstraction in multiple different contexts (cf. Washington and McLoyd 1982).

Borrowing from Niels Bohr's complementarity principle in physics, we may be able to relate discontinuous and mutually exclusive perspectives of "observation and definition" as one slips "from one plane of objectivity to another" and between "different conscious experiences," including "consciousness as the object of description and the subject consciousness which experiences it." This depends on "different placing of the section line between the observing subject and the object on which attention is focused." One possible path is development of "the analogy of the situation to multivalued functions of a complex variable." In this analogy, "each complex number can be represented unambiguously as a point on a two-dimensional plane, but the multivalued function may have potentially an infinite number of values, each a complex number, for each value of the independent complex variable" (Folse 1985, 113, 175–77, 180. See also Bell 1987a; Rasmussen 1987).

OPTICS

Variants of validity earlier appeared like different combinations of shadings of the faces of Janus. One formulation suggests that "certainty about natural phenomena . . . tends to vary inversely with proximity to the scientific work." Thus, "proximity to experimental work . . . makes visible the skillful, inexplicable and therefore potentially fallible aspects of experimentation, it lends salience to the web of assumptions that underlie what counts as an experimental outcome. . . . Distance from the cutting edge is the source of what certainty we have."[5]

The covariation of certainty and proximity suggests that we view validity through different types of glass with varying focal lengths. Longer scientific foci present a window into the distant outside environment. A closer, medium-range political focus mirrors the scientists as actors. It is important for the investigator to distinguish between these and that he or she "avoid mistaking a mirror of his (or her) own mind for a window into the minds of others" (Schuman 1986, 438). The shortest focal lengths, the most minute microscopy, display the glass itself—the character, idiosyncrasies, and effects of our language, our psychology.

A sophisticated political science should have control over these optics, consciously and systematically choosing the section—adjusting, comparing, and synthesizing mutually exclusive views to achieve a more pluralistic, exhaustive density of description. Perplexing as they are, we cannot escape from the paradoxes of validity. The implications of validity suggest not a single mirror but a whole corridor of them that produces images whose ultimate source is hard to trace and whose forms appear inconsistent. The political scientist and the broader political community that he or she observes appear to be not in separate rooms but in the same one. We are surrounded top and bottom, forward and backward, right and left, by a floor-to-ceiling glass corridor at which we look and which we have created. In different lights, the glass seems either to allow a view into other spaces, to reflect back our own image, or to provide a picture of itself. We cannot know for sure which glass or which light currently exists; we do not have an independent measure of the glass's fidelity or its identity—be it a window onto politics, a mirror of ourselves, or a kaleidoscope. This is glass that is ahead of us and behind, on all sides, above and below. It creates illusions and delusions with varying extension and distortion. Recursive, regressive images stretch into infinity. Relaxing customary constraints makes us uncomfortable and uncertain at first. The images change with each step that we take. When we first see this, we are dizzy and disoriented. And yet, as we walk, we do not fall through the glass. We can take steps with our feet that our eyes tell us are impossible. Once we proceed some way down this corridor with our eyes opened, we discover rich new areas for the attention and investigation of political science. The glass is invisible to the naive observer, but a sophisticated political science—reflective and reflexive—must increasingly take account of it. This political science, including the political science of war and peace, must recognize and include its existence and importance, its limits and its power, its validities.

A clearer appreciation of our reflected, refracted situation opens new dimensions of political reality. Eventually in an incremental way, we can expand our comprehension and expertise so that we can make more educated guesses, more informed wagers, in our scientific game with the political nature of war and peace. We cannot leap the final ontological barriers and resolve all the paradoxes. Yet as our scientific discourse, our epistemology, evolves, we can appreciate and use multiple methods in a more precise and powerful manner. We can switch and adjust our foci to specific purposes. We can develop a broader, more consistent, and higher-order lattice of belief. We can reorient our perception of science and achieve a more comprehensive and complex understanding, differentiating levels of analysis for scientific observers as well as scientific phenomena. In this conception, science can be simultaneously and alternatively an objective product and a subjective process, a material artifact and a human action, a language of nature and a topic of human rhetoric and discourse. Such a sophisticated science becomes a critical, multidimensional component in our complex, emerging understanding of international reality and of the worlds of meaning embedded in war and peace.

PART II

Rhetorics

The preceding section on semantics focused on the way in which the meanings of individual words central to our understanding of war and peace—and to war and peace themselves—vary. In that section we examined in detail the critical words *war, reason,* and *validity.* We explored the way in which their surrounding verbal microcontext produced variations in the meanings of such words and, by implication, in the meaning of other war and peace terms and concepts, facts and thoughts, actions and interactions. That section illustrated, in close-up detail at a high level of magnification, the larger theme of this book: how words of war and peace index worlds of meaning.

We now extend this idea to a larger arena. In this section on rhetorics we shall show how words also frame the meaning of war and peace in a larger sense, within a broader political macrocontext. When aggregates of words are used persuasively in this extended arena, they go by the name of rhetoric. When they are used by multiple actors with multiple styles for multiple purposes, they are called rhetorics. The rhetorics work through various devices. One set of mechanisms is constructional, the creation of general theories and specific arguments. The theories and arguments build and build on the meanings of the terms and concepts. They use and form particular definitions of war and peace; they use and form reason; they use and form scientific and political validity. Beginning from such foundations, words reflect and create the rhetorical frames that we call theories and the arguments that convey and shape the larger meaning of war and peace.

Earlier work developed the importance of rhetoric in the theory of international relations (Beer and Hariman 1996). It began with realism, the standard theory of international relations, and showed how it operated not only as science but also as a powerful scientific and political rhetoric. It then advanced a new theory, postrealism, with a more self-consciously rhetorical perspective. It concluded with a three-tiered strategic model, the capstone of which was interpretation—the discernment and construction of meaning. In this view, theory not only reflects but also constructs the meaning of war and peace: Theory itself achieves new meaning as a politically powerful form of rhetoric. Chapter 4, "Postrealism, Just War, and the Gulf War Debate," begins at this point. It briefly recapitulates the theoretical debate between realism and postrealism and summarizes the postrealist strategic model. From there, it shows how congressional participants in the Gulf War debate used a particular structure of argument—the just war doctrine—to argue for and against specific policies and actions and to interpret their meaning.

Chapters 5 and 6 shift focus a bit to what rhetoricians might designate as an element of style or what political scientists might see as a verbal strategy—the rhetorical use of metaphor and the way in which such use reflects and constructs the meaning of war and peace. Although metaphors can be individual words, they are linked to larger clusters of terms: They also help orient and structure larger discursive aggregates like theories and arguments. Metaphor is a crucial stylistic device and tropic form, leveraging powerful meaning shifters within the verbal context of war and peace.

Metaphor involves a different strategy for meaning transformation than we have so far considered. Our examination of the semantics of crucial terms and concepts showed how context helps determine variation in their meaning. Context creates textual meaning by envelopment, surrounding the central term. Metaphor works in a narrower sense by substitution, replacing key elements. At the same time, metaphors—like terms and concepts, theories and arguments—are a major part of the larger rhetorical context, helping rhetorically reorient cognition and behavior of war and peace (Beer and de Landtsheer 1999; Chilton 1996; Lakoff 1991; and Beer 1986, 1981a, 1981b, and 1979).

Chapter 5, "Body, Mind, and Soul in the Gulf War Debate," starts from the standpoint of realist theory, again showing realism in actual political discourse. There is, at the same time, much more than realism to foreign policy debate. Part of the behavioral meaning that we bring to the discourse lies in our existence as embodied beings, the experience of our bodies. This chapter shows how bodily metaphors were used in the Gulf War debate. It suggests that such bodily metaphors may indeed reflect and form a deep structure, a symbolic generative grammar that lies within foreign policy discourse, a separate stratum of meaning.

Chapter 6, "Women's Words: Gender and Rhetoric in the Gulf War Debate," considers a particular aspect of the body—gender—and its relation to the discourse of war and peace. Using the Gulf War debate again as an example, this chapter takes a self-consciously feminist perspective. Not only do different bodily metaphors influence linguistic meaning within speeches, differences in physical bodies also affect both speakers' words and audience reactions. Our research demonstrates gender effects with regard to both text and analysis. In this chapter a female coauthor helps shape the interpretation of rhetorical similarities and differences between female and male speakers. Bodies are important, and female bodies, minds, and words are particularly significant here as elements of meaning.

4

Postrealism, Just War, and the Gulf War Debate

FRANCIS A. BEER AND ROBERT HARIMAN

Realism is the traditional, historical theory of international relations, reformulated in recent years as neorealism.[1] It includes important narratives, among which are stories of itself and of the world. Realism presents itself as the primary actor in the world of theory, with greater power than other theories. Its taut story of world politics includes the following important elements: (1) nation-states are the primary characters of world politics; (2) nation-states are ranked by their power, measured mostly in terms of material capabilities, especially military force; (3) nation-states conduct their foreign policies on the basis of national interest defined in terms of power, calculating and comparing the benefits and costs of alternative policies and actions, using all available means, including war; and (4) the competition for power is permanent and ubiquitous. The story of realism continues indefinitely, often with consequences that are tragic in human terms.

Postrealism

With the end of the Cold War and the transformation of the international environment, critics have increasingly attacked this view. They believe that realism has serious deficiencies as positive theory, failing fully and accurately to describe, explain, and predict international behavior. Postrealism makes the same charge and goes on to challenge the very positivistic bases upon which realism rests. Postrealism takes a linguistic turn and suggests that realism is not only scientific positivistic theory but also—more significantly—a form of rhetoric representing itself as scientific positivistic theory. Realist theory thus is not only detached scientific observation but also speech action. As realism describes, explains, and predicts the world, it also constructs, shapes, forms, and controls it (Beer and Hariman 1996).

Postrealists go beyond criticism to construct world politics persuasively in other ways. There is more to the story than realists admit, and postrealists supply missing parts of the tale. Elements of the postrealist narrative include the following:

(1) Nation-states are not the only important characters in international relations. International organizations such as the United Nations, domestic political factions, public opinion, and individuals all affect global events.

(2) Power does not grow just from the barrel of a gun. International interactions are complex, and nonmaterial capabilities can be significant. Power is difficult to generalize and project and has very important dimensions that are embedded in specific issues and places.

(3) Foreign policy cognition is thicker, denser, and hotter than realism believes. There is more to decision making than simple motivations of national interest defined in terms of power, benefits and costs, ends and means. National elites have singular memories of history and its lessons, unique perceptions that shape their views of policy situations and their political decisions. They are concerned with the legal, ethical, and moral rules of their communities, and they can be emotional.

(4) Decision makers are not necessarily bound by realist narrative, by its characterization or plot. Decision makers appear in many different forms; they can construct themselves in many different ways. They can and do make a difference.

Postrealism, like realism, recognizes logic and facts. However, unlike realism, postrealism also recognizes rhetoric. Taking a linguistic turn, it emphasizes narrative as an important means of persuasion with realist and postrealist narratives being primary examples. Postrealism relies on criticism and the formulation of alternatives. It involves deconstruction and reconstruction, a rereading of texts, and the rewriting of concepts and practices to achieve a thorough revision of realist discourse. The turn into postrealism also involves an emancipatory dynamic; a renewed emphasis on agency, action, and freedom; and the belief that a postrealist can affect his or her world. While sensitive to the claims of objective science, determinant structures, and processes, it sees at the same time that these are human creations—the resultants, the emergent properties, of scientific and political practice. Postrealists broaden scientific inquiry to include a complex field of analytical frameworks. These frameworks are shaped in such a way that they are suitable for analyzing not only an objective Other, but also the more important subjective Self. Postrealism thus implies reflexivity; it suggests self-awareness that is enhanced by a heightened sensitivity to speech. Finally, postrealism combines strategy and ethics, power and prudence, cultural context and interpretation, and persuasion and psychology. These combinations emerge more clearly from a reconsideration of the realist doctrine of strategy, to which we now turn.

Postrealism incorporates these concerns in a three-tiered pyramid model of strategic action that includes competition, control, and criticism. The first level, and the broadest, is the competitive calculus. The actor in this primitive situation is similar to Hobbes's natural man, driven by basic needs or instincts or drives. In the state of nature where "man is a wolf to man," the actors compete with each other for scarce resources. This level is pure realism, with its heavy reliance on self-interest and the strategic interaction of self-interested actors as they are typically represented in rational choice and game theoretic formulations.

The second level is control, particularly self-control. Whereas the first level of competition emphasizes interaction with the Other, the second level of control emphasizes the construction of the Self. The Self, like Machiavelli's prince—or the modern head of state or political decision maker—recognizes the chaos and unpredictability of the competitive situation in the guise of *fortuna*. In response, the Self focuses on controlling what is most controllable: persona or *virtu* (Hariman 1995). This persona is always calculating, manipulating, and reacting to the competitive environment while—first and foremost—constructing itself as an imposing and intimidating character that others will obey. It is better for the prince to be feared than loved, or so believes Machiavelli. One wonders if, in contemporary times, this also applies to princess and courtier equivalents—Margaret Thatcher or Hillary Rodham Clinton, Henry Kissinger or Madeleine Albright, for example. In any event, self-control is the attribute of this character that is essential to produce the desired outcome.

The argument to this point reflects and is consistent with classical and modern realist discourse. The third level of strategic action, critical judgment, takes us into new territory, well beyond modern realism's comfort zone. It is the critical turn, the defining move of postrealist strategy. It draws upon the work of strategist Carl von Clausewitz, particularly his elaboration of the importance of *Kritik*, which can be roughly translated as "criticism." As Clausewitz defined it, *Kritik* is the process of moving strategic analysis through a hierarchy of perspectives that incorporate ever more diverse criteria and standards for judgment. The application of *Kritik* does not deny the validity of lower-level analyses, but it does allow the strategist to reintroduce previously bracketed considerations. Furthermore, from the perspective of *Kritik,* no account of the action is ruled irrelevant simply because it does not fit with a lower-level analysis. Thus, this form of critical thinking, which seems unnecessary to explain actions in simple competitive situations, allows us to compare and translate different, perhaps incommensurable, accounts that may question the very nature of such situations.

This idea develops more fully when it is restated as part of the linguistic turn. After the move to the highest level, strategic thinking becomes explicitly a form of interpretation. The strategist has to be able not only to assess the array of forces and to gauge political objectives and constraints, but also to understand different accounts of the situation stated in different ways. Instead of presuming that outcomes are determined by the logic of a primitive strategic situation and the natural laws of coercion in a static political environment, the strategist knows that the meanings of strategic conflicts are not easily predicted from any one set of variables. Instead of an autonomous mode of analysis and a single language of calculation, the strategist recognizes that different languages offer different realities, different meanings, and different means for motivating reactions. Thus, the strategist has to be able to translate, learn from, and perhaps act in accord with discourses that reflect cultural practices and communal interests different than those explicitly represented in the typical formulations of grand strategy.

Law, ethics, and religion become more serious concerns at the highest level of strategy because they are now understood in a different way. Where realists saw irrelevant distractions, postrealists recognize important and accurate maps of complex social formations. This wide screen also captures previously neglected discourses of the peoples caught in the field of conflict, whether they are there as enemies, collaborators, or bystanders and regardless of their level of "civilization." We cannot presume that any of their perspectives is inadequately informed or inconsequential but have to look to each separate viewpoint for knowledge, symbolic resources, and constraints potentially at work in the situation. Likewise, we cannot rule that an argument is not sufficiently "military" or "geopolitical," for the strategist has to consider whether success on those terms could be damaging to broader political, social, or ecological objectives.

In short, many levels of discourse impinge upon the strategic situation, and the strategist will be more likely to succeed by recognizing how the "horizontal" means-end calculus within any account of the situation also has to be matched by a "vertical" attempt to gain maximum interpretive power. One's thinking will always be bracketed; questions of utility and effectiveness, of speed and impact, will be paramount. But strategic genius lies in the ability to discern which discourses for interpreting the scene shall be maximized and which set aside at any particular time.

This formulation reevaluates the normative dimension of world politics. From their bracketed, marginal position in realist theory, values, ethics, and morality reemerge as significant parallel discourses, the return of the repressed. Normative discourse has its own important strategic implications depending on the actors, the situation, and the number of people who believe it to be important.

Normative discourse exists in the schemata of the mind, to return to our introductory discussion of the vocabulary of contemporary psychology. Schemata are internal cognitive frames, mental software programs that run in people's minds. As dynamic structures of past experience, they provide guides to future action, helping actors interpret environmental cues, framing current issues of peace and war within a particular context of previously learned meaning. The cognitive process begins when initial cues from the environment stimulate or prime the actors to recall a particular schema. The schema frames events in a particular structure of perception and interpretation that leads to specific policies, decisions, and actions. Sound strategic analysis recognizes the critical importance of such cognitive processes, and of alternative cognitive schemata, in the heuristics of decision making.

Just War

The doctrine of just war is a clear example of an alternative cognitive schema at work in the formulation of foreign policy. Just-war doctrine provides a nonrealist schema or framework to structure the global struggle for power and the massive violence that goes with it, indexing a complex network of related narratives. Public speakers articulate and evoke these narratives in public discourse to reflect and shape public consciousness of political issues. They frame these issues to give them a particular intention and meaning, sense and direction, goal and purpose.

Just war has deep and broad historical roots. Some of its sources lie in the work of non-Western scholars, for example, the classic Islamic scholar Shaybānī. Western origins include the classical churchmen and lawyers whose Latin words index many of the terms in contemporary usage (see Welch 1993;

Beer 1987, 1981a; Walzer 1977). The doctrine of the just war has two major branches: justification for going to war, or *jus ad bellum,* and justifiable acts in wartime, or *jus in bello.* The justification for going to war in turn depends on four principal elements: proper authority, just cause, right intent, and peaceful end (Johnson 1975, 26). Once war begins, international law helps define its limits. Contemporary limits on the level of violence employed, articulated through the doctrine of *jus in bello,* include two major elements: proportionality and discrimination (Johnson 1975, 26). Despite claims of military necessity, the doctrine of *jus in bello* helps us say whether the means are appropriate to the ends.

Modern proponents of just war suggest that it serves as a set of international norms or rules that are part of the prevailing international legal and ethical regime. Yet the political mechanisms through which just-war theory operates in the real world have not been well developed. For just-war theory to be politically effective, actors must bring the theory to the concrete level of politics. International decision makers and attentive international publics must have a material interest in promoting it, believe that it is important, be well informed about it, and attempt to apply it in specific international situations.

This happens in policy discourse. Proponents and opponents of particular policies related to peace or war use elements of just-war doctrine to support their own policy positions and attack those of political opponents. The motivation to use just-war doctrine comes not only from the abstract, general desire to rein in international violence but also as part of the rhetorical weaponry of policy argument.

The rhetorical use of just war is talk, but it is also more than that. One can never be certain that words accurately reflect the real thoughts of the speakers or that all of the important motivations for action are spoken. Yet one can safely assume that public rhetoric reflects what is in somebody's mind. Speakers would not say the words if they did not believe that an audience would properly receive and appreciate them. Political actors speak theory to maintain and mobilize support, to articulate and refresh the beliefs of supporters, to neutralize or convert opponents, or to construct and dissolve domestic and international coalitions.

The Gulf War Debate

Between January 10 and 12, 1991, the U.S. Congress conducted the most extensive public peace/war debate in American history. Most members of the

House and Senate spoke for the record. All of this is in a compact body of text that is self-contained and locally accessible.

Analysis reveals an outline of how the speakers used arguments asserting claims and counterclaims that were traceable back to the elements of *jus ad bellum*. For example, one facet of the debate concerned the president's authority to undertake the war and the role that Congress should play in that decision. Senator George Mitchell (D-Maine) succinctly described the conflict between presidential and congressional authority.[2] On one hand, he noted the president's valid claim to authority: "The Constitution designates the President as Commander in Chief of the Armed Forces. With that designation comes the authority to direct the deployment of those forces." On the other hand, he advanced a counterclaim, limiting presidential authority: "The Constitution also grants to the Congress the authority to raise and support armies and to declare war" (lines 104–109).

The proper authority of the United Nations was also important. Senator Patrick Leahy (D-Vermont) noted that "President Bush's leadership in securing a U. N. authorization of the use of force if necessary to compel Iraq to leave Kuwait is a triumph for the role and authority of the United Nations in establishing collective security as a basis for international relations" (lines 554–57).

Some senators challenged Saddam Hussein's proper authority to wage war. His claim hinged partly on the acceptance or rejection of his historical claim that Kuwait was properly a part of Iraq and therefore within Iraq's sphere of sovereign internal action. Senator Daniel Patrick Moynihan (D-New York) implicitly recognized Saddam's argument: "Iraq as such is an artifact of the Treaty of Sèvres which ended the First World War with Turkey and the allies in 1920. The precise borders of Iraq were drawn in a tent in 1925 by a British colonial official" (lines 1141–43).

Most of the senators did not believe that Iraq had a reasonable historical claim to Kuwait. They asserted instead that Kuwait was an indeed a proper, independent sovereign state, and that, therefore, Iraq did not have proper authority under international law to use military force. Senator Jesse R. Helms (R-North Carolina) asserted: "The principle of national sovereignty is the very basis of our independence and national survival. It follows from the rule of national sovereignty that legitimate governments have the right not to be disturbed by foreign aggression." By itself, this statement might have justified the proper authority of Iraq to use force within its sovereign borders, including Kuwait. Senator Helms, however, explicitly rejected this claim when he asserted

Kuwaiti sovereignty: "These principles are of particular importance to the United States when the victim whose sovereignty is violated is a country such as Kuwait, which has a key role in economic and diplomatic relationships with the United States" (lines 40658–64).

Iraq's lack of fundamental democratic processes also raised the question of Saddam's own legitimacy as a leader, further undermining his claim of proper authority. This issue, however, was complicated by Kuwait's lack of the political, economic, and social freedoms that Americans took for granted. Senator Kent Conrad (D-North Dakota) did not favor military intervention. He tried to lighten the challenge to Iraq's proper authority by claiming: "the sovereignty of Kuwait is a secondary issue. A well-crafted compromise can restore Kuwaiti independence. Freedom, at least as Americans understand it, is not an issue in the Gulf. Americans serving there aren't free to observe their religious holidays nor enjoy their favorite beverages" (lines 27509–14).

The questions of just cause and right intent hinged partly on resolution of the prior issue of proper authority. As we have noted, Saddam Hussein's argument rested on his reading of the history of the British Empire. If Saddam did not have proper authority or just cause, as U.S. and allied decision makers insisted, the legitimacy of the U.S. *casus belli* was stronger. It was also clear that Americans and their allies had just cause and right intent because the U.S. effort was part of a collective self-defense project legitimated by the UN charter. Alleged Iraqi human rights violations further strengthened the allied case.

Similarly, the question of peaceful end also depended on whether one interpreted the conflict in a short-term peacekeeping frame or a longer-term imperialist one. Senator Robert Dole (R-Kansas) strongly asserted the peaceful end of American policy: "I have implored the President, who also has been there in World War II, that what we are attempting to do in the Congress of the United States is to strengthen his hand for peace, not to give him a license to see how fast we can become engaged in armed conflict" (lines 37475–78). Senator Conrad challenged this interpretation of allied motivation: "The sand that Saddam wants, and the oil under it, aren't worth the sacrifice. And there should be no mistake; the oil is what the war is about" (lines 27504–507).

Important issues were also raised by the theory of *jus in bello.* Concerns of proportionality and discrimination centered on legitimate war aims—for example, embargo costs to the Iraqi population and the possible occupation of Baghdad. Other questions included uses of inhumane weapons—atomic, biological, and chemical—distinctions between civilian and military targets, and protection of the sick and wounded. One example of such issues was expressed by Sen. Tim Wirth (D-Colorado), who urged: "If force must be used we would be well advised to restrict offensive action to air attacks, using armored forces defensively to deter any attempt by Iraq to widen the conflict on the ground. We could, for example, assert the sovereignty of Kuwaiti air space quickly and without great casualty. Then any Iraqi attack on Kuwaiti-sanctioned aircraft in Kuwaiti air space would be dealt with immediately and decisively" (lines 17548–54).

Talking Theory

The Gulf War debate was a war of words that came before the actual war. Realist concerns of power and efficient application of force were as substantial in the debate as they were later on the battlefield, yet postrealist ideas were also important. The debate clearly showed the significance of factors going well beyond the realist model: nonnational actors (legislators), nonmilitary actions (rhetoric), and ethics, law, and morality (just war). The constraints of international competition and the discipline of self-control remained important in formulating strategy. At the same time, criticism and interpretation played crucial roles. During the Gulf War debate, political actors engaged in critical thinking as they debated just-war doctrine. Just war framed, justified, and interpreted the acts involved in fighting the war on the battlefield and in constructing the subsequent peace (see Vaux 1992).

Just-war doctrine is one of the important ways that political and scholarly actors construct contemporary collective meaning. Just-war doctrine provides an ethical, normative frame to structure and limit massive violent actions. Speaking just-war discourse is part of how political actors go about creating both war and justice. Writing just-war text, and testing its existence in the real world, is an important scholarly contribution to public policy and political understanding. Our analysis illustrates how political actors use just-war doctrine to supplement realism in foreign policy discourse. Actors accentuate or diminish different elements of just-war doctrine to support and oppose the use of coercive force. Just-war doctrine is not only part of the international and domestic struggle for power but also a separate, independent theme in political discourse and culture that helps shape real-world conflict and cooperation. At the same time, the speakers' use of just-war categories feeds back into just-war doctrine itself. Just war rests on a long historical tradition and is usually expounded in general, abstract terms. By grounding it in a specific, contemporary debate, scholars have a much better sense of its relevance and importance in a contemporary context. Just-war analysis is not just an abstruse branch of public international law of war but a dynamic part of collective political life.

Political debate in a democratic forum is part of a process of complex practical reasoning that articulates logics of international competition (realism) and cooperation (just war). This process is explicitly normative, thoroughly strategic, and essentially symbolic. Just war is used as a template for integrating interest and justice; for building alliances, domestic and foreign; and for instilling a bias toward the long view into decision making (in part by tending to slow down decision making; in part by implying that just acts are the most strategic in the long term as they produce stability, reduce domestic dissent, etc.). The just-war schema also operates as a "moving category system," that is, a basic device for sifting, organizing, and evaluating information and perspectives, particularly when they come from disparate (seemingly contrary, contested, or incommensurable) sources or discourses. Hence, just-war theory is not just a set of principles applied "from above" and fitting poorly on the realist practice of foreign policy decision making. It is instead, postrealism suggests, an important dimension of the meaning of war and peace.

5

Body, Mind, and Soul
in the Gulf War Debate

FRANCIS A. BEER AND BARRY J. BALLECK

On August 2, 1990, Iraqi military forces entered Kuwait.[1] A period of concentrated diplomatic activity followed in which the United States and other allies of Kuwait attempted to persuade Iraq to withdraw. At the same time, an intense American domestic debate occurred in the general public, the media, and in the U.S. Congress, culminating in the middle of January, 1991, when Congress voted to authorize the president to use military force.

Peace/War Consciousness

We may take the Gulf War debate as one reasonable reflection of the state of collective American consciousness about peace and war. Talk is not pure thought, yet it also is not random. It implies a thinking speaker and a thinking audience who try to communicate through conversation. If our words do not completely reflect our ideas, they still suggest how we attempt to represent our thinking and create ourselves for our fellow citizens. It may be naive to think that congressional words accurately reflect congressional thoughts about the real issues at stake. At the same time, however, such words probably reflect congressional thoughts about constituents' thoughts. Congressional rhetoric thus attempts to justify congressional votes to the folks at home (see Campbell and Jamieson 1990).

If there is a collective consciousness about peace and war, such consciousness may be imagined as a unified field. However, its reality may be much different than the one imagined by the traditional realist theory of international relations (see Beer 1992). Indeed—in contrast to the simplicity of a few realist decision-makers calculating on the basis of power maximization and cost-benefit—collective consciousness of peace and war as it is reflected in the Gulf War debate appears extremely complex and multiplistic. We may think of multiple actors using multiple forms of reasoning in multiple rhetorics.

The Gulf War debate provides a rhetorical self-portrait of the collective American mind at work thinking about peace and war. The thickest texture of description is the talk itself, captured either in video or text. We infer collective peace/war consciousness out of this discursive raw material. We imagine such collective consciousness as an emergent property of a massively parallel, multidimensional system including multiple interconnected minds. These minds perceive, decide, and influence issues of peace and war on very different grounds in very different ways. The various minds individually contain multiple images. Each war activates old images—land mines in the minds (Beer and Boynton 1991). Each war also creates new images waiting to be activated in new wars at some future time.

When we constitute peace/war actors—individual or collective—as massively parallel, multidimensional systems, we can do no less for peace/war observers. Using the raw data, observers categorize the talk according to their own schemata. Thus, one possible coding scheme in which we may understand the Gulf War debate is standard realist theory with its emphasis on national interest defined in terms of power. An alternative coding scheme, to which we turn our attention in this chapter, is metaphor, particularly the metaphor of the body.

The Theory of Embodied Understanding

Metaphorical reasoning is one of the many accepted prisms of human observation and reasoning. Just as one can talk of case-based, model-based, rule-based, explanation-based, and other forms of reasoning as general approaches to problem solving and planning, so it is also possible to think of metaphor-based reasoning in these terms (cf. Sylvan and Voss 1998; Hybel 1993; Mefford 1991). In an important sense, each spoken or written word is a metaphor, creating a system of metaphors, composing the language by which we understand our world. And language is the medium by which understanding is achieved and shared by its participants. Thus, metaphor contains important keys to human thought processes. Research in this area has helped us achieve a more stable and structured understanding of the metaphoric dimension of cognition (see Goatly 1997; Mio and Katz 1996; Steen 1994; Ortony 1993; Van Noppen and Hols 1990; Greiner 1988; Lakoff 1987; Lakoff and Johnson 1980; Black 1962).

Metaphor also provides a powerful rhetorical tool. We propose to think of the mind constructed as a densely interconnected lattice of nodes and links. In this conception, the mind merges with the body. Cognition and emotion are joined through the central nervous system. In the phrase of Boynton and Lodge (1993), we have "hot cognition." If we have hot cognition, metaphors appear as hot buttons. There is an infinite number of hot buttons with varying strengths and connectivities. Actors may approach these buttons strategically, consciously attempting to construct and manipulate their audience to produce desired political effects.

When each word is a metaphor, and each metaphor has an infinite number of meanings, it is hard to know where to begin a metaphorical analysis of politics. Fortunately, a set of metaphors centering on the body offers a plausible and powerful way for us to begin to think about peace/war decisions. We are, after all, physical beings "bounded and set off from the rest of the world by the surface of our skins, and we experience the rest of the world as outside us" (Lakoff and Johnson 1980, 29).

We have long been accustomed to the metaphor of the body in politics. The "body politic" is an old figure of speech, stretching back to the origins of political theory. Plato, for example, held that the state absorbed and included the entire collective activity of its citizens— that the state was, moreover, the citizen writ large. Aristotle, too, believed in an "organic" theory of the state, viewing it not merely as an aggregation of parts but as a separate entity with its own immanent teleology. Cicero saw the state as the product of man's fundamental social nature. Perhaps the most famous use of the body politic as metaphor is the frontispiece of Thomas Hobbes's *Leviathan,* where the state is depicted in the form of a man composed of homunculi.

Only recently have we begun to appreciate the fundamental importance of the human body in a more detailed way for our understanding of the political world. Our bodies provide the basic relational system that guides our understanding of the world and our place in it. We distinguish between bodies and things, yet we also understand things in terms of our bodies. We distinguish between bodies and minds, yet despite Cartesian dualism, modern science understands very well that the mind is in the body. We are only now beginning to appreciate that the body is also in the mind. *Pace* homunculism, there is indeed a little man—or woman—inside.

In this view, the key notion is embodied understanding, since meaning cannot be independent of a human being's conception of the world. The body is a key to the deep structure of consciousness, cognition, and rhetoric. We are never separated from our bodies; nor are we separated from the forces and energies acting upon us that give rise to our understanding of "being-in-the-world." A general understanding of the world, including its political aspects, in terms of our physical body has specific implications. Bodily "image schemata are pervasive, well-defined, and full of sufficient internal structure to constrain our understanding and reasoning." Embodied understanding implies "spatial orientation like up-down, front-back, on-off, center-periphery, and near-far" (Lakoff and Johnson 1980, 25; Johnson 1987, 126, 206. cf. Brooks 1993; Gilman 1991; Hunt 1991; Berman 1989; Scarry 1985; Brown 1966; Burke 1966). A list of some of obvious, direct bodily referents includes attraction, balance, block-age, center-periphery, collection, compulsion, contact, container, count, counterforce, cycle, enablement, full-empty, iteration, link, mass, matching, merging, near-far, object, part-whole, path, process, removal, restraint, scale, splitting, superimposition, surface. These words compose a partial list of sche-mata—embodied structures of understanding—that constitute a large part of what we mean by form itself in our experience.

An Embodied Understanding of the Gulf War Debate

The Gulf War debate offers a case in which we can see the political importance of embodied understanding. Prior work has already begun such an interpre-tation. Lakoff (1991) suggests the importance of the anthropomorphic "State-as-Person" metaphor and the "Ruler-for-State" metonymy. Voss, Kennet, Wiley, and Engstler-Schooler (1998) also discuss a diverse sample of specific meta-phors used in the Gulf War debate with some of their discussion specifically incorporating a bodily orientation. For example, during the Senate debate sev-eral Democrats characterized America's position as "in a hole" (Joseph Biden [D-Delaware]), "boxed in" (Brock Adams [D-Washington]), "painted into a cor-ner," or "like lemmings marching into the sea" (John Kerry [D-Massachusetts]). Republicans, in contrast, saw the situation as a "window of opportunity" (William Broomfield [R-Michigan] and Thomas Craig [R-Wyoming]), although one Democrat, Senator Adams, referring to the lack of attention given to the situation in the Baltic states, said, "we are looking out the wrong window." Further evidence of spatial perspective during the debate can be seen by use of the word "path" and its synonyms. Democrats frequently referred to follow-ing a particular path to reach an acceptable conclusion—for example, we should "stay the course" of sanctions (George Mitchell [D-Maine]). Senator

Edward Kennedy (D-Massachusetts) utilized a literary reference to "path" by quoting from Robert Frost's "The Road Not Taken." With only one exception—Sen. William Cohen (R-Maine), who stated that "the path is dark and dangerous"—Republicans did not utilize the path metaphor.

One approach to understanding embodiment theory as it was manifested during the Gulf War debate is through a simple frequency count of bodily references and their cognates. Of course, frequencies alone are too crude and simple to tell us very much about decision-making processes. For such language to "count" in more than the sense of descriptive statistics, it must be translated into the standard lexicon of international relations discourse. The extent to which particular words have bodily content depends, moreover, on the context in which they appear. Furthermore, one ought to distinguish between diverse literal and figurative denotations and connotations. Space does not allow for a full explication and translation of each bodily referent listed above. Nevertheless, we can present raw citation frequencies for a small sample—attraction, balance, blockage, center-periphery, collection, compulsion, contact, container—in the text of the U.S. House and Senate debates.

ATTRACTION

Attraction and its cognates appear relatively little in the debate text. Perhaps it is well to start here. Reference paucity induces some healthy skepticism and modesty. At the same time, it also encourages ingenuity, like the famous Sherlock Holmes case of the dog that did not bark. The infrequency of *attraction* is all the more surprising because President Bush mobilized a grand international alliance against Saddam Hussein. *Attraction,* we believe, is properly translated into the lexicon of international relations as *alliance.* Allies in general, and in the particular case of the Gulf War, were supposedly *attracted* to each other through either past history and shared values, or common interests. As evidence of this, the common international relations term *alliance* and its cognates appear quite frequently, a total of 701 times.

BALANCE

Balance, of course, is a central term in international relations. *Balance of power,* enshrined in two millennia of realist theory beginning with Thucydides, is also part of the common folklore—the shared wisdom of foreign policy. The congressional Gulf War debate reinforces the privilege of this term. It and its cognates occur in the debate a total of 107 times. Like the famous earlier Peloponnesian debates, the Gulf War debate helps us to achieve a more complex understanding of the way thought is structured and language is used (Alker

1988). In the case of *balance,* we come to understand more clearly an entire complex of related applications. In the following passage, for example, Rep. Peter De Fazio (D-Oregon) uses *balance* to lay out the national pieces of the Gulf region and attempts to structure the forces of that region on a very complex board: "if we think about what is the long-term effect here, we have embraced Iraq to *counter* Iran. Now we are embracing Syria to *counter* Iraq. After we decapitate Iraq in this war, if that is what happens, what then is next in the region? How do we instill a new government in Iraq? How do we *balance* the forces in the region? Will we have to occupy Iraq? Will we have to defend Iraq against Syria or Turkey or Iran in the near future in order to gain so-called or restore so-called *balance* in the region?" (CR, H-132)[2]

BLOCKAGE

Blockage encourages us to explore the semantic field or network in a bit more detail. Cognates include *block, blockade, blockaded, blockading, blockages, blocked, blocking,* and *blocks.* Related words are *embargo, force, intervention, penetration,* and *sanctions.* An extended family of antonyms might include *freedom, liberation, release,* and *unblockage. Blockage* itself appears relatively infrequently in the debates. Yet a cognate, *blockade,* is used sixty-one times. *Blockade* has such a specific strategic connotation that we should not ordinarily think of its association with *blockage.* However, once the association is made, we have enlarged and enriched our understanding. A blockade is, of course, a form of blockage. Indeed, in the case of the Gulf War, blockage in the form of an economic embargo was the major alternative strategic option. *Embargo* and its cognates, by the way, appear 260 times.

It is said that opposites attract. Through the dynamic of difference suggested by Saussure and Derrida, an analysis of *blockage* implies consideration of *unblockage. Unblock* does not appear at all in the debates. But *liberation,* particularly the liberation of Kuwait, figures strongly. The word *liberation* itself and its cognates only occur forty-six times. When we widen the net a bit, however, we catch more fish. For example, *free* and its cognates appear 167 times.

Penetration is the opposite of blockage in another dimension. Where liberation relieves or dissolves the blockage, penetration pierces it. This line of argument has obvious sexual connotations that have been well explored in Freudian interpretation. This is a hotter cognition button, much more powerfully embodied than the words we have been considering. Yet it seems too hot for those in Congress to touch directly. There are only two direct references in the debates. A cooler version is *intervene;* there are 374 references to it or its cognates. Intervention, like blockade, is a standard means of foreign policy and is densely connected in the theory and practice of international relations. It was, of course, the major strategic alternative to an embargo, and the option finally chosen by the United States.

The center-periphery distinction has had wide play in international political economy. Theorists like André Gunder Frank and Johan Galtung, their associates, and followers have used the differentiation, sometimes substituting *core* for *center* to distinguish between the international elite and mass. In this sense, the discussion is very much linked to *mass,* another important bodily term. Nevertheless, the key metaphorical orientation is different. *Center-periphery* implies a Euclidean circular geometry. *Mass* evokes the world of Newtonian physics. The words are tools that can be used to perform the same operations— distinguishing between the privileged center and exiled periphery or mass— but they are different tools, forged on different anvils, used in different ways. *Center* emerges as the key term in this dyad, appearing thirty-seven times compared with periphery's three. *Center* evokes a very clear circular spatial grid. Indeed, as Sen. Steven Symms (R-Idaho) used *center,* he conjured up an image of a spider—Saddam Hussein—sitting at the center of a web of domestic power: "The Iraqi dictator sits at the *center* of a web of state, party, military, and secret police organizations. As President and Chairman of the Revolutionary Command Council, Saddam controls all government bureaucracies. As Secretary General of the Regional Command of the Baath Party, he leads 50,000 Baath Party members and 1.5 million sympathizers. As Commander in Chief of the armed forces he leads Iraq's one-million-man army" (CR, S-380).

When the web spreads outward, beyond the national boundaries of Iraq, it entangles an ever-growing number of participants, including the international world of terrorism. However, as in a real web, control always remains at the *center* with the spider. Indeed, as Sen. Orrin Hatch (R-Utah) suggested: "We all know that the world's most vicious terrorists have taken up residence in Baghdad. But while we have been waiting and debating, they have been preparing for cold-blooded killing. Our embassies and bases on three continents have been cased by likely terrorists. Terrorists are on the move, and weapons and equipment are being put into place. Iraq stands at the *center* of these actions, providing the crucial support—false passports, sophisticated equipment, vast sums of money—that only a state sponsor of terror has available" (CR, S-385).

During the course of the debate, it became evident that the allied counter-strategy could be plotted on the same circular grid. Indeed, Sen. Daniel Akaka

(D-Hawaii) invoked the *center* referent to describe contemplated actions against Saddam Hussein: "Following Iraq's illegal takeover of Kuwait, the United Nations has adopted 12 resolutions over the past 5 months in an attempt to resolve the crisis peacefully and without the use of force. The *centerpiece* of the U.N. initiatives was an agreement to apply economic sanctions against Iraq, which would result in its peaceful withdrawal from Kuwait" (CR, S-396).

Periphery, of course, is an opposite of *center* and its textual use illustrates another important dimension of bodily orientation. For example, Sen. Paul Sarbanes (D-Maryland) distinguishes between vital (or central) and peripheral components of the national interest: "Of course we have interests in the Gulf. But it is essential to distinguish between *peripheral* interests and vital interests. Vital interests exist when our national security is truly at risk. Vital interests are those you kill and die for" (CR, S-154).

Peripheral interests of the state may be sacrificed in order that its more vital central interests be maintained. In much the same way, peripheral elements of the human body—such as skin or even limbs—may be sacrificed in order to maintain the "center" of the body—the life essence, or "soul."

COLLECTION

Collection shows up most frequently in the text as *collective.* In this form it sharpens a dichotomy between the individual leader or nation and common activities taken in concert by democratic societies, allies, and international institutions. Power is not individual but collective. The American president acts as the collective representative of a democratic people, mobilizing and applying their united force and strength. As Rep. Frank McCloskey (D-Indiana) pointed out, "Such power ultimately is not up to one man, but the collective wisdom of the people through their elected representatives" (CR, H-152). Democratic judgment, conscience, and decision are collective. Indeed, as Rep. Patricia Schroeder (D-Colorado) pointed out: "That is what this democratic principle is all about. This is not a country where we recognize that one person has all the wisdom. Every one of us has feet of clay, and the best judgment we can have is a lot of *collective* judgment in this wonderful Republic" (CR, H-153).

International security and defense are also collective and are buttressed by the norms of international law. Within this collective, America has a leadership role and "bears the brunt of our *collective* security burden" (Rep. Henry Waxman [D-California]; CR, H-156).

Compulsion is used as a frame to distinguish between free and slave societies, the free American Self and the enslaved Other. One of the marks distinguishing the evil regime of Saddam Hussein is the use of compulsory labor. The theme of compulsion also enters the democratic debate in Congress. Senator Joseph Lieberman (D-Connecticut) made it clear that he did not wish to create an unseemly compulsion of the president to go to war. Rather, he wanted Congress to share the collective responsibility for the actions that must be taken: "I make my choice today to support the President of the United States, to give him not a *compulsion* to go to war, but an authorization to commit our troops to battle should he determine it necessary to protect our national security. Mr. President, by doing so, we do not pass the buck of responsibility. In fact, we in the Congress share in the responsibility of leadership and that is part of the price of public service" (CR, S-376).

CONTACT

The network of political life is constructed through contact. The world of international relations is bound together through contact. As Sen. Trent Lott (R-Mississippi) noted: "The world is united—and I have to commend President Bush for the effort that he made through the United Nations and with personal diplomacy, personal *contacts* with leaders all over the world to bring the world together, unite against the aggression of one man, really, Saddam Hussein" (CR, S-376).

In contrast, the evil nature of Saddam Hussein appears clearly in his lack of contact with others in his society: "Saddam lives and works in isolation, shunning *contact* with his people, probably out of fear of assassination. He is believed to have survived several attempts on his life and is heavily guarded during his rare public appearances. Saddam is extremely distrustful, even of his closest associates" (CR, S-380).

The great issues of war and peace also depend on contact. During the Gulf War debate Sen. Daniel Patrick Moynihan (D-New York) recalled the wise words of the great Prussian chief of staff Helmuth von Moltke: "No battle plan ever survived *contact* with the enemy" (CR, S-394). Likewise, Sen. Hank Brown (R-Colorado) evinced belief in contacts by stating his hope "that economic sanctions and diplomatic *contacts* would convince Saddam to restore Kuwaiti sovereignty. Namely, that these efforts [would] show that the world is committed absolutely to his withdrawal from Kuwait" (CR, S-396).

Container obviously translates into *containment,* one of the major orienting terms of postwar international relations. The Gulf War debate evokes new nuances. Iraq is a *container* that contains Kuwait, and Kuwait is a *container* that contains significant territory and oil. As Senator Symms reported: "When Kuwait was annexed as Iraq's nineteenth province on August 8, a swathe of northern Kuwait that the Iraqis named the Saddamiyat al-Mitlaa was incorporated into Iraq's Basra province. According to maps distributed to Iraqi embassies, this territorial enclave consists of Kuwait's Northern Province, which *contains* approximately one-third of Kuwait's territory and one-fifth of its oil. Refugees fleeing Kuwait report that border posts and a concrete wall are being constructed along the new border" (CR, S-380).

Containment, in contrast to *container,* suggests a state of being rather than an actual object. Of course, the policy of containment—pivotal to realist theory—draws its inspiration from George Kennan. As Senator Kerry of Massachusetts pointed out: "We sustained our fight against the Soviets for 40 years after Stalin took over Eastern Europe. We *contained* Stalinism, and in time, an isolated and decaying Soviet Union has been going through a process of caving in. Iraq, a far less powerful nation than the Soviets, will be ground down even more surely, and far more quickly, if we only have the patience to stay with our original policy" (CR, S-249).

In the Soviet case, containment had an important military dimension. The North Atlantic Treaty Organization's (NATO) doctrine in Europe was based on strong military forces opposing massive Soviet conventional might but relied on nuclear weapons to make up for conventional force shortfalls. In the Iraqi case, the context was somewhat different. The proposed strategy of containment in this context took on a more economic flavor. As Senator Sarbanes spoke of the Iraqi case, the assumption of those who supported a sanctions policy was that over time "as the bite of these economic sanctions were felt and the punitive *containment*—the embargo, the blockade, the use of force to make the sanctions effective through the blockade—as that bite [became] stronger and stronger with the passage of time, it would over time lead to his departure from Kuwait" (CR, S-151).

There was, of course, a fear of a wider political and military containment failure if narrower economic containment was not effective. Indeed, as reported by the *New York Times:* "the conflict would thus become regionally destabilizing, on a scale that is difficult precisely to define but that could become also impossible to *contain.* Moreover, if Arab emotions were to become aroused by military action against Iraq, that is seen as largely American in origin, the ensuing radicalization of the Arab masses could eventually even produce upheavals in those more moderate Arab states that the United States is currently seeking to protect" (CR, S-155).

Farther Reaches of Embodiment

The analysis of bodily metaphor in the rhetoric of the Gulf War debate only begins to suggest the potential richness of this approach. Subsequent research may examine bodily form and structure, process and motion in more detail. Such work will treat more intensively the terms already discussed, as well as additional terms that we have not had the space to examine. Words of the body offer only one avenue into this world.

The large majority of these words are generic, ignoring such critical differences between bodies as gender. A special analysis of engendered terms might begin to spell out more clearly and specifically the grammar of male hegemony and privilege, female subordination and repression (cf. Peterson 1992; Grant and Newland 1991; Elshtain and Tobias 1990; Sylvester 1994; Enloe 1990).

Finally, the language of embodiment brings us from the physical to the metaphysical, from the profane to the edge of the sacred. With some exceptions, mythology and theology have not, to put it gently, been favorite areas of contemporary political science, psychology, or international studies. Yet, as political beings—citizens and decision makers—we do not escape the human condition. Indeed, as suggested earlier in chapter 4, we cannot remove ourselves to some higher ground where total objectivity and neutrality reign. Rather, we are bound by our own time and our own space to understand the world in which we participate through a shared way of understanding. We are, therefore, necessarily subjected to the limits of our existence, including our use of language, which allows us to participate in a human community. It is our political language, of course, that expresses the various dimensions of our humanity (Vaux 1992).

Embodiment theory provides some tools through which we can examine the language reflecting this dimension of our consciousness. A focus on the body helps us to see and code the words that express the struggle against death with its field of stasis, despair, end, decomposition, loneliness, and sorrow. It captures the words of life, involving breath, joy, verve, community, flow, vitality, and hope (Gerhart and Russell 1984, 32, 125). Peace and war are ultimately about millions of people engaged in enormous, perhaps apocalyptic, struggles of life and death on a global scale.

Peace, War, and the Body

The strong program of modern Western civilization, beginning with the Enlightenment, sought to establish a realm for the mind separate from the body and the soul. Philosophers constructed strong dualities of mind and body, state and church, science and religion, reason and emotion. In this way, they sought to establish separate identity, space, and freedom for the privileged terms—mind, state, science, and reason. Modern ontology, the philosophy of being, is the result of half a millennium of this program.

Contemporary realist theory of international relations is very much a part of this effort. International relations theory aspires to the rigor and status of science. According to this science, states are the main actors in international relations. Political leaders use reason to decide the weighty issues of peace and war. Free from religious superstition and emotion, they simply calculate the costs and benefits. When war has greater expected utility, within the formal constraints of strategic interaction, states fight.

Our approach to the Gulf War debate shares some aspects of this modern program—particularly its concern with a scientific approach. Yet, paradoxically, the resulting research shows something quite different than one might have expected. The debate occurred within the formal institutions and processes of a modern secular democracy. It was conducted in the language of states and reason. However, in a certain interpretive lens, the debate takes on a very different aspect. We see not only states but also individuals. We see the figurative language of metaphor—the metaphor of the body, the body politic. If we looked a bit farther, we should see very specific body types and body parts appear vividly in the debate. We should see the profane, the devil in the details. We should see the divine, God's vicar on earth, in the secular garb of the president. We should also see the sacred. Death is there, but so are birth and rebirth, life and eternal life. The devil appears and also the deity. The story of the Gulf War, in this light, might resemble a medieval passion play.

Embodiment theory enriches our understanding of international consciousness. Many key realist concepts can be traced back or translated to bodily referents. For example, the previous discussion suggested how realist theory projects humanoid attributes onto the nation-state, drawing strict boundaries between the national Self and Others, between those inside and outside national identity and property (cf. Burch 1997; Walker 1993). It discussed the way in which attraction is connected to alliance; balance to the balance of power; blockage to blockade; center-periphery to core and marginal interests; collection to collective interests as well as collective defense and security; compulsion to the use of force and coercion; contact to diplomatic discourse and military friction; container to containment. At the same time, this analysis suggests dimensions of international consciousness beyond realism. Indeed, it attempts to understand through metaphor the conceptual systems of the key actors involved—be they individuals, institutions, or states. Embodiment theory is thus both a frame for and a supplement to conventional realism.

A better understanding of collective consciousness is important as part of the evolution away from war and toward more stable peace. The language of the body is a key to such progress. It includes the complex interaction between rhetoric and psychology in deciding and mobilizing for peace and war. It allows our experience of physical objects to provide the basis for further understanding. Constructive collective learning depends on our ability to understand the structure and dynamics of existing collective myths, and to form effective new ones. In such myths, the language of the body is a part of the language and the meaning of peace and war.

6

Women's Words

Gender and Rhetoric in the Gulf War Debate

FRANCIS A. BEER AND LAURA BRUNELL

Realism, as we have seen, proposes that national decision makers decide issues of war and peace on a standardized basis. Their central criterion for peace/war decision is national interest defined in terms of power. Yet, as we have suggested, and as an enormous body of research makes clear, war and peace are decided in a much more complex way than the simple realist view implies. In modern states, particularly democracies, power is diffused and shared by multiple actors. These actors have different attributes that influence the way they approach and the meanings they give to war and peace.

One of these attributes is gender. In contemporary democracies, a growing number of political scientists and political decision makers are women. A wave of literature suggests that gender needs to be included in a sophisticated understanding of politics.[1] Feminist theorizing about international relations has been an important part of this movement.[2] This wide array of work on gender differences strongly supports the idea that women and men policy makers may reason and deliberate about war and peace in very different ways. For example, men and women have very different orientations toward peace settlements in an environment of intractable conflict. Women appear more concerned with relationships, men with retribution. In the presence of a prior peace settlement, women are more forgiving about an opponent's future conflictual actions. Men react in the opposite way; violations of a peace agreement provoke more extreme conflictual responses than if there had been no agreement (Bourne, Beer, Sinclair, and Healy 1996).

The gender hypothesis suggests that men and women have significantly different affective, cognitive, and rhetorical orientations that affect peace/war decisions—that women feel, think, speak, and act differently than men about war and peace. We investigate this hypothesis through an analysis of gender differences in the rhetoric of the 1990 congressional Gulf War debates. We assume that different individuals in Congress emphasize different rhetorical themes. These rhetorical themes either reflect accurately what they feel and think or their articulation of the feelings and thoughts of their constituents. In either case, we believe that the words of decision makers are important aspects of the foreign policy decision process and that women's rhetoric will have its own separate identity that expresses and shapes the meaning of war and peace.

Framing the Gulf War Debate:
Gender Differences and Rhetorical Themes

The Gulf War debate has already given evidence of just-war argument and bodily metaphor in foreign policy discourse. It now provides a rhetorical portrait of the gendered American mind at work thinking about peace and war. It offers a case in which we can see the political importance of gendered understandings of peace and war.

Our analysis of the role of gender in the congressional Gulf War debate focuses on the extent to which female members of Congress framed the debate differently than their male counterparts. Twenty-eight female members of Congress participated in the Gulf War debate. Twenty of these women were Democrats and eight were Republicans. Of the twenty Democrats, seventeen advocated that the United States continue sanctions against Iraq, while seven of the eight Republican women argued for more immediate forceful intervention. In order to make comparisons by gender, we selected a random sample of twenty-eight men who spoke during the debate. The sample consisted of fourteen Democrats and fourteen Republicans. All of the Republican men and six of the Democratic men supported going to war.

We constructed four scales to measure rhetorical themes that we believed important. We used these four dimensions to determine whether the debate was framed differently by female and male speakers. Specifically, we asked: (1) Are there significant differences in the usages of each dimension between female and male speakers? And (2), Do any of these dimensions significantly influence policy makers' decisions about war? The first two scales, realism and idealism, measured themes derived from international relations theory. Realism, as we have discussed, is the dominant form of reasoning and rhetoric in international relations. Realist theorists and decision makers conceive of international relations as the anarchic interplay of unrestrained actors for whom military force is a primary form of international action. Idealism is often juxtaposed to realism in the language of international relations. Idealism stresses the importance of international due process in the form of international organizations and agreements modeled on domestic democratic institutions.

The rhetorical approach and the scales for realism and idealism are based on earlier work on the rhetoric, semantics, and psychometrics of realism and idealism. Prior scaling analysis was used in searching canonical international relations texts for prototypic realist and idealist words (cf. Beer and Hariman 1996; Balleck 1994; Beer and Balleck 1994). Expert coders then evaluated the words for goodness of fit along realist and idealist dimensions. The resulting realist and idealist items included a short list of key words and their cognates. For realism, the words of interest included *anarchy, balance, defense, force, interests, nation, power, security, sovereignty,* and *state.* Idealist words included *agency, agreement, democracy, disarmament, environment, government, institutions, justice, order, organization, peace, reform, regulation, security, structure, transformation,* and *welfare.*

The first question of interest was whether women and men used words differently in the Gulf War debates. In the case of realism, men generally used realist words more frequently than women. In particular, men tended to use specific words such as *force, interests, military,* and their cognates more often than women did. Interestingly, women used some realist words—such as *defense* and *state*—more frequently than men did. Other realist words had balanced gender profiles—*nation* and *power,* for example. Finally, some words in the realist lexicon—*anarchy* and *balance of power*—were used more sparingly than international relations theorists might have suspected. Idealist words, taken as a whole, were used less than half as often as realist words. The use of specific idealist words was generally more balanced between genders, though men again used them slightly more. Men emphasized specific words such as *agreement, peace,* and *security.* Women stressed *democracy.*

The other two thematic scales derived more directly from our concern with gender. These scales centered on the body and the family. We have already discussed the relevance of metaphors, particularly metaphors of the body, for the theory and rhetoric of international relations.[3] The physical body seems particularly important to a concern with gender.

The defining characteristic of the words in the body scale is their physical grounding. Each of them emerges from the attempt to orient human bodies in the material world. At the same time, there is some overlap between the body words and the realist words that we discussed earlier. For example, both the realist and the body scales include the words *balance* and *force*. The body scale also includes the word *intervention*, which has both realist and hawkish connotations. The body scale also has an idealist or dovish dimension—for example, *freedom*. In order to strengthen this idealist strand and to balance the scale's realist, prowar implications, we also included in the body scale the words *embargo* and *sanctions*. Although less directly related to the physical body, they appeared to be reasonable international applications of *blockage* and *container*. Men used these body words more frequently than women. The largest differences occurred with words that were less metaphorical and more political.

Finally, a set of words was derived from Ruddick's (1989) idea of "maternal thinking," or familial metaphors and references.[4] According to Ruddick, maternal thought comprises "the intellectual capacities [a mother] develops, the judgments she makes, the metaphysical attitudes she assumes, [and] the values she affirms" (1989, 24). Ruddick argues that anyone engaged in maternal work must provide for three demands of all children: preservation, growth, and social acceptability (1989, 17). She asserts: "Conceptually and historically, the preeminent of these demands is that of preservation. . . . Preserving the lives of children is the central constitutive, invariant aim of maternal practice; the commitment to achieving that aim is the constitutive maternal act" (18–19).

Ruddick further notes that the maternal commitment to preservation is in direct conflict to the aims of military actions: "It seems obvious, even without resorting to war memoirs and analyses, that military endeavors endanger what a mother seeks to preserve. . . . Treasuring lives, holding them and the material that sustains them, seems directly opposed to the conquest of battlefields, the destruction of wills, bodies, landscapes and artifacts, expected of soldiers" (1989, 240).

Ruddick also explores connections between gender and the epistemology of war. She believes that conceptions of peace and war are stratified by gender. In her view, "The rhetoric that pervades dominant understandings of war and peace is dichotomous and split along gender lines—a perfect illustration of standpoint theory. Within militarist thinking, as well as within larger militarist cultures, a warrior's death—and murder—is set against a child's birth; male violence against feminine connection; military destruction against preservative love" (1989, 141).

This line of reasoning led us to expect that mothers and those most socialized to practice maternal thinking (women) would oppose war based on the maternal commitment to preservation. We expected that the rhetoric surrounding the issues of peace and war would be differentiated along gender lines.

The list of words in the maternalist scale includes *brother, children, daughter, family, father, growth, husband, kid, life, love, mother, parents, preserve, protect, sisters, son,* and *wife.* As we expected, women used these words more often than men—about twice as often. This tendency was uniform across each and every one of the maternalist words. The result was the strongest gender difference that our four thematic scales—realism, idealism, body, maternalism—revealed.

The following excerpts from several of the women's speeches are exemplary.[5]

Representative Nita Lowey (D-New York), advocating continued sanctions, said: "As I prepare to vote, I must ask myself, as the *mother* of three grown children, could I accept their deaths in battle, with the justification which has been made at this point. As a Member of this Congress, I have a responsibility to consider the lives of the American men and women serving in the gulf as if they were my own *children.* To use any other standard would be unthinkable. For now, my answer to those questions is no" (emphasis added).

Representative Patsy Mink (D-Hawaii), also arguing for continued sanctions, observed: "Before we commit our *children* to this violence I ask that Congress tell our *children* why declaring war against Iraq is necessary for peace in the world, and that Congress advise our *children* that they go to war because their Government has exhausted all other avenues to peace" (emphasis added).

The passages above highlight two different aspects of the maternalist dimension. First, Lowey framed her decision in terms of her own experience as a mother and whether she would be willing to risk her own children's lives in the Gulf War. Second, Mink talked about the responsibility she felt for all of America's children—that is, for the young men and women who would serve in the Gulf.

Relationships and Clusters

We have discussed qualitative gender differences in word frequencies. These rhetorical findings are interesting, but they still need to be related to the broader political dimensions of the Gulf War. The exemplary texts just cited, for example, lead immediately to a question about the relationship between maternalist thinking and policy position. Did women, and men who used maternalist thinking, disproportionately support economic sanctions rather than military intervention? Some data relevant to this question are embedded in the body scale; men made greater use of the words *embargo* and *sanctions* than did women. Nevertheless, men also disproportionately used the word *force,* and the data do not reveal whether the men, who tended to favor war more than the women, were positively or negatively disposed to harder or softer policy alternatives.

We did not follow this lead in the direction of a more qualitative, contextual analysis, although it strongly beckoned. Instead, we chose to push farther in the direction of more quantitative, systematic, comparative relationships. Each speaker in our samples of women and men was given an overall score on each of the four thematic dimensions associated with the realism, idealism, body, and maternalism scales. These scores were based on the total number of key words (and cognates) she or he used during the debate, with the frequencies collapsed by deciles into five ordinal categories ranging from zero to four.

This manipulation led to dramatically compressed variance. Most speakers fell at the lower end of the collapsed scores, using the words from all of the scales relatively little. There were strong, statistically significant ($p = .001$) overall relationships between usage frequencies in all of the themes. Relevant correlation coefficients included realism-idealism (.67), realism-body (.72), realism-maternalism (.48), idealism-body (.59), idealism-maternalism (.51), and body-maternalism (.48). Large or small users of items in any one of the scales were more likely to show similar usage frequency patterns for the other scales. It is unclear whether this was a function of the condensed scale structure or a measure of cognitive/linguistic complexity.

In addition to the rhetorical measures already discussed, we developed comparable measures of political ideology based on American Conservative Union (ACU) ratings, using a similar zero–four ordinal scaling metric. We also used binary measures of political party and the individual's final vote on the use of military force. Ideology, party, and vote, as one might have expected, were significantly ($p = .001$) related to each other. We further coded the speakers' parental status. With one exception, there were no significant relationships between the political measures, gender, parental status, and the rhetorical scales. That one exception—a negative association (-.3495, $p = .01$) between maternal rhetoric and the vote—provides an answer to the question that we asked earlier about the association between maternalist rhetoric and the final vote. Speakers emphasizing family narrative in their talk tended to be more dovish and to vote against the use of military force.

The analysis so far has been variable-based rather than case-based. In order to get an additional perspective, we conducted a cluster analysis, organizing our data by speakers.[6] The most theoretically significant of the resulting clusters was one that included sixteen individuals whom we call realist-maternalist-liberals. What set this cluster apart from the rest was its particularly high mean scores on both the realist and maternalist dimensions: more than twice as high as the general population mean on realism and three times as high for maternalism. It was also the most liberal cluster, with ten of its sixteen members scoring below twenty on the ACU rating. This cluster was also the most male dominated, with men comprising 63 percent of its members. In terms of hawks and doves, it was almost split with seven members advocating war, including three Democrats, and nine members voting against war.

The one member who probably typifies this cluster best is Rep. Dick Gephardt (D-Missouri). He sponsored the Gephardt-Hamilton resolution that advocated continuing sanctions against Iraq. Gephardt justified his decision in both realist and maternalist terms, as one can see in the following passages from his speeches:

REALISM

Mr. Speaker, let us be clear about the lines being drawn in this debate. This is not a choice between those who want to force Saddam Hussein out of Iraq and those who want to talk him out. All Americans agree: Saddam Hussein must be driven out of Kuwait. And driving him out will take more than words. It will take *force*. I realize that. The President realizes that. The entire world recognizes that (emphasis added).

Thus, the choice was not between action and inaction, it was a choice between two different courses of action—two different methods of applying force. It was a choice between the headlong rush to combat, and the policy of patient strength.

MATERNALISM

We owe it to those courageous *young men and women* to try every other alternative before we sacrifice even a single American life. As former Defense Secretary Robert McNamara has said: "Surely we should be prepared to extend sanctions over a 12-or 18-month period if that offers an opportunity to achieve our political objective without the loss of American lives. Who can doubt that a year of blockade will be cheaper than a week of war."

Yes, sanctions do take time—there's no doubt about it. Can it be that we are not willing to ask the American people to wait for success, but we are willing to ask them to sacrifice their *sons and daughters* to achieve success? Is our patience really that thin? Is our resolve really that frail (emphasis added)?

It is evident from the previous passages that Representative Gephardt justified his decision rhetorically in terms of both the metaphors of realism and maternalism. He did not portray continuing sanctions as a passive strategy but one of action and forcefulness. He used maternalist rhetoric in order to cast the decision of going to war in human terms, terms that would cost some people the lives of their children.

Ironically, those in the realist-maternalist-liberal cluster who advocated going to war also used maternalist rhetoric. They argued that not going to war would ultimately cost more human lives and cause further suffering to children in the Middle East. Comments by Robert Lagomarsino (R-California) demonstrate the point: "Saddam Hussein has used chemical warfare on numerous occasions against both the Iranians and his own people in Iraq. Without reservation he gassed entire Iraqi villages indiscriminately killing innocent men, women and *children,* most of whom belong to Iraq's sizable Kurdish minority. He has made no secret of his desire to literally annihilate Israel, which includes Jews, Christians and Moslems, with chemical and nuclear weapons. Again, there are many frightening similarities to Hitler" (emphasis added).

Different people used realist and maternalist rhetoric in different ways, depending upon what actions they preferred. Those wanting to go to war pointed to the suffering of Iraqi children. Those preferring to avoid war pleaded for the lives of America's young people.

A second interesting cluster was one that we call, somewhat inelegantly, idealist-unmaternalists. The name is justified by the counterfactual definition of the cluster—a lack of maternalist rhetoric. All nine members scored a zero in this dimension. Surprisingly, this was also our most female dominated cluster—seven of its nine members were women. In terms of party, six of the nine were Democrats, but they were more mixed ideologically, scoring close to the population mean, which was moderately liberal. The strongest dimension for this cluster was the idealist one, averaging about 50 percent higher than the rest of the population.

Representative Louise Slaughter (D-New York) provides an example of an idealist-unmaternalist speaker. She stressed the idealist root human in advocating continued sanctions against Iraq. In all, she used the word *human* seven times stressing *human lives, human suffering,* and international agreements on *human rights.* She also used the root word *peace* seven times. The following passage suggests the idealist tone of her talk: "Today, we must deal with the future—and we must do so with a full realization that diplomacy and economic sanctions still offer opportunities for *peace* that may be lost forever if we vote to engage in war" (emphasis added).

Slaughter and the other women in this cluster put faith in diplomacy and the ability of international organizations to control Iraq. They tended to frame the debate in terms of treaties, agreements, and rights. This cluster was outstanding for its use of idealist rhetoric and for its domination by women.

Conclusion

This analysis reinforces the idea that war and peace have multiple meanings for different people. There are many ways of reasoning and talking about peace and war. Realism is certainly important. At the same time, women and men come to international relations with many other perspectives and emphases that influence both their rhetoric and their willingness to commit their nation to war. During the Gulf War debate, realist words were used more frequently than words from the other scales, but certainly not to their exclusion. Words from the other dimensions that we measured—idealism, body, maternalism—both supplemented and complemented realist rhetoric.

Maternalism, the family narrative, emerged as a particularly relevant rhetoric. The raw frequency data showed the clearest differences between men and women of any of our scales. The compressed maternalist scale showed a significant association with antiwar voting. Our cluster analysis associated maternalism with realist rhetoric and more general liberal political ideology, as indicated by past congressional votes.

What have we learned about gender and the meaning of war and peace? Gender differences exist but should not be overstated. There is some rhetorical variation between men and women. At the same time, political party affiliation and ideology may be more important than gender in how men and women finally vote. The evidence suggests that there are gender differences in cognition, language, and behavior—but there are also gender similarities. The sets of meanings of war and peace incompletely intersect: Men and women inhabit partly joint and partly separate worlds of meaning.

PART III

Audiences

The meaning of war and peace, as we have seen, depends partly on small-scale semantic effects of individual words and partly on larger-scale rhetorical effects of word aggregates. The semantic and rhetorical effects of speakers' or writers' words do not, however, exist in isolation but in connection with those who hear or read them. The meaning of war and peace thus also depends partly on audience effects, on pragmatic relations with different communities. Having moved from the linguistic microcontext of particular words to the macrocontext of masses of words, we now shift to the cognitive and behavioral macrocontext of masses of people. While still centering on language, we adjust focus to bring into view the dynamic interaction between those who speak the words and those who hear them and the effects of this interaction on the meaning of war and peace.

Chapter 7, "Talking About Dying," begins with an insight by Anthony Downs (1972) about an "issue-attention" cycle in public policy. Using as an example the case of the U.S. military intervention in Somalia, this chapter shows how different rhetorical tropes flow and ebb as political leaders attempt to move their citizen-audience into and out of military involvement. The rhetoric of the body—bodies living and dying—is the tactical tool that political leaders use to shift meaning and achieve their larger strategic purposes with their audience.

Rhetoric, as we have seen, is important for manipulating the preferences of audiences. In his later work, William Riker (1986) labeled such political manipulation "heresthetics," and his last book focused on Constitutional Convention rhetorical strategies. The next chapter, "Beer and Quiche in the Fast Lane," follows Riker into the intersection where the dynamics of rhetoric meet the theoretical narrative of rational choice. This chapter again uses material from the Gulf War debate to demonstrate how political rhetoric expresses and creates simultaneous but very different meanings of war and peace for internal and external audiences.

The last chapter in this section, "Between Maastricht and Sarajevo," further expands the focus. The lens here is a wide-angle one with a particular filter. It returns to the metaphor of the body and uses it to reinterpret the broad narrative structure of world politics during the Cold War. This shared narrative expands the identity of the audience from a collection of discrete, separate, physical individuals to a more general, collective, virtual community. As narrative blends with individual identity, shared myth, and collective culture, language merges with cognition and behavior to reflect and shape the meaning of war and peace.

7

Talking about Dying

Rhetorical Phases of the Somalia Intervention

FRANCIS A. BEER AND G. R. BOYNTON

The meaning of war and peace involves many elements. One of the most important is dying. Large numbers of people die in wars, famines, and various other catastrophes that cross national boundaries. Members of the U.S. Congress who specialize in foreign policy must, therefore, speak about dying on a regular basis.

Rhetorical Evolution: From the Cold War to the New World Order

During the Cold War, "in harm's way for the cause of freedom" was a formulaic idiom that distanced the speaker and the audience from some of the harsh reality of dying. "Whenever we put Americans in harm's way, life or limb, it has been for the cause of freedom, either our own freedom or that of our allies and our friends," said Sen. John Warner (R-Virginia) (Hearing 1987). He was talking with members of the Reagan administration about sending U.S. naval personnel to protect Kuwaiti oil tankers in the Persian Gulf during the war between Iran and Iraq. "Harm's way" objectifies and distances; U.S. leaders were not sending Americans to be killed and maimed, they were putting them in harm's way. With euphemisms, the speakers protected themselves from the harsh reality of what they felt they had to do. Why it had to be done was also part of the formula: "for the cause of freedom." Every conflict was brought within the domain of the Cold War. The United States was not protecting the world's richest hereditary monarchy when it protected the Kuwaiti tankers; it was keeping the Soviets out of the Persian Gulf. Every conflict, even that one, became "for the cause of freedom."

The Cold War is over, but its legacy remains. Representative Donald Payne (D-New Jersey) pointed out that the guns of Somalia are one of the sequelae of the Cold War. "Many of us have forgotten," he said, "that for 40 years we've had a Cold War. Many of us have forgotten that African countries were really the pawns in this Cold War. Many people may have forgotten that for 10 years the United States supplied the aid and weaponry and so forth that is in the hands of these thugs and warlords" (Hearing [1992b]). In 1991 and 1992 Somalia's "thugs and warlords" went on a rampage that produced famine and the deaths of hundreds of thousands of Somalis. The guns with which they fought were a legacy of the Cold War, but "the cause of freedom" was no longer available as a rationale for U.S. action—which eventually led to the death of U.S. soldiers. During the Cold War, members of Congress could have spoken about Somalia as "putting in harm's way for the cause of freedom," but that formula was less relevant.

How will death be spoken of in the emerging new world order? Four brief congressional hearings dealing with Somalia begin to provide an answer to this question. The first was a hearing of the Africa Subcommittee of the House Foreign Affairs Committee held in September, 1992, just after President Bush agreed to augment U.S. support for the United Nations Operation in Somalia (UNOSOM I)—the security force that was formed to protect UN humanitarian operations in Somalia. The House Foreign Affairs Committee conducted the second hearing in December, 1992, after the formation of the U.S.-led Unified Task Force (UNITAF). The UNITAF was created to bring the heavy weapons of organized factions under international control, disarm the irregular gangs, and extend its operations to the whole of Somalia, prior to handing over operational responsibility to UNOSOM II, a new peacekeeping force under United Nations command. The Senate Foreign Relations Committee held another hearing in July, 1993, about a month after Pakistani troops serving with UNOSOM II were ambushed and twenty-four were killed. The fourth hearing we looked at was held by the Senate Foreign Relations Committee in October, 1993. A key speaker was U.S. ambassador to the United Nations, Madeleine Albright, who talked about U.S. and UN peacekeeping operations. One focus of that hearing was the failed raid by the U.S. Quick Reaction Forces in which eighteen U.S. Army Rangers and a Malaysian peacekeeping soldier were killed (United Nations 1996, 93).

Words and Phrases about Death and Dying

The language used to talk about dying is an important dimension of the rhetoric of war and peace. As peace/war activity moves through time, political rhetoric molds itself to fit changing motivations and circumstances.

The successive stages or phases of war initiation, war fighting, and war termination produce a shifting distribution of different kinds of words and phrases along an emotional distance gradient. War initiation rhetoric, at the first stage, implies hot cognition. It uses direct, concrete, emotional language to attract political attention and move the issue to the center of the political agenda. A physical rhetoric powerfully evokes human atrocities and mobilizes the political support necessary to spill blood and spend treasure, to send sons and daughters for a distant cause in a far-off land. As the war moves along, the language modulates according to changing political objectives. Strong political rhetoric becomes less useful and appropriate over time. The most powerful images have already been used; they gradually lose their force through repetition. Context and contingency muddle the message; there are atrocities and casualties on both sides. Other issues demand priority. Finally, whatever the justification for the conflict, there comes a time for decreasing the commitment of military forces and the termination of hostilities. Just as political reasoning and rhetoric drive entrance into war, political reasoning and rhetoric eventually also move toward an exit.

We examined each of the committee hearings with such concerns in mind. We extracted words and phrases that seemed to us directly related to dying from the talk and listed them in the accompanying tables. A systematic, rigorous thematic content analysis was beyond our ambition. Instead, the objective was more modest, more exploratory: simply to begin to construct a glossary of talking about dying in a peace/war context. Often the reference to dying is implicit. *Tragedy*, for example, is frequently used in the hearings. It almost always refers to hundreds of thousands of Somalis starving to death. Thus, *tragedy* is one way to characterize the death of Somalis. Not all deaths are equal in the testimony. Some references are more indirect. The deaths of participants in the clan wars, for example, are explicitly referred to only once in the first two hearings. Assistant Secretary of State Herman Cohen said that as many as thirty thousand people died in the fighting. We have not extracted *insecurity, fighting, looting,* and other terms that characterize the fighting between the clans because they did not seem to be talking about dying in this context. That does not mean the committee members and witnesses were unaware of the deaths of the fighters, but they did not focus on them.

The Africa Subcommittee of the House Foreign Affairs Committee met on September 16, 1992 (Hearing [1992a]). President Bush had increased the U.S. commitment of aid and assistance to Somalia through the UN during the previous month. The committee met to learn about these actions and the results to date. The witnesses were Herman Cohen, assistant secretary of state for African affairs, and Andrew Natsios, assistant administrator of the Agency for International Development (AID).

Representative Mervyn Dymally (D-California), who chaired the hearing, had just returned from Somalia. In his opening statement he spoke in vivid human detail about what he had seen:

> Baidoa has become, as has much of Somalia, a land of the living dead. The situation there has become so desperate that the living cannot survive on bread alone. If we had all the food in the world, many people would die because they need medicine and care in addition to food. The women of Baidoa and the children that they revere are so weakened from the prolonged famine they have endured that without urgent medical attention all the food in the world would not save them. Over 25 percent of all Somali children under the age of five have already died. Four and a half million people out of a population of six million are in danger of dying from starvation or a violent death. In the refugee camp I visited—and this was not really a camp; we shouldn't call it a camp. In the refugee place I visited, relief workers told me that the death rate there was between 200 to 300 people a day. Their bodies are hauled away every morning in trucks as they prepare for another day of hell in Somalia.[1]

Notice the powerful words and phrases he used: "land of the living dead," "desperate," "the living cannot survive," "people would die," "weakened from the prolonged famine," "25 percent of all Somali children under the age of five have already died," "dying from starvation or a violent death," "death rate," "bodies are hauled away," "another day of hell in Somalia." This is direct, strong language, a far cry from "harm's way." It is compelling language; it requires the audience to confront the tragedy of Somalia.

The direct language did not end with Representative Dymally's opening statement or with Representative Dymally. It ran throughout the hearing in the talk of members of the committee and the testimony of the witnesses. Much of the hearing was about what relief agencies, the United States, and the United Nations were doing or hoped to do. But references to the depth of the tragedy

TABLE 7.1. SOMALIA, PHASE I

Mobilizing Attention and Support, Exemplary Phrases: Senate Foreign Relations Committee, Africa Subcommittee, September, 1992

Agony

Anarchy

Bodies are hauled away

Casualties

Chaos

Conditions in Somalia the worst they have seen

Could kill more people

Crisis

Crisis looms

Day of hell

Death

Death rate

Desperate

Desperate need

Desperate search for food

Die

Dire need of immediate assistance

Dying

Dying from starvation

Dying nation

Emaciated bodies of the living

Ending starvation

Escalating the warfare

Faced with starvation

Fighting forces

Food gets to the starving

Greatest tragedies mankind has ever experienced

Haunted by that experience

Horror

Increase the violence

Innocent lives

Land of the living dead

Living cannot survive

Man-made tragedy

More at risk

More people would die

My staff has been shot at and had guns put to their head

None of the television footage prepared me for what I saw and experienced

Not going to be peace

On the firing line

Over 25 percent of all Somali children under the age of five have already died

Pawns in their struggle for personal power

Peacekeepers

Peacekeeping forces

Peacemakers

People are dying

People dying every day every minute

People who are about to die

People who need the food

People would die if

Personally at risk

Politically motivated bloodshed

Prey on the starving population

Putting at risk foreign troops who risk getting killed and wounded

Risk

See the tragedy there in stark terms

Sight of women men and children dying

Starvation

Starvation and malnutrition are widespread

Statistics of those people who are dying

Taken the risks

Terrible things happening there

Those who need it

Too weak to bury their beloved ones

Tragedy

Troops

Unwarranted and unprecedented atrocity

Using people as pawns

Violent death

Weakened from prolonged famine

Witnessed there will haunt me for the rest of my life

Exemplary Phrases from Andrew Natsios's Statement

1,000 to 2,000 people could be dying daily

11-year-old girl . . . scrounging for food for her five-year-old sister

25 Percent of the children under five have already died

Five-year-old child died

Avert disaster

Bodies of two elderly women who had just died lying in the corridor

TABLE 7.1. PHASE I *(cont.)*

Body of a teenage boy who had just died in front of me being carted out of the	Great tragedies	Mass starvation
	Half the refugees who move toward these refugee camps die of starvation	People are dying now
		People are hungry
Collected 1,334 bodies of young and old victims of starvation		Risk of starvation
	Her family's lone and only survivor	Staved off starvation
		Tragedy
Continued violence	Images too horrific and too numerous for the mind to fully absorb	Unspeakably tragic human suffering
Dying of starvation		Violence
Facing, in all its horror and wasting, mass starvation	Lifesaving work	
	Magnitude of the tragedy today is staggering	
Feeding center in a wheelbarrow	Malnourished children	

never faded from the talk. Table 7.1 presents a list of the most relevant words and phrases about death and dying.

The tragedy was elaborated with stories about children dying, estimates of the number of deaths per day, and the starkest of characterizations. These phrases were used to describe the plight of the people of Somalia. The deaths of combatants in the clan warfare were not discussed; the deaths of "thugs" and "bandits" did not warrant comment. A few phrases described the risks faced by relief workers and the potential threat to UN or U.S. soldiers if they were to be sent to Somalia.

Talk is always addressed to an audience. The audience for this talk was in the room: the committee members and the witnesses. But they talked about other audiences they were addressing. Congressman Dymally began and ended with an appeal to the State Department to permit members of Congress to go to Somalia. The State Department was discouraging trips to Somalia by members of Congress because of the danger. However, Representative Dymally said they must be encouraged to go because, "Unless they see this, they will not be moved as they were in previous experiences . . . they need to go to see the tragedy there in stark terms."

Andrew Natsios from AID talked about holding press conferences attempting to encourage interest in Somalia in the news media: "I held five press conferences this year. I might add that the first three, two people attended earlier this year. No one took any interest in this subject in the press. The last two were attended by about 50 people." Congressman Dymally reiterated the lack of interest in the press when AID was starting its work in Somalia. The press who "are now blaming us, blaming the United States for not being there, did not cover the stories of our presence there." From January through July, 1992, there were approximately two stories a week in the *Washington Post*. The number jumped to one a day beginning in August and then soared in December and January as the U.S. sent troops to Somalia. Even as the committee was holding hearings the press had begun to pay attention to Somalia in a sustained way.

President Bush was also an audience for the hearing's speakers. Natsios told the committee how the president first learned about the deteriorating situation in Somalia: "That assessment trip (an AID mission) coincided with the President's reading of a cable by the U.S. Ambassador to Kenya, Smith Hempstone, on the current situation along the Kenya-Somalia border. The President, deeply disturbed by what he read in the Ambassador's report and heard from the Kunder mission, ordered an expanded U.S. initiative." Thus, the efforts of the diplomatic wing of the U.S. government reached President Bush indirectly and convinced him to increase the level of U.S. involvement.

Committee members and witnesses were pulling out all the stops to expand the audience, to increase concern about what was happening in Somalia. Vivid descriptions and stark characterizations punctuated the language they used. However, they also knew how to use language that distances death. Congressman Dymally began the hearing by saying, "Before we begin this Hearing today, I want to express my deepest sympathy to the family and friends of Congressman Ted Weiss, who passed away yesterday. . . . The Congress has lost a noble and courageous man." "Passed away" and "lost" was not characteristic of the language they used to describe the death and dying in Somalia.

Committee members and witnesses were in full agreement until the end of the hearing when, Rep. Amo Houghton (R-New York) asked about sending in a large number of UN and U.S. troops to protect the trucks carrying food. Cohen and Natsios answered that such a move would put both troops and volunteer workers from private organizations at risk of death and injury. It would also be quite unprecedented for the United Nations to send in troops over the objection of the local government or clan organizations, and the clans were not willing to accept large numbers of foreign troops, Cohen stated. Finally, Cohen said he did not believe there "is a sentiment in favor of that, either in Congress or in the general public." Peacekeeping troops were one thing; peacemaking troops were a very different matter.

The House Foreign Affairs Committee met on December 17, 1992, shortly after President Bush sent U.S. troops to Somalia (Hearing [1992b]). Even though one Congress had ended and another had not yet started, committing twenty-eight thousand U.S. troops to restore order in Somalia was important enough to warrant this extraordinary meeting of the committee. The witnesses were Herman Cohen, assistant secretary of state; James Woods, deputy assistant secretary of defense; and Lois Richards, AID deputy assistant administrator.

The hearing began, as had the September hearing, with a recounting of the tragic events in Somalia. Representative Toby Roth (R-Wisconsin) stated that "the suffering is almost beyond comprehension, 300,000 have starved to death, one in four of the youngest children is dead . . . and the faces of the children—who can ever turn away and do nothing?"

Several features of this hearing differentiate it from the September hearing. One is self-congratulation. Representative Roth concluded his recital of the suffering with "Somalia has cried out in agony, and America has opened its heart and reached out its hand."

In September, Ambassador Cohen had argued that the United States and the United Nations could not send large numbers of troops into Somalia over the objection of the local clan leaders. It would be unprecedented, he said. In December that objection had disappeared: "Why did we come to this decision? Simply put, the relief system was not working, it was broken. Someone had to fix it or tens of thousands more would die. Only we could do it." Only the United States (and its twenty-two coalition partners) could bring order to Somalia and ensure the delivery of food to the starving—exactly the argument Representative Houghton had made in September.

Representative Payne noted that for the first time in years America was helping "the powerless and the homeless, and without a Cold War agenda." Representative William Goodling (R-Pennsylvania) was doubly proud. He was proud that his president had not used Somalia for political purposes when other Republicans had suggested that Bush should send in the troops before the election. He also said he was proud that the United States was taking the lead for a humanitarian cause: "And I don't know how anybody can turn on a television set and see what has been happening there and say that we, the greatest nation on the earth, have no business there whatsoever."

Representative James Oberstar (D-Minnesota) brought his constituents to the dialogue: "I think most people that I've talked to in my Congressional district have said we had to do this. When they saw the torment, the torture . . . there's no other course for America to take than to use its preeminent position in the world to bring relief to a suffering people." He spoke of his constituents' horror at seeing the torture of starvation and the sense of responsibility that went with America's preeminent position in the world: "President Bush committed us, and the members of the committee were proud that the United States had taken its rightful place leading the nations of the world in the humanitarian mission."

A second difference in this hearing was in the talk about suffering. References to the tragedy did not disappear: Representative Roth's expression of concern has already been quoted. But the tragic tropes are much less prominent in the talk. Table 7.2 contains a list of phrases that refer directly to death and dying. The list is much shorter than the list for the first hearing—even though the transcript of the first hearing was slightly shorter (9,200 words) than the second hearing's (10,700 words).

The difference between the two hearings is one of quality as well as quantity. Compare the testimony of AID's Andrew Natsios at the first hearing and to that of the same organization's Lois Richards at the second hearing. Natsios began with "unspeakably tragic human suffering," whereas Richards began with "death rates dropped" and "death rates soared again." She talked about individuals starving and mass starvation. She talked about "severe impact on malnourished populations." Natsios used general characterizations of the suffering, but he also spoke about specific individuals—women and children—who died as he watched. Richards used only abstract language to characterize the suffering. American troops were in Somalia at the time of the second hearing, and the Somalis' suffering and starvation were no longer the central focus of the talk.

President Bush was sending twenty-eight thousand U.S. troops into a dangerous situation; a mission necessitated by escalating war between clan military groups. "Risk" was the only straightforward reference to the danger in which the troops were placed. If committee members and witnesses did not speak bluntly about the danger the troops faced, how did they talk about it? Assistant Secretary Cohen characterized the situation leading to sending in the troops: "The situation in the country continued to deteriorate." He described events in Mogadishu after the troops arrived: "There have been no major encounters." He discussed moving the troops outside of Mogadishu to the "Somali interior, where the security situation has been unstable," and where they had "secured Baidoa's airport and established a security cordon around the town." He further distinguished the U.S. mission of "peacemaking" from the UN mission of "peacekeeping." Richards described the relief effort: "The primary obstacle to achieving our relief and rehabilitation objective in Somalia was lack of security. Today that problem is being rectified by the deployment of U.S. and coalition troops."

TABLE 7.2. SOMALIA, PHASE 2
Self-Congratulation, Exemplary Phrases: House Foreign Affairs Committee,
December, 1992

1.5 million people are at risk

2 million more face starvation

25 Percent of children under age five have already died

250,000 have starved to death

3,000 Somalis could be dying every day

300,000 Somalis have starved to death

Another 30,000 may have died in the fighting

Brutalized by the ruthless warlords

Can turn on a television set and see what has been happening

Desperately seeking

Dimensions of the suffering are almost beyond comprehension

Don't worry about being attacked by someone else

Faces of the children—who can ever turn away and do nothing?

Factional fighting

Fear that someone else will attack them

Figures are numbing

Food and safety

For those at risk in Somalia

Helping the powerless and homeless and without a Cold War agenda

Horror and misery in Somalia

Mission not without risk

Nearly a million have abandoned their homes and land

Of the youngest children . . . one in four is dead

Saving hundreds of thousands of lives

Seen the faces of Somalia's children

Seen the horrific images from Somalia

Somalia has cried out in agony

Starvation has begun to decline

Tens of thousands more would die

The starving people of Somalia

Torture that they're suffering

Tragedy in Somalia

UN is there in force to help protect

When they saw the torment

The torture

Women and children too weak to speak for themselves

Exemplary Phrases from Lois Richards's Statement

Crude mortality rate in the displaced population

Death rates dropped

Death rates soared again

Incredibly high mortality rates

Reduce death rates

Severe impact on malnourished populations

Senator Warner's favorite phrase—"harm's way"—was never used. Instead of "harm's way," "deteriorate," "encounters," "unstable," "secured," and "the problem is being rectified" were used. But these were, at best, oblique references to the fighting and dying in Somalia—into the middle of which U.S. troops were being deployed. They were verbal tools for skirting the danger.

What the participants in the hearings did talk about—perhaps in lieu of talking about the danger—was when and how the troops would leave Somalia. Every representative, save one, wanted to impress on the administration witnesses the importance of a quick transition from the U.S.-led peacemaking coalition to the UN peacekeeping force. "It is quickly becoming a U.S. problem," said Representative Roth. "Can you guarantee that no U.S. troops will remain after six months?" How the decision about when the situation was "secured" would be made was gone over in fine detail. Who would decide? Would UN troops be ready? Could the United Nations overrule U.S. commanders who reported their area had been secured?

Finally, the audience was also less important in this hearing than it was in the first hearing. The news media had become a voice rather than an audience. There were references to turning on the television and seeing the faces of starving women and children. They had seen them, their constituents had seen them, and the citizens of other countries had seen them, the participants stated. The news media no longer needed to be encouraged to focus on the story. They were bringing the pain of Somalia into living rooms around the world. As the news media picked up the story, the audience shifted to the American people and constituents. Members of the committee spoke for them and spoke to them as they asked questions and responded to the answers. In addition, Representative Payne said, America's actions were speaking to the world. President-elect Bill Clinton's endorsement of President Bush's actions "demonstrated to the world that our country is united." Payne also said that the United States was speaking to African nations, and had to act with "maximum sensitivity to Somalia's sovereignty and pride."

The focus had shifted. No longer were members of Congress and witnesses concerned about getting in. They were now concerned about getting the United States out.

PHASE 3: CRITICAL REFLECTION

In December, Assistant Secretary Cohen characterized the UN peacekeeping force that was to take over from the U.S.-led coalition: "It's not going to be a traditional UN peacekeeping force—lightly armed with very, very passive rules of engagement. We expect it to be heavily armed with very robust rules of engagement. And we are now actively promoting this point of view within the Security Council." That was indeed the basis of the United Nations's multinational peace enforcement effort under chapter 7 of its charter. Somalia was setting precedents in the new world order.

By July, 1993, the UN peace enforcement effort was in trouble with U.S. politicians (Hearing [1993a]). Senators were questioning U.S. participation. As Sen. Nancy Kassebaum (R-Kansas) said, "I worry, Mr. Chairman, that so often as the cameras move on, our own interests move on." Starvation had been alleviated, the tormented faces no longer filled the television screen, and some senators could think of more reasons for the United States tò move on than to stay.

The Foreign Relations Committee met and did what it often does (Boynton and Dozark 1993). It talked to administration witnesses: Undersecretary of State Peter Tarnoff and Marine Corps Lt. Gen. John Sheehan, representing the Defense Department. It asked questions that were being asked with more feeling elsewhere, and, in the process, managed to reconstruct much of the history of U.S. and UN involvement in Somalia.

Table 7.3 presents a chronology constructed from the Phase 3 talk, a list of events referred to by committee members or witnesses. Dates are included only when they were in the text. No one set out to recount systematically the events of Somalia's past. As in other hearings, international relations were talked about as a historical stream, with the country of the moment as the focus of the stream (Boynton and Dozark 1993). Events were mentioned within the nonlinear texture of statements, questions, or answers about the current situation: Historical sequences served as an underpinning for discussion of the current situation.

The chronology begins with Italy's colonial role in Somalia and shifts quickly to the Cold War and the weapons brought into Somalia during that period. It then skips forward to 1992, when clan warfare resulted in famine and the starvation of three hundred thousand Somalis. President Bush ordered U.S. troops into Somalia in December, 1992, as part of UNITAF, and twenty-two other nations joined the coalition that was put together to end starvation. The United Nations's political reconciliation work led to an agreement signed at Addis Ababa and UN Resolution 814, outlining the mission of UNOSOM II, which would take the place of UNITAF. In May, 1993, UNOSOM II replaced UNITAF and the United States withdrew most of its military personnel. One month later, Gen. Mohammad Farrah Aidid's forces attacked Pakistani UN peacekeepers. That was followed by UN Resolution 837, which authorized members of UNOSOM II to detain persons responsible for the attack. Between June 5 and the end of July, the date of the hearing, the UNOSOM II command concentrated on Aidid's military forces in Mogadishu. That focus included a raid on Aidid's headquarters in which the U.S. Quick Reaction Force participated. And it led to consternation in Italy and the U.S. Senate.

What questions were being answered in Phase 3, and who was doing the asking? The overarching question was: Should the U.S. stay in Somalia? This was the question asked by those who criticized the Clinton administration's actions. Only Sen. Robert Byrd (D-West Virginia) was named, but when problems are encountered, a plentiful supply of critics can be found in Congress,

TABLE 7.3. SOMALIA, PHASE 3
Critical Reflection, Chronology of Events: Senate Foreign
Relations Committee, July, 1993

Italy as colonial power in Somalia	Aidid breaks agreement he signed at Addis Ababa
Weapons into Somalia as result of Cold War	UN resolution 837 authorized UNOSOM to detain Aidid; raid on Aidid command and control center by U.S. Quick-Reaction Force
Support of Said Barre before 1986	
Weapons as result of Eritrean campaign from "other side"	
300,000, 5 percent of Somali population, starved to death before Bush decision	Italians unhappy about peace process and command arrangements in Somalia
December, 1992, Bush decides to send troops to Somalia—UNITAF	Tarnoff met with Italian military to work out UN-Italian relations
December, 1992, 8,900 U.S. troops move into Somalia	Senior Italian military officer appointed to work with UN in New York
January, 1993, U.S. force in Somalia reaches 25,000	U.S. working with UN to "refine, modernize, and make smoother" arrangements by which multinational force works
22 nations join U.S.-led coalition December–May	
Addis Ababa agrees to forge national reconciliation	Defense Department team stops in Italy to consult with Italians
UN Resolution 814: mission of UNOSOM—political reconciliation, rehabilitation of Somali economy	Debate in Senate on U.S. participation in UN peacemaking
Repatriation of refugees and restoration of local police force	"Let's run; let's leave Somalia" questions raised by Senator Byrd
May 4, 1993, U.S.-led UNITAF turned over to UNOSOM; improvements since December, 1992; famine over	Current U.S. troops in Somalia: 3,000 logistics, 1,000 Quick-Reaction Force
Feeding centers turned back to schools	Current UN troops in Somalia: 21,000
Substantial reduction in violence (other than South Mogadishu)	UN force will grow to 28,000
June 5, 1993, Aidid attack on Pakistani peacekeepers	End of 1993, U.S. force level will drop to 1,400

both among foreign policy experts and in the news media. Senator Claiborne Pell (D-Rhode Island), chairman of the committee, noted the critics in the Senate and answered that he continued to support U.S. involvement. Senator Paul Simon (D-Illinois), chairman of the Africa Subcommittee, was rather more biting in his response. "There are those in the Senate now who say 'Let's run; let's leave. . . . We have asked other nations to join us . . . [but] 'we're going to high-tail it out of here.' I think [that] would be absolutely irresponsible." Senator Kassebaum, who had been the ranking Republican member of the Africa Subcommittee, reminded the critics that real progress had been made in

Somalia. It was essential, she said, that the United States "stay the course in Somalia. . . . Too much has been accomplished to give up now." Senator Jim Jeffords of Vermont, the ranking Republican member of the Africa Subcommittee, reminded critics that the United States did not want to be policeman to the world. And if it did not want to be the world's policeman, then it had to support the United Nations when it assumed that role. Senator Christopher Dodd (D-Connecticut) echoed Senator Jeffords's statement. Only Sen. Larry Pressler (R-South Dakota) identified himself as being opposed to U.S. involvement in Somalia. Senator Paul Coverdell (R-Georgia) said that although he thought Presidents Bush and Clinton had acted correctly, he also believed that the critics' objections should be addressed. The committee was not ready to give up on the Bush-Clinton initiatives in Somalia.

One of the objections of critics was that U.S. troops were no longer under U.S. command. The witnesses answered this question by reviewing the status of American troops. The three thousand engaged in logistic activities were under UNOSOM II command, but the Quick Reaction Force remained under the Defense Department's control. Moreover, Undersecretary Tarnoff noted, "the United States, of course, retains at all times ultimate control over our forces."

The United Nations's ability to command a military force had been questioned. Senator Dodd and other members of the committee responded to this criticism with: "This—these missions are—always have their problems, you know, but I think the fact that the UN is taking on this role is long overdue in my view. And the fact that they're willing to take some risks is something we ought to be willing to stand behind. And the minute the ground gets a little shaky, we head for the hills on this stuff. I mean, the alternative is us doing it alone." The witnesses also recounted what the United States was doing to help the United Nations improve its procedures.

The breach between the United Nations and the Italians was a matter of concern to critics and a number of the committee members as well. Were they negotiating secretly with General Aidid, as was rumored? Undersecretary Tarnoff answered, "Mr. Chairman, I don't believe that the Italians are deviating from the general understandings that we all have with respect to the mission . . . but in every way, I think the Italians are playing a loyal and supportive role in the execution of the mission." He also described what the United States was doing to resolve the differences between the United Nations and Italy.

General Aidid shattered what had been for seven months a rather uneventful UN intervention in Somalia. Twenty-three Pakistanis were killed, and the United Nations committed itself to bringing Aidid to justice. That situation introduced uncertainty into the scenario. Critics spoke out about the shortcomings they discerned in the way the United States and the United Nations were handling the situation. The committee met to ask administration witnesses the questions that critics were asking.

What the participants talked about very little was death. Senator Pell talked about "a short-run military action." Senator Simon spoke about mistakes being made. Senator Kassebaum raised her "concern about the many aspects of the situation in south Mogadishu." Undersecretary Tarnoff spoke about a "flagrant violation of the accords" and "restoring order in south Mogadishu." One or another variant on "secure the situation" was used thirteen times during the hearing.

Language in Phase 3 that touched somewhat more directly on suffering and death is listed in table 7.4. Four times a participant referred to the suffering and starvation that was being overcome. The phrasing was not as strong as in earlier hearings; everyone was happy that the tragedy was going away. There were four statements that characterized the attack on the Pakistani UN troops. The language used was "unprovoked attack," "Pakistanis who were killed," "shooting of the 23 Pakistani peacekeepers," "flagrant violation," and "attacks on UNOSOM." They spoke of death bluntly, but there was very little elaboration in their talk. The same was true when speaking about the Americans wounded in the attack on General Aidid's headquarters. "Wounding of," "attack on," "attack against," and "casualties suffered" were the phrases used. The conflict with General Aidid was characterized with the words "military opposition," "military challenges," "defied the UN," and "indulged in armed opposition." Senator Coverdell asked a hypothetical question: What if Aidid had been killed or wounded in the attack? That led to responses about this hypothetical. At one point General Sheehan characterized the Aidid forces as being limited to two hundred or three hundred individuals who intimidated, murdered, and attacked other clansmen. Senator Pressler asked another hypothetical question: What would the United States do if civil war reoccurred?

These were the first signs of danger to U.S. and other UN troops in Somalia. Until June 5, the operation had proceeded with little opposition. It was important to the committee to consider this new factor in the UNOSOM operation, but it discussed the issue rather matter-of-factly. It was not treated as an occasion for hyperbole.

PHASE 4: POLICY MAKING

The Foreign Relations Committee met again on October 20, 1993 (Hearing [1993b]). Chairman Pell made the introductory remarks: "Today the air is thick

Accomplished either quickly or bloodlessly

Ambush of the Pakistanis who were killed

Attack against Aidid's forces

Attack on Aidid's command center

But in southern Mogadishu, there's [*sic*] 200 to 300 hard-core Aidid supporters who derive their strength from carrying weapons, from intimidation, from murder, and attacks on other clansmen. As long as that type of activity exists,

Casualties suffered on Aidid's side as well as the UN side

Defied the UN and its missions in Somalia

Flagrant violation of the accords and attacks on UNOSOM will not go unpunished

General Aidid had been wounded, captured, or killed

If he had been a casualty in the attack

Incident in which Aidid's forces engineered the shooting of the Pakistani peacekeepers

Large-scale starvation has been eliminated

Lessening of the threat to UNOSOM forces

Military challenges to the UNOSOM forces

Pockets of suffering remain

Reduce the levels of suffering and starvation

Restore order to southern Mogadishu

Resumption of lawlessness and violence

Return of famine

There does not seem on the scene, Senator, any likelihood of the kind of generalized violence in the country which could be characterized as a civil war

They have indulged in armed opposition to the UN presence and the UN mission

UN faced with military opposition

Unprovoked attack on the Pakistani peacekeepers

What if this—what if the attack had resulted in his (Aidid's) death?

World rife with humanitarian crises caused by armed conflict

Wounding of the American peacekeepers

---

with cries to pull American troops out of Somalia, to abandon the UN peacekeeping operation of which we, the United States, were the major architect." In the background was another failed attempt by UN forces and the U.S. Quick Response Force to capture General Aidid. American servicemen died, and Aidid escaped. America's UN ambassador, Madeleine Albright, was a key witness at the hearing.

Ambassador Albright began her testimony by talking about Somalia, but much of her testimony was about a new U.S. policy on the relationship between U.S. and UN peacekeeping operations. At the end of her statement she put this policy development into historical perspective: "Mr. Chairman and members of the Committee, I think some of you know that I have been a professor in my past life and have studied history fairly closely, and it is my sense . . . that we are living in one of the major watershed periods, that what we are looking at is what the world was like in 1815 or 1945.... I think this is the most challenging job for all of us, and I consider it my major challenge and, frankly, a major honor to be one of those that is in a position to be present at this recreation of an international framework, and I hope very much that we're able to do this work closely together because the world is really looking at us for answers."

She went on to say that, at this major juncture in history when the Cold War had ended and with it Soviet obstruction in the Security Council, the Security Council was at last able to undertake the business that people had in mind when they set up the United Nations. There had been more UN peacekeeping operations in the previous five years than in the preceding forty-three. Some had worked very well. Some, like Somalia, had been less than successful. She did not mince words in assessing the current state of readiness: "Unfortunately, the UN emerged from 40 years of Cold War paralysis overweight and out of shape, and since the fall of the Berlin Wall, its responsibilities have grown faster than its capabilities."

The United States was, she said, necessarily recreating the UN peacekeeping mission at that very moment. As she articulated the Clinton administration's responses to a world looking to the United States for answers, she turned many of the assumptions of earlier hearings on their head: "The secretary-general always says there are thousands of people dying or starving in other places and we're not paying attention to them. And the question is, what is the selection process? Do we—which ones do we do and how?"

The secretary-general, she implied, is always able to find another country where people are dying by the thousands. It was more than the United States could handle. Criteria for deciding where to intervene and where to stay out needed to be developed. This did not sound like the first Somalia hearing, where the problem had been how to get people to pay attention.

Ambassador Albright focused on the role of television in producing immediate engagement: "Television's ability to bring graphic images of pain and outrage into our living rooms has heightened the pressure both for immediate engagement in areas of international crisis and immediate disengagement when events do not go according to plan. Because we live in a democratic society, none of us can be oblivious to those pressures, but regular consultations between us can nevertheless contribute to steadiness of policy and purpose."

Television was the enemy. It brought images of pain "into our living rooms" and with them demands for doing something immediately. Conversely, when something went wrong, the televised images produced demands for immediately getting out. Television made "steadiness of policy" almost impossible in a democracy. This was not the celebration of television found in earlier hearings.

Furthermore, events were televised in such a way that they promoted dramatic reaction rather than thoughtful public discussion, she noted: "Events in Somalia and, to some extent, Bosnia and Haiti over the last few months have also caused dramatic swings in American public opinion. Depending on the month or the place, the UN is accused of attempting to do too much or of not doing enough, of relying too heavily on force or of reacting passively to the use of force by others, of trying to run things or of failing to be assertive enough."

Institutional learning from hard experience was not reflected in the "dramatic swings in American public opinion." "This is all very new," she said at another point, "and doing too much or too little, using too much force or too little force is not the learning that we need if we are to re-create a UN peacekeeping organization that is effective." Only a year earlier, Representative Dymally and Andrew Natsios surely would not have agreed with her.

Nine months on the roller coaster was enough for Ambassador Albright and the Clinton administration. What was needed was a new policy that could produce a steadier course.

Ambassador Albright's presentation of the administration policy was carefully reasoned and impressively articulated. She began with some very general principles: The United States must remain an active leader in world affairs; multilateral peacekeeping is a potentially valuable foreign policy tool; current UN capacities are not adequate and must be strengthened; the United States should provide technical assistance for improving UN capabilities; the U.S. share of the cost should be decreased; the United States should participate in UN peacekeeping only when it is in America's best interest to do so; the United States should be sure that there is competent command and control before committing U.S. personnel; there should be regular consultation with Congress on UN peacekeeping activities. Each was elaborated in her statement and many were discussed during questioning.

Ambassador Albright also outlined the criteria that would be used by the Clinton administration for evaluating UN peacekeeping: "Does there exist a real threat to international peace? Does the proposed mission have clear objectives? Can an end point be identified? What are the projected costs? If it is a peacekeeping as opposed to a peace enforcement operation, is there a cease-fire in place, have the parties to the conflict agreed to a UN presence?

In an answer to Sen. Jesse Helms (R-North Carolina), she said that the administration was already using those principles when voting on UN peacekeeping operations. While answering a question from Chairman Pell she said that when she had served as president of the Security Council in August she had convinced the council to use the same principles.[2]

Much of the talk in the Phase 4 hearing was about principles. It was about capabilities that needed to be improved. It was about criteria that should be used in making decisions. It was about financing. Where does talk about death fit in such a context? Ambassador Albright spoke directly. Senator Hank Brown (Colorado), a Republican member of the committee, said that if she ever wanted to go over to the Defense Department—whose representatives did not speak with such directness—she would find many supporters on the committee. When talking about events in Somalia, she rarely used euphemisms that distance death. Ambassador Albright did not mince words about the events in Somalia in Phase 4. "Murder," "ambush," "killing," and "tragic death" were the words she chose to characterize the deaths of UN peacekeepers, as outlined in table 7.5. "Violence in Mogadishu" was her characterization of the situation in the Somali capital. When she talked about Cambodia she invoked the celebrated phrasing "fields that were once red with blood." Senator Helms mentioned a helicopter that had been shot at the day before; Senator James Jeffords (R-Vermont) referred to "harm's way."

However, when talk centered on policymaking, even for Ambassador Albright, it took a turn toward the abstract. Policymaking is, after all, a generalizing activity, and the language of policy must be abstract to be general. The language of policy distances human beings, their pain, and their deaths. It centers on decision criteria, capabilities, and finances. The text is filled with abstract characterizations. The threat was "civil strife" and "cross-border aggression." The U.S. response would include both multilateral and unilateral "means." Responses would be determined by whether there was a threat to international peace, what the cost would be, and so on. Human beings were replaced by "forces," "servicemen and women," "peacekeepers." The benefits were the prevention of "tremendous loss of life in various places."

The talk signaled that it was time for a midcourse correction—even if it was somewhat earlier than midcourse. Ambassador Albright reminded the committee that "the Clinton administration took office intending to provide strong support for UN peace operations, but concerned about the potentials for problems." She also quoted from her own testimony at her confirmation hearing to reinforce the point that the plan she was suggesting in this hearing was not simply a response to the criticism of the month. But the hearing covered both the administration's policy and United Nations problems. The mission of U.S. forces as part of the UN forces in Somalia was reviewed. How UN peacekeeping should be reformed was covered as well.

TABLE 7.5. SOMALIA, PHASE 4
Policy Making, Exemplary Phrases:
Senate Foreign Relations Committee, October, 1993

Actions that clearly violate
Active military presence
Ambush of UN peacekeepers
Assassination attempt on Mr. Bush
Bitter civil war
Chaos
Conflict
Conflicts are going to continue
Covert military means
Covert operations
Dangerous situations
Death by starvation
Difficulties of peace operations in
Engaged in a dangerous situation
Events of October—early October
Far riskier and far more complicated
Fields that were once red with blood are
   now green with crops
Graphic images of pain
Harm's way
Has prevented the starvation of hundreds
   of thousands of people
Here strife has taken place
Huge danger to the population
Involvement in hostilities
Killing of these Pakistanis

Loss of life
Mistakes or shortcomings
Murder of 24 Pakistani peacekeepers on
   June 5th
Outlaw behavior
Renegade behavior
Responsible for killing the Pakistanis
Return to anarchy in Somalia
Rights of people
Shock of October 3rd
Shot that was fired at another helicopter
   and missed
Situation where fighting resumes
Starvation and deaths
Sustained military action
Tragic death of American servicemen
Tremendous loss of life
Vast tragedy
Violence in Mogadishu
Violent confrontations
War
When events do not go according to plan
Where there's cross-border aggression
Young person who is willing to die to
   protect his country

Who was the audience for this talk? More than was true for the three earlier hearings, the audience seemed to be those in the room. Most Americans, even most American politicians, are not prepared to spend several hours on improving UN peacekeeping. One sign of the attention the hearing received is the coverage of it in the *Washington Post*. The report about the hearing was tacked onto the end of a news story about senatorial resolutions asking President Clinton to consult with Congress before doing anything in Bosnia and Haiti, which received top billing. The hearing's twenty-five thousand words were reduced to three hundred—without even a headline to call their own.

The Policy Cycle, Rhetoric, and Audiences

The four congressional hearings can be understood as outlining a policy cycle. The first hearing was about mobilizing attention and support. It was followed by self-congratulation at having taken action. The third began critical reflection. The circle was closed with the fourth hearing, which generalized about what had been learned through the first phases of the cycle. We should not expect this cycle to be played out as neatly for other policies as it was in the case of Somalia. The cycle resulted from a particular confluence of events: a new administration thinking through its own views in the policy domain, and an international organization in need of reform. If the United Nations and the United States are successful at developing UN peacekeeping capabilities, questions about organization and capabilities will not surface again until attention shifts to some other aspect of UN action. Future administrations will need to develop their views of UN peacekeeping in relationship to U.S. foreign policy, but they will do so as they struggle with a different set of events or crises. The individual phases can, however, readily be found in other committee-administration deliberations. What we have learned about the language of death and dying by studying this cycle is probably applicable to much of U.S. deliberation about international affairs.

When speaking about dying, committee members and witnesses used language appropriate to the context. A colleague "passed away," was "lost." When mobilizing attention and support for U.S. engagement, the language was concrete, full of the details of suffering, shaped for political impact. The language characterized the depth and breadth of the suffering in personal, emotional, and involving terms—appropriate to catching our attention and to enhancing our feeling that something should be done. In later phases, after U.S. engagement, committee participants did not speak like this about Americans wounded and killed in Somalia. On the floor of the House and the Senate they may well have—especially critics of the Clinton administration. In later phases, senators and representatives spoke in other terms as they reviewed the actions that had resulted in the death and wounding of many Americans. Critical reflection raised questions about policies. Why was that done? What else could have been done? The dying helped precipitate the questions, but it moved into the background for the deliberative talk. Generalizing what has been learned—policy making—involved more abstract language, the language of principles and structure. Concrete instantiation may return later as the principles are put to use.

Each phase of the policy process has its own appropriate talk. Talking about dying is an important dimension of the meaning of war and peace. People think about dying; people kill others and are killed. The talk mediates these thoughts and actions. It reflects the meanings that exist and also shapes new meanings. It makes them visible and accessible. As people move through the complex policy process of war and peace, the talk connects speakers and audiences, political leaders and followers, conveying and shaping at every phase the meaning of war and peace.

8

Beer and Quiche in the Fast Lane

Signaler's Dilemma, Democratic Debate, and the Gulf War

FRANCIS A. BEER, MARK I. LICHBACH,
AND BARRY J. BALLECK

Semiotics, sign language, has long been recognized as an important subject in international relations. A rich theoretical and historical literature in perception and misperception, deception and disguise, and strategic communication has highlighted diverse possible signals in the sender's repertoire, various possible recipient perceptions and interpretations, and the multidimensionality of international communicative interaction as it reflects and shapes the meaning of war and peace (e.g. Hybel 1986; Jervis 1976; Wohlstetter 1962; Schelling 1963).

Signaler's Dilemma

Democratic politics, by their constitution, imply a signaler's dilemma. Democracies like to talk; it is hard to imagine democracy without discourse. At the same time, democracies do not like to fight. As Harold Lasswell's work on the garrison state pointed out half a century ago, democracies tend to be dominated by specialists in persuasion rather than coercion. Such political communities are complex and cumbersome. They are difficult to organize and slow to mobilize. They prefer to associate and ally with each other, and they do not like war, particularly against other democracies. Even the generals in a democratic society, where the parents of slain soldiers vote, do not like to bring home high casualties (Manchester 1978).[1] The domestic structures and cultures of democratic regimes thus tend to send mixed signals that foreign opponents may misinterpret as weakness in specific contexts and situations. Normal democratic procedure may encourage an opponent to discount the potential cost, undertake reckless actions, and thereby raise risks for both sides. Democratic dynamics may weaken the virtual defense of psychological deterrence and necessitate actual physical defense when deterrence fails.

The Signaling Game

THE POWER BREAKFAST

Work in the tradition of game theory suggests a metaphor for democratic signaling dynamics (Cho and Kreps 1987. Cf. Fearon 1997, 1993; Lohmann 1993; Banks 1991; Davis and Arquilla 1991). The signaler's dilemma is set in a context somewhere between Alexandre Dumas's *The Three Musketeers* and Robert Altman's *The Player.* In the world of the power breakfast, gender-based gastronomic stereotypes are political markers. One player, the sender of the signal, chooses from a limited menu of beer and quiche. The other player, the receiver, interprets the opponent's choice as either strength or weakness. In this politically precorrect world, real men do not eat quiche for breakfast. If the sender drinks beer, the receiver is intimidated and withdraws; if the sender eats quiche, the receiver is encouraged and duels.

PREFERENCES AND SOLUTIONS

The breakfast metaphor is easily translated into the language of international relations.[2] Nature, the breakfast's environment, makes the democracy either militarily weak or strong. Eating quiche or drinking beer translates into the presence or absence of democratic debate; strong states and leaders do not debate. Dueling becomes war between states. The adversary interprets the presence or absence of debate as a sign of capability and uses that information to help assess the risks of fighting.

Other things being equal, the democratic peace hypothesis suggests that the strongest preference for democracies is for peace. The preference for peace probably dominates the preference for debating in both strong and weak democracies. It is the first criterion for sorting policy preferences. Democratic politicians who like to get reelected, in both strong and weak situations, place a high value on not shedding electoral blood.

Going further, we propose that military strength or weakness influences democracies' desire to debate. Leaders of strong democracies would rather not debate. Militarily strong democracy follows the logic of power maximization inscribed in theories of international realism and domestic governmental centralization. Leadership relies on the privilege of a directly elected powerful executive and commander in chief, with established prerogatives to deal effectively with other nations. Leaders of strong democracies see little constructive reason to share with domestic opponents the credit for the victory that will come from military superiority.

Strong democracy's best outcome is executive peace. This involves no war in which the democracy might suffer casualties, and no war debate, which would affect the military discretion of the foreign-policy elite. In a second preference, democratic peace, a strong democracy would rather debate than fight. The third choice is executive victory, which involves fighting a war without extensive discussion. This scenario avoids the agony of potential battle casualties even if it means having to go through rigorous discussion. A strong democracy's worst outcome, democratic victory, involves a divisive debate, with domestic power sharing, that is potentially constraining and humiliating, followed by hostilities. This was the actual immediate outcome of the Gulf War.

Like its stronger brother, a militarily weak democracy would prefer not to fight. Its first choice would be a democratic escape. This best outcome includes an extensive war debate, but then not having to follow through with hostilities. The next best choice is executive escape. This avoids fighting, which risks defeat, but it forgoes debate. If a weak democracy has to fight a war that it might lose, prior discussion should at least legitimate and justify its third choice, a democratic defeat. The weak democracy's worst fear is an executive defeat, which lacks debate to spread responsibility and mobilize domestic support and yet includes hostilities and defeat. In this scenario, the weak democracy's leaders will be alone in telling their conservatives why the war was lost and the liberals and socialists why the soldiers died.

The model draws the opponent differently than democracy. First the opponent is conceived as the classic unitary, power-maximizing decision maker of realist international theory. The opponent is oriented entirely to the international arena. It also has an authoritarian regime. The logic of such a regime suggests a military profile in which the leader, a man of action, is strong, decisive, and firm, presiding over unified and effective command and control. Leaders from such cultures may interpret extensive public debate in other polities as an indicator of governmental division, internal opposition, and weak national resolve to use force. The opponent, on the basis of its prior information about the strength or weakness of the democracy and the new evidence provided by the occurrence or absence of debate, decides whether to fight or withdraw. The opponent's preferences are simpler than those of a democracy, falling into two groups. In the first group of preferences, the opponent chooses either not to fight with a strong democracy and escape from a likely loss, or to fight with a weak democracy, which implies a probable victory. The second group of less preferable options includes fighting with a strong democracy, a probable loss, or not fighting with a weak democracy, a foregone victory.

Given this array of preferences, game theory suggests different outcomes. In the case of a strong democracy, the equilibrium is executive peace: no war and no debate. Strong democracies deter their opponents and do not have to fight them. Nor do the leaders have to talk to the opposition; they are strong, silent types. The weak democracy, in this formulation, is likely to achieve debate, war, and democratic loss. Weak democracies cannot deter and have to fight. As Thucydides said long ago, the strong do as they will, whereas the weak do as they must.

The Gulf War and Beyond

The signaling game is a model for some of the interactions between the United States and Iraq in late 1990 and early 1991 that led to war in the Persian Gulf.

A STRONG OR WEAK UNITED STATES?

Prior information about U.S. strength or weakness was mixed. On the positive side, the United States was the sole remaining world superpower. Over the prior century, beginning with the Spanish-American War, the United States rose to a position of unchallenged global preeminence. The American century finally culminated, after the collapse of the Soviet Union, in a unipolar moment. The American superpower, however, was heavily constrained. Vietnam clearly showed that the United States had neither the desire nor the ability to impose its will in distant geographical areas with a complex relationship to the American national interest. American guns, moreover, had been bought at a heavy price in butter. Former adversaries with lower military expenditures, like Germany and Japan, challenged the United States for technological dominance. Low-cost producers in various parts of the third world were formidable business competitors in the international marketplace. Two world wars and almost half a century of cold war had contributed to massive indebtedness, made all the more difficult by popular resistance to further taxation. The American infrastructure and social fabric needed serious investment attention.

American military strength or weakness was also uncertain within the particular context of the Persian Gulf crisis. The historic geopolitical struggle between Russian and Anglo-American interests centered on oil. Contemporary U.S. policy in the region turned on opposition to Iran. The fall of the shah, the accession to power of the Ayatollah Khomeini and a radical fundamentalist Islamic regime, the holding of American hostages in Teheran, and Iranian support for international terrorism all threatened the United States and American interests. Iraq had been a U.S. ally in this struggle against Iran, and the United States had supported it during the long, bloody years of the Iran-Iraq war. America had resisted direct military involvement, and it needed Iraq to oppose Iran. April Glaspie, the U.S. ambassador to Iraq, in a fateful July 25 interview with Saddam Hussein, failed to convey a strong message that the United States would militarily resist an Iraqi invasion of Kuwait (Sifry and Cerf 1991, 122–33). This specific diplomatic ambiguity reflected the long-term complexities of the U.S.-Iraq relationship. Ironically, it had been foreshadowed by a similar situation in the Falklands/Malvinas during 1981, where American and British diplomats had sent mixed signals to Argentinian president Galtieri (Freedman and Gamba-Stonehouse 1991, 33). In spite of the conflict, the United States still needed Saddam Hussein to block possible Iranian moves to the west and fundamentalist challenges to the Gulf state regimes. Such reasoning probably influenced President Bush's decision at the end of the war not to push on to Baghdad and finally dispatch Saddam Hussein.

THE DEBATE OVER DEBATE

The rhetorical war before the shooting war included a debate over debate. The two sides of the formal signaling game were clearly reflected in this debate.

Misrepresenting Strength. The American administration clearly followed the line of a militarily strong democracy in the Persian Gulf crisis. President Bush stated that he did not wish to fight the war. Again and again, he and Secretary of State James Baker publicly urged Saddam Hussein to withdraw his forces from Kuwait without bloodshed. Yet President Bush and Secretary Baker believed that the United States was militarily strong enough to impose its will on Saddam Hussein. The United States commanded the greatest concentration of military power assembled in several generations. Bush and Baker had mobilized an overwhelming allied coalition operating under the banner of a virtually unanimous United Nations reminiscent of the grand alliances of World Wars I and II, with the most advanced military equipment (see Woodward 1991).

In light of this strength, the administration sought to convey resoluteness. It wanted to send a clear signal to Saddam Hussein. Nobody wanted to leave any doubts. President Bush called on the mythic memory of British prime minister Neville Chamberlain's pact with Hitler at Munich in 1938. "Appease-ment does not work," he said. "Standing up for our principles will not come easy. It may take time and possibly cost a great deal, but . . . America has never wavered when her purpose is driven by principle" (Weekly Compilation of Presidential Documents, Administration of George Bush 1990, August 8, 1990).

A week later, speaking to Pentagon employees, the president continued in a similar vein: "no one should doubt our staying power or determination. . . . A half century ago, our nation and the world paid dearly for appeasing an aggressor who should, and could, have been stopped. We are not going to make the same mistake again" (*New York Times,* August 16, 1990).

General Colin Powell, chairman of the Joint Chiefs of Staff, was even more graphic. Testifying before the Senate Armed Services Committee, General Powell stated: "We will use our strengths against their vulnerabilities, and we will avoid their strengths. . . . [The] only question the Iraqis will have to consider is, do they move it, or do they lose it?" (*Washington Post,* December 4, 1990). He continued the same theme to the members of the 354th Tactical Fighter Wing stationed in Saudi Arabia. "If we go in," he said, "we go in to win, not to fool around" (*Washington Post,* December 22, 1990).

As part of the strategy of signaling strength, the administration also sought to limit congressional participation during the period leading up to the Gulf War. The administration made it very clear that it did not wish congressional hearings, debates, or votes. Secretary Baker appeared eventually before the Senate Foreign Relations and the House Foreign Affairs Committees. Yet his heart was not in it. "I really think it would be self-defeating," he said, "if we have days and days of discussion about what we should or should not do" (*Washington Post,* October 19, 1990). Secretary of Defense Richard Cheney echoed Baker's sentiments before the Senate Armed Services Committee: "I do not believe the President requires any additional authority from Congress. Of the more than two hundred occasions in American history when presidents have committed U.S. military force, on only five of those occasions was there a prior declaration of war" (*Washington Post,* December 4, 1990).

In spite of administration opposition, there were congressional hearings, and high administration officials appeared reluctantly before congressional committees. Congress conducted the most extensive public debate in American history over a peace/war issue. Even as congressional deliberation moved forward, however, members of Congress themselves sought to limit debate. Senator Strom Thurmond (R-North Carolina), for example, exhorted his colleagues to exercise good judgment and self-restraint and to end the discussion: "The time to end the debate is now. I implore this body to demonstrate to the world—and especially Saddam Hussein—that we are behind our President and the United Nations. . . . A vote in support of the President is a vote for peace. I urge my colleagues to stop the debate and show our solidarity with the President and resolve to get Saddam Hussein out of Kuwait. Solidarity, we need it now. Not division, but solidarity" (*Congressional Record*, January 10, 1991).

The president got neither of his wishes to avoid debate or to avoid war. Debate occurred and war followed. The outcome was the lowest ranked of a strong democracy's preferences. Why did it occur?

Members of Congress took great pains to signal Saddam Hussein that he should not misinterpret the proceedings. Senator Arlen Specter (R-Pennsylvania) urged the Iraqi leader not to confuse democratic deliberation with weakness and indecision:

[I]t is obviously a matter subject to great misunderstanding by Iraq and President Saddam Hussein about what our processes are.

I believe that the value of our democratic system and our open debate is worth every bit of the cost and more. If Iraq and its leaders do not understand this, then that is regrettable. . . .

It is easy for President Saddam Hussein to misunderstand the Congressional and other public discussions on U.S. policy in the Persian Gulf. Without considerable understanding of our democratic processes, he could easily misunderstand our disagreements on prospective policies and the controversy on constitutional authority to authorize the use of force. But this debate is an indispensable part of our democracy and is well worth whatever President Saddam Hussein may think about our lack of will and unity (*Congressional Record*, January 10, 1991).

The game metaphor suggests that Saddam saw the debate as a signal of weak American resolve. Senator Daniel Moynihan (D-New York) questioned American willingness to bear any burden:

[A]s we go about this collective exercise—an exercise under chapter VII of the UN Charter—what possesses the President to declare that "no price is too heavy to pay for it!" No price? Five million Arab civilian casualties, for example? Conflagration in the Middle East? The exhaustion of American military resources?

It is enough simply to ask the question to realize the answer. The answer being that we are prepared and ought to be prepared to pay some price, but not any price. (*Congressional Record*, January 12, 1991).

Senator Joseph Biden (D-Delaware) emphasized even more strongly the unwillingness of many Americans, in the post-Vietnam environment, to make the supreme sacrifice: "Let me just say this, Mr. President: President Bush, if you are listening, I implore you to understand that even if you win today 46–54, you still lose. The Senate and the Nation are divided on this issue. You have no mandate for war. Mr. President, President Bush, the debate to punish Saddam Hussein, the impatience you feel, the anger you feel are all justified, but none of them add up to vital interest and none of them—none of them—justify the death of our sons and daughters" (*Congressional Record,* January 12, 1991).

The public and congressional debate was a massive and complex tapestry, containing many crosscutting strands of rhetoric and argument, some obvious, others subtle. We do know that Saddam Hussein observed them, but we cannot know the extent to which they informed and influenced his thought and action. In his message to President Bush on January 16, 1991, President Hussein asked: "Do you have no qualms of conscience coming from the man that is still inside you . . . ? Do you not experience nagging qualms of conscience that may deter you from evil . . . ?" His statement about the public discussion provided at least a clue to the answer. "We refuse to attribute to the American people anything that is not positive," he said, "for those people . . . rose to meet their humanistic duties and went out in their hundreds of thousands to denounce your aggressive policies" (Bangio 1992, 164–71).

According to this analysis, American debate and dissent sent the wrong signal and undermined deterrence. The wrong war was fought in the wrong place because the misleading signals created a false consciousness that resulted in an inappropriate and suboptimal political reality. Democratic debate, added to mixed perceptions about America's general and local power, increased uncertainty about U.S. strength. The subjective illusion of weak political democracy dominated real elements of strong military democracy and led to the worst possible outcome for both parties.

In this logic, war initiation was the direct result of misrepresenting American strength by debating. If Congress had originally supported the president's ability to act alone, decisively, and without a long and divisive debate that signaled weakness, the war would not have had to be fought. This was a war that was not necessary.

Representing Weakness. A second line of reasoning suggests that the United States was better modeled as a weak instead of a strong democracy. Opponents of the war had serious doubts about the ability of the United States to project military power into the Middle East and the Persian Gulf for an extended period of time, and they expressed those doubts in the debate. Senator Paul Sarbanes (D-Maryland) stated that he believed the administration was "paying insufficient attention to these inherent uncertainties of war. The war could prove more destructive, more bloody, and more difficult to terminate," he continued, "than administration spokesmen, not to speak of sundry private advocates of war, seem to think. . . . An American military invasion of Iraq would be likely to set off a chain reaction that could bog America down in a variety of prolonged security operations in a setting of intensified political instability" (*Congressional Record*, January 10, 1991). Senator Sam Nunn (D-Georgia) spoke in the same tone: "What will be the effect on Islamic fundamentalism throughout the region? What will be the effect on terrorism? Will friendly Arab nations be destabilized over time?" (*Congressional Record*, January 12, 1991).

The weak-democracy argument is counterintuitive if one considers the subsequent military outcome. The *casus belli* was resolved in favor of the United States. Iraq withdrew from Kuwait. The Allied air attack on Baghdad demonstrated a destructive power similar to the fire-bombing of Dresden. Allied casualties were minimal, whereas hundreds of thousands of Iraqis died and the country's infrastructure was destroyed. Yet, viewed from a later perspective, the picture looks more complex. The allies did not achieve all their war aims; Saddam Hussein remained in power; the allied coalition disbanded; the United States withdrew most of its military forces from the area and began the process of massive demobilization following half a century of Cold War with the Soviet Union; and President Bush lost the next election.

The weak-democracy argument is given some additional weight by decisions made near the end of the hostilities. General H. Norman Schwarzkopf, the allied ground commander, wanted to push forward to Baghdad, capture it, and deal with Saddam Hussein in the same way that American forces did with Gen. Manuel Noriega in Panama. But President Bush refused to press his advantage. Why? Because certain aspects of the situation may have seemed less like Panama and more like Vietnam. If he killed or captured the Iraqi leader and installed a friendly but weaker regime, he ran the risk that a hostile regional power, Iran or Syria for example, would move militarily and politically into the vacuum—perhaps all the way to the Persian Gulf, thus risking the ultimate loss of the oil fields for which the war had been fought. Saddam Hussein lost the battle, but not the war. He calculated properly. The game modeled for a weak democracy correctly predicted the ultimate outcome of the Gulf War.

According to this line of argument, the debate sent the correct signal. The United States was, in important ways, ultimately the weaker power in this context. The divisive debate and relatively close initial vote were strong and important signals of real American political, military, and economic problems. Weighing all these factors, and adding in a loss of strength gradient for distance, Saddam Hussein may have believed that the United States would not fight. Alternatively, if America did fight, the Iraqi president may have believed that he had the advantage in staying power and would eventually emerge victorious. The equilibrium solution of the weak-democracy signaling game correctly predicted the ultimate outcome.

Signaler's Dilemma and Multiple Audiences

There are important differences between the simple world of the signaling model and the much more complex reality of international relations. Nevertheless, the application of this model to the case of the Gulf War helps sharpen our understanding of both the model and the war. The analysis also suggests some more general conclusions about the relationship between domestic democratic values and the requirements of international security.

In the signaler's dilemma, democracies must choose between augmenting or limiting democratic values through greater or lesser debate. Their domestic audience and their international allies presumably value democratic procedures. Democratic due process may, however, send the wrong signal to the audience of adversaries. Depending on their prior situation, democracies will either represent or misrepresent their physical strength or weakness, with important consequences for deterrence and defense. One of the lessons of this analysis is that democracies may be able to avoid the paradox of signaler's dilemma by fostering either learning or conversion of potential opponents. Democracies may win wars, like the Gulf War, following domestic debates. The lesson of the Gulf War, taken with other democratic military successes, may enhance the learning of nondemocratic decision makers. The perceptual linkage between debate and weakness may thus be attenuated. Debates, if properly framed, need neither indicate weakness nor misrepresent strength. Alternatively, democracies may help resolve signaler's dilemma by converting their international opponents to democratic procedures. Such a happy outcome would merge, at least theoretically, considerations of cultural consistency, self-interest, and international security.

International signaling and democratic debate are important components of political life. Such activities link producers of signs and messages with the multiple audiences that receive them. In the modern age, leaders and followers at home and abroad are all watching the same television screens and hearing the same sound bites. Signaling and debate are important in themselves, and are strongly linked with other elements of thought, language, and action in a larger process that conveys, communicates, and constructs the meaning of war and peace.

9

Between Maastricht and Sarajevo

European Identities, Narratives, Myths

FRANCIS A. BEER AND JEFFREY S. KOPSTEIN

The fall of the Berlin Wall and the end of the Cold War, political difficulties over the ratification and implementation of the expansion of Europe, pressures of migration, and the intractable Balkan War have been a few of the major events that have stimulated a growing literature on the future of Europe. Mostly situated within politics and political science, this literature constructs itself and Europe using standard categories of conservative or liberal, realist or functionalist discourse. It enriches our understanding of the stream of unfolding historical experience and helps to place it in received traditions that give it shared meaning.[1]

There are, at the same time, other traditions and *topoi* available to frame the same events. There has been a good deal of contemporary concern, for example, coming from various disciplines, with problems of identity and difference. Much of this has focused on the individual, but wider aspects of political identity and difference have also received attention.[2] We feel that the politics of identity will help determine the ultimate trajectory of Europe. What is meant by political identity is quite simple: who we think we are, and what are the basic assumptions about political life that we bring with us into politics. Underlying this line of analysis is the assumption that the subjective side of political life cannot be easily dismissed or reduced to other "variables." If modernity engenders wider and more inclusive definitions of boundaries and membership, then we can expect that over time this will lead to larger political units. If, on the other hand, modern identity is rife with particularisms, then we may be far less sanguine about the entire project of "Europe."

The concern with identity intersects with narrative. Narrative is far from simple although it is popularly understood in simple form. In linear essence, it focuses on stories—characters undertaking actions and interactions structured in plots (Miller 1990). To some, such stories may seem trivial or juvenile, developmentally restricted or disabled, but this impression is deeply misleading. Indeed, narrative is a fundamental way in which we define our understanding of reality and ourselves. It helps us bring closure—even though artificial, arbitrary, and temporary—to the infinite indeterminacy of our worlds and our selves (cf. Roe 1994; Schleifer, Davis, and Mergler 1992). The seriousness of the narrative enterprise is illustrated, for example, in the work of Mircea Eliade and Claude Lévi-Strauss. For such authors, stories of everyday life and religious myths embody and maintain the structure of society. For distinguished historian William McNeill, narrative is at the center of the historian's craft, and the dominant narratives become "mythistories" for their societies (cf. Mali 1992; Barthes 1972). For psychologist Jerome Bruner (1990, 84, 77), the narrator is "a form of Self," and "the 'push' to construct narrative" provides an "entry into meaning." In the work of computer scientist Roger Schank (1990), stories structure computational models of human cognition; frames and scripts are major building blocks of artificial intelligence. More to the present point, Paul Ricoeur (1988, 247) states that "individual and community are constituted in their identity by taking up narratives that become for them their actual history." Self is thus embedded in narrative, which is the matrix that identifies, locates, indexes, specifies, and recognizes the emergent pattern of the Self (cf. Digeser 1995; Kerby 1991; Edel 1984; Spence 1982).

These concerns with identity and narrative inform our discussion of Europe. We argue that European identity emerges from historical narrative. The Cold War is a special kind of narrative, a hegemonic narrative, or myth, whose authority was embedded in that of the dominant Cold War regime. The end of the Cold War has lessened the narrative's appeal, increasingly opening it to revisionist interpretations and releasing previously suppressed competitors. Other stories now contend in a more pluralistic, multivocal European environment. The winner, if there is one, of this contest will be the future of Europe.

Historical Europe and Cold War Europe

Historians—political, economic, social, and cultural—positioned at different expanses of space and time with different visions, have constructed the identity and narrative of "Historical Europe." They have embedded its long anchor in sedimented depths of oriental and occidental tradition, Judaic and

Islamic experience, the classical heritage of classical Greece and Rome, medieval Christian and feudal orders, the humanism of the Renaissance and Enlightenment, the growth of nation-states, colonialism and imperialism, and democracy and capitalism. Wherever Europe is spoken, monasteries, archives, and libraries thickly describe the tapestries of Historical Europe for contemporary heirs waiting to claim their legacy. Europe's identity is lodged in these multiple stories, emerging from the past, but maintained in the present. Historical Europe is the collective name of all of these European stories.

One story from this group, placing Europe in the great frame of world politics, is of particular recent importance. The century of total war, in the telling phrase of Raymond Aron, nurtured the myth of the Cold War and Cold War Europe. Cold War Europe, in turn, constituted itself through a particular view of the world and itself. We formulate its central elements as follows:

> The Cold War was a struggle between ultimate evil, represented by the Soviet Union, and the forces of good, represented by Europe and its allies.

> The Atlantic Alliance between Europe and North America provided a wider umbrella of association and security.

> Europe had a center, defined geographically by northwestern Europe and functionally by economics. Europe also had a periphery that blended into Central and Eastern Europe.

This narrative, reinforced by events, has been the hegemonic discourse, the dominant and interpretation, the mythical superframe of European politics for the last half century.

THE COLD WAR AND THE COMMUNIST ENEMY

Common knowledge and common sense of the Cold War constructed the world as a story of the Manichaean struggle between good and evil. Archetypal memory and millennia of historical enmity reinforced powerful distinctions between two hostile groups: a white, Christian, occidental Self, and a dark, oriental Other.

A system of concentric circles defined the essential Other, the Enemy. At the periphery of the outer ring, were the neutral nations even though, in the stark world of John Foster Dulles, there were no neutrals. In the next ring came the opposing Communist nations formally tied together through formal and informal political, military, economic, or cultural bonds, for example the Warsaw Pact; Council for Mutual Economic Aid (COMECON); and agreements for military assistance, trade, and aid. Near the center of this Russian doll was the Soviet Union, and, successively, the Communist Party, the Kremlin, the Politburo, Joseph Stalin, and his successors.

This narrative was strongest and most persuasive during the early years of the Cold War. The Sino-Soviet split, combined with other differences in the camp of Communist nations; the death of Stalin and Nikita Khrushchev's renunciation of part of his legacy; the stresses and strains of peaceful coexistence—all of these gradually weakened the definition and credibility of the Enemy. As the half century of what John Lewis Gaddis called "the long peace" waned, Westerners had less and less reason to believe, based on their personal lives, that the fundamental choice was between being Red or dead. Yet, anchored in the primacy of earlier formative experience, the Cold War and the Communist Enemy continued to frame and orient Europe's post–World War II identity.

THE ATLANTIC COMMUNITY AND DEMOCRATIC ALLIES

Cold War history already fills whole libraries with sources and details. We can here only sketch out brief elements from the standard account. The story begins with the Allied victory over the Axis powers, a combination of triumph and tragedy. The Allied achievement led, paradoxically, to the disintegration of the grand alliance that had successfully prosecuted World War II. Allied agreements at Yalta dividing Europe into Eastern and Western spheres of influence; tensions at Potsdam, particularly surrounding the political implications of the first atomic bombs; and Allied conflicts over the administration of Berlin all prefigured what was to come.

Central to the account were the ruthless suppression of democratic institutions and dissent and the construction of Communist national regimes in Central and Eastern Europe, particularly highlighted by the Czechoslovakian coup. These, combined with the terrible winter of 1946–47, encouraged Western fears of Soviet penetration and violation. Historical memories of invasion and conquest—the Moors in Spain, the Turks at the gates of Vienna—were an element of the deep background of Western response.

One of the foundational texts was George Kennan's 1946 "Long Telegram," the essence of which was published in *Foreign Affairs* under the pseudonym "Mr. X" and was the basis for National Security Council document NSC 68, which defined American strategic doctrine (see May 1993; Jensen 1991). These writings developed the ideas that came to be associated with the metaphor of containment. Containment constructed an updated and protracted version of the siege script, which had figured so prominently in European military history, against walled castles and cities both in Europe itself and the Middle East. Containment promised to reduce the costs of resistance. The postwar allies had little stomach for a conventional war against masses of Soviet ground troops in Europe. During the war, the unwillingness of Gen. Dwight D. Eisenhower as supreme allied commander to allow Gen. George Patton to push forward against the Russians to the east reflected Allied military concerns. Moreover, memories of losses from two world wars that had begun from the "cult of the offensive" warned both the Soviet Union away from adventurism and the Allies away from military engagement that was not absolutely necessary (Snyder 1989).

The balance of terror was an important metaphor. Balance of terror took a standard stratagem of European historical diplomacy, balance of power, and added to it. Nuclear weapons supplemented the conventional historical arsenal. An important psychological dimension was also mixed in. Just as fire had produced panic in crowded medieval fortresses, atomic bombs served to induce terror in the Enemy. Indeed, they were dropped on Hiroshima and Nagasaki for their "shock" effect on both the Japanese and the Soviets (cf. Bundy 1988, 80; Alperovitz 1985).

Western leaders also had the task of alleviating the terror of their own populations and encouraging their will to resist the Enemy. The North Atlantic Treaty Organization (NATO) thus entered the narrative as the house in which allied nuclear weapons would be kept. Within NATO, the United States, together with Britain and France, provided the nuclear umbrella against potential Soviet nuclear weapons. Under the strategic doctrine—a genre of military narrative—of the sword and the shield, the institutions of NATO grouped and coordinated Western military capabilities, including nuclear and conventional forces and other related activities (see Beer 1969).

The developing story of the postwar order, and the pressures it implied, thus included the Atlantic Community as a protective habitat for European integration. The interior of the Atlantic Community comprehended not only military elements, but also economic and political dimensions. In the early stages of Atlantic economic cooperation, the Truman Doctrine and Point Four program aimed specifically at assisting Greece and Turkey and the Marshall Plan at the reconstruction of Western Europe. Formal economic institutions subsequently fleshed out the design. The Organization for European Economic Cooperation (OEEC), later the Organization for Economic Cooperation and Development (OECD), led to the creation of its Enemy double, COMECON. The NATO Parliamentarians Conference never attained the flowering of the advocates of full

Atlantic union. Nevertheless, it contributed to the institutional superstructure of Atlantic Community. Atlantic institutions, including United States political, military, and economic power fit together with and buttressed Europe.

EUROPE: BOUNDARIES, CENTERS, AND PERIPHERIES

The Iron Curtain and the Berlin Wall bounded Europe to the east. Winston Churchill, in his defining speech at Fulton, Missouri, in March, 1946, described the eastern perimeter of Europe: "From Stettin in the Baltic to Trieste in the Adriatic, an iron curtain has descended across the continent" (Yergin 1977, 176). The Iron Curtain was the Eastern surface of Europe. It defined Europe's limits and liminality. The eastern boundary was the farthest extension of European identity. It had physical location, like the North Cape, and it had texture. Instead of ice, it had the texture of steel. The hardness and finality of the Iron Curtain warned away any who would be daring or foolhardy enough to traverse it. The boundary of Europe never lost the character that Churchill gave it. Yet gradually it was redefined and resymbolized. Guard dogs, barbed wire, land mines, and the Berlin Wall extended it in space and time.

The Atlantic and the Mediterranean opened Europe to the west and south. Within the Cold War's negative frame and the sheltering umbrella of the Atlantic alliance, the positive dynamic of European cooperation and integration could occur. Inside these boundaries, Europe tended its garden. The center of Europe lay in the northwest. In the face of the Communist threat, France and Germany had a dominant national security interest in putting behind them their historical enmity. The spatial center of Europe consisted of the original six countries, bound together by a foundational skeleton also laid down in iron metaphor, the European Coal and Steel Community (ECSC). Building on this core, another organization, the Western European Union, allowed the major European powers to control possible German rearmament.

As we have recounted, Western leaders needed to help restore the confidence of Western European publics in their abilities to reconstruct their world in the light of their own visions and dreams. Just as the military pillar of nuclear weapons balanced the conventional forces of the Soviet Union, so the political pillar of the European Community balanced the economic force of Central and Eastern Europe. The early steps of the European Community constructed the economic dimension of the counterweight to the Soviet Union. The ECSC was solidly based on converging economic self-interests of France, Germany, Italy, and the Benelux countries. The "spill-over" of these interests in peaceful "security communities" implied the constructive evolution of ECSC institutions, tasks, and membership through the integrative learning of a dynamic European regime (cf. Puchala 1984; Lindberg and Scheingold 1970; Haas 1958; Deutsch et al. 1957).

An outer circle of European cooperation originally consisted of those states outside the original six that desired a looser form of association. The European Free Trade Area initially provided an institutional setting for European fellow travelers. This periphery of European space and activity was gradually pulled in as many of these reluctant partners were brought into closer relations with the center. The center came to include additional layers of states and tasks. Formal neutrals like Switzerland, Austria, and Finland developed networks of relations with Europe. The West was also able to fish successfully at the edges of the Communist bloc, helping Hungary and Yugoslavia to become more independent and prosperous.

The periphery of Historical Europe had always blended into central and eastern Europe. This was also true for Cold War Europe, and the magnetic pull of the center, embedded in the Atlantic Community, eventually helped to bring down the Berlin Wall, the alliance of Eastern European states and their Communist parties, and the Soviet Union.

Post–Cold War Europe

Europeans toast the end of the Cold War story, but there is a residue at the bottom of the wine glass. The myth of the Cold War has lost much of its power with the disappearance of the Enemy. Paradoxically, the fall of the Berlin Wall and the disintegration of the Soviet Union have also helped to undermine Europe's collective belief and purpose and, with them, Europe's common identity. Cold War Europe contained within itself the seeds of what would emerge, but the new identity of post–Cold War Europe remains unclear. We can, however, try to sketch certain important parts of an emerging narrative. This story contains three major components, the death of the *ancien regime*, the Cold War; the legacy of the legitimate heir, Europe-Maastricht; and the dark shadow of the half-sister taken from the brothers Grimm, Europe-Sarajevo.

COLD WAR EUROPE IS DEAD

The Cold War has come to an end. It is over as an experienced myth, even if historical narratives continue to be written (e.g., Brinkley 1992; McCullough 1992). The war between good and evil is finished. The democratic Western allies won the Cold War. The myth of the Cold War is generally accepted as a true story, cosmologically and practically. The theory was confirmed by hard evidence. A deadly, evil Enemy—concrete and observable—was finally destroyed.

Western leaders had political virtue. Their wise policy of balancing and containment, prudence and perseverance, was vindicated (Isaacson and Thomas 1986). Their truth finally brought the Cold War to a close. As the myth predicted, the truth has made us free.

The Soviet regime collapsed like the czarist regime that preceded it. The Soviet Union has dissolved into the Commonwealth of Independent States, a loose collection of the former Russian empire's component parts. The arms race and the threat of nuclear war have receded. Totalitarianism has disappeared in the European context. Lenin and Stalin have finally passed away, their heirs and legacy scattered. The Soviet Union is gone; the Communist Party has disintegrated as a dominant political force. If contemporary empirical research in international relations tells us anything, it is about the close relationship between democracy and peace. We are, so popular writers tell us, in the springtime of democracy and at the end of history. As the superordinate category of evil itself—defined in the Cold War narrative—has disappeared, so the litany of subordinate evils, particularly war, should soon follow into the dusty archives of past narratives.

Yet the end of the Cold War has created a crisis for Atlantic institutions, particularly those involving military security. The Atlantic Alliance has lost its raison d'être, the external Enemy; it has lost the cohesive power of hate and fear produced by the threatening Communist Other. The friends are still friends—after all, they are democrats. And NATO can even expand. However, as it does so, its purpose and identity disintegrate. In the absence of compelling danger, friends often go separate ways. They have separate interests that are not always easy to coordinate, even in the face of security problems like the Balkan War (Levine 1992).

EUROPE-MAASTRICHT BECKONS

Churchill dramatized the balance of terror in the metaphor of two scorpions in a bottle, each poised to sting the other to death. One of the scorpions has disappeared, not with a bang but a whimper, not through nuclear devastation but from economic exhaustion. The other is deeply damaged. The Soviet Union is America's vanquished foe, but also a possible prophecy of America's future. The United States is, at least briefly, the sole remaining superpower. Yet America's unipolar moment is troubled by the enormous economic and social sequelae of the Cold War. The collapse of the Soviet Union and the weakening of the United States have increased the relative weight of all other players, especially Europe. In this context of exhausted adversaries, Europe is, in Johan Galtung's phrase, an emerging superpower.

The center of Europe reborn is Europe-Maastricht, named after the city where a central agreement leading to the common European currency was forged. Maastricht is the living symbol of the new Europe, embodying hopes for a common European identity born of rational self-interest and positive reinforcement. The treaty of Maastricht speaks the language of instrumental rationality, of a currency union that will rationalize resources and lead to greater wealth for all, but the more important issue is that of identity. Behind the Europtimists lies the idea that giving up national control over currencies reflects a more fundamental shift in political identity away from national to supranational units. For the Europtimists it is not a matter of economics being less important than identity. Nothing could be farther from the truth. It is precisely because material life and its institutional substructures are so important that the willingness to begin changing the locus of control must symbolize the potential for a shift in center of political authority. Europe's emerging identity is shaped by instrumental rationality but has much greater ambitions for the creation of a new Europe and new Europeans. Self-interest will lead to a new European Self, dare one even say a new European Soul?

Nevertheless, the new European narrative and identity are increasingly fragmented. Without the dynamic, focusing power of fear, greed alone may not be enough to structure completely political reality. The European superpower emerges, but with deep political problems of its own. Europe is no longer compressed, constrained, distorted, diminished, dwarfed, and stunted by the Cold War and the Atlantic Alliance. The earthshaking fall of the wall has loosened and disturbed other structures. The same post–Cold War dynamic of exhaustion and deconstruction that destroyed the Soviet Union and has seriously weakened the United States is also at work in Western Europe.

Even with the excitement of the new Eurocurrency, a major event, the European Community labors heavily in troubled waters. European moviemakers and farmers resist harmonization into the World Trade oranization (WTO). The future of the new money is still not entirely clear. The potential economic benefits of deeper union have met obvious strong resistance from some groups inside the Community and some European states outside of it.

Europe-Maastricht is an heir of the Cold War; it implies centers and peripheries similar to those that have gone before. The core states remain poles of power and growth. Interestingly, France, Germany, and the Benelux nations— in the core of the original six—have wished to move ahead most rapidly with the steps toward enhanced monetary cooperation after Maastricht. Around the latest turn in the track, the same racers, joined by some others, still lead the pack. But European Monetary Union has been transformed into a multi-speed vehicle where the historical sovereign governments of many individual European nation-states will continue, at least partly, to determine their own trajectories and velocities.

The two Germanys have finally achieved reunification, but its future and consequences are unclear. The effects of the new Germany on wider European relations run in different directions. German vision and economic strength help to pull Europe forward. Yet this Grossdeutschland frightens many of its neighbors whose long historical memories of the kaiser and the führer do not always match those of some Germans. Germany's current situation has a similarly ambivalent impact on Germans themselves (Kopstein and Richter 1992). Germans dreamed of reunification for half a century; now they are reunited and families have been brought back together. Yet the wall has left lasting scars; pains balance joys. The German family is one of richer Wessi uncles and aunts and poorer Ossi cousins sharing the same house. West Germans have paid the price of reunification in higher taxes, unemployment, and inflation, as well as refugees and racist violence. East Germans, who enjoyed the dignity, security, and distance of their own state and society, have ironically also paid many of the same costs. In addition, they have had to accept their inferiority and subordination, a new living situation and lifestyle that does not always seem better to all than what went before (cf. Priewe and Hickel 1991; Maaz 1990).

Elsewhere in Western Europe, political scandals, scattered violence, resurgent nationalism and subnationalism, and group identification along ethnic boundaries all indicate continuing serious divisions (Moynihan 1993; Greenfield 1992).

EUROPE-SARAJEVO THREATENS

At the far eastern end of Cold War Europe's periphery, the repressed and denied world of Central and Eastern Europe lurks as Europe-Sarajevo. It is the remainder, containing everything missing from Europe-Maastricht. Europe-Sarajevo is the world without—without borders, without electricity. The nations of Central and Eastern Europe continue an earlier imperial collapse, the deconstruction of the Austro-Hungarian Empire. Czechs and Slovaks, Ruthenians and Ukrainians, Rumanians and Magyars, Croats and Serbs, Bulgars and Pomaks—each has more weight and freedom. These groups and others struggle for the separate identity, the autonomous narrative, the emotional satisfaction, that was earlier denied to them through the long centuries of imperial history, the long preceding history of Balkan crises, and, in this century, the Cold War.

Sarajevo, calling on the deeper heritage of Historical Europe, symbolizes something altogether different from Europe-Maastricht: Balkan crises redux. The images of division and subdivision, the bodily rhetoric of physical destruction, of brother killing brother tell us that the "United States of Europe" is a story that is a long way from pan-European adoption. If there is an underlying instrumental rationality in the Balkans, then this only indicates that rationality does not always lead to peaceful, unified, or even humane political outcomes. A further possibility runs to the core of all assumptions of European unity. Not only are the cultural commonalities of the European heritage not as binding as many might like them to be, but the dissection of Bosnia is only the latest demonstration that identities bend slowly to the iron logic of instrumental rationality.

The map of Cold War Europe could be drawn as it was because Central and Eastern Europe were defined as at least partly Asiatic and, therefore, out of Europe. Yet, Central and Eastern Europe were not only more Asiatic, they were also more authentically European. They were more Asiatic because of the great eastern reaches and autocratic history of the Soviet Empire. They were more European because of their distance from another Other, a repressed Enemy within, more potent for being integrated with the Self. This Enemy was the United States, whose dominant postwar position allowed an ongoing military, economic, and cultural penetration. It was more powerful for being unacknowledged, avoided, and denied. Cold War Europe was an identity imposed at least partly from the outside—based on a victor's justice, inscribed in a victor's story. Cold War Europe, in this light, identified with the aggressor. Central and Eastern Europe remained more alien and more alienated. They were farther on the distance gradient, less violated, more pure.

With the Soviet collapse, Central and Eastern Europe offer the possibility of an ethical fiction (Booth 1988). They present at least the symbolic opportunity to dissolve the morass of manipulation, the web of fear and greed, the moral corruption articulated by Böll and Fassbinder. Following Grass, it may now be possible to reverse the standard Cold War escape story, to escape to the east. In that light, East Germany is the real Germany; Dresden is a city that looked as German cities would have looked if Germany had won the war; Budapest is a more authentic Vienna. Ironically, Historical Europe has survived Cold War Europe. Historical Europe still lives in the east, separate from American-occupied Europe, its purity protected from the protracted rape of the last half-century by the superficial veneer, the apparent ugliness, of oriental despotism.

New and Old Worlds in Order and Disorder

Today's Europe appears in shades of postmodern darkness and scattered light, worlds of virtual reality connected as hypertexts, bricolage in a cyberpunk *nouvel roman, sans clef, degré zéro.* The Cold War was a war, but it was not a shooting war—except occasionally in the alleys and subterranean passages of *The Third Man* and Smiley's world, the streets and squares of Warsaw or Prague, the mountains of Afghanistan, the jungles of Angola or Nicaragua. The dominant mode of Cold War was "virtual warfare," an Orwellian twilight zone where peace was war and war was peace. War was not "hot war" but "cold war." Not the Clausewitzian war of physical friction but Virilio's and Lotringer's war of pure fiction. In a sense, the Cold War was fought on television; in the United States it existed just after *Jeopardy* and before *The Brady Bunch.*

In the post–Cold War period, peaceful coexistence is transformed to take new referents and meanings. Europe is multiple coexisting worlds in constant internal change and external motion. There may be a New World Order, but it is ordered in much different, more complex, and discontinuous ways than what preceded it—with both too many and too few characters and plots. In contemporary European narratives, the boundaries and locations of images transform and displace each other. Criteria of identity and difference, production and reproduction, economics and psychology, appear and disappear, shift and blur, come together and move apart dissolving any attempts at closure (cf. Bourdieu 1993; Derrida 1992; Attali 1991; Baudrillard 1983).

Europe's worlds are past, present, and future all in cohabitation. Cold War Europe now settles as one among many narratives and identities in the archives of Historical Europe, its orthodox received wisdom to be sifted with all the other lessons of European history. Present Europe contains the past, but not necessarily in the orderly linear form, sorted neatly by ideological keys, with which we are familiar. For example, the symbolic lexicon contains multiple entries under Sarajevo. If these are organized by reference to standard major events and put in sequential chronological order, a partial list might look something like this:

1429. Fell to the Turks.

1878. Awarded to Austria-Hungary at the Congress of Berlin.

1914. Site of the assassination of the Austrian Archduke Franz Ferdinand and his wife and the immediate cause of the chain of events leading directly to World War I.

1918. Incorporated into Yugoslavia.

1988. Site of winter Olympics.

Merely to begin making such a list exposes its arbitrariness. There is no law that specifies historical experience as a list, or Gregorian dates as major organizing categories of such a list. Lived experience and life worlds are broader and deeper, more and less continuous than such a list-narrative suggests.

Zbigniew Brzezinski (1993) writes that the modern world is out of control, lacking the coherence of either internal or external discipline. It is fashionable to believe that the center cannot hold. Perhaps. But one must ask which center, out of whose control? The Cold War myth is gone, leaving challenges of adaptation and evolution. The corseted realist stability of Cold War Europe was a frame for the European Community. It contained the rational logic and enhanced the empirical probability of functionalist linear progress toward European integration. Whether the elites that dominated the Cold War can maintain and continue the myth, and the Europe-Maastricht identity that follows from it, through the next generations remains to be proven in the order and disorder, continuity and discontinuity, of a rapidly changing post–Cold War world.

We have not reached the end of history, but rather the end of a particular interpretation and episode of history. The myth and identity of Cold War Europe have ended. New worlds and new Europes are, as always, struggling to be born. As the stories and identities of the compelling Europe-Maastricht and the repellant Europe-Sarajevo move forward though hyperspace, the new post–Cold War Europes jettison and leave behind the shards of Historical Europe, already receding from the distant horizons of memory. Yet, as Historical Europe remains in its own ash heap, it is simultaneously recycled. The new worlds carry history forward as memory at the same time that they leave it behind as experience. Monnet, Schuman, Adenauer, De Gasperi, and Spaak are permanently inscribed as icons of supranational identity in the canon of the new Europe. Yet de Gaulle and Thatcher, articulating the continuing pull of traditional national identities, are also new European prophets. The new Europes approach the millennium carrying also the ghostly epiphanies of Augustine and Aquinas, Saint Peter and Saint James, Saint Francis and Saint Cyril, Luther and Zwingli; the imperial dreams of Charlemagne and Attila; Ferdinand and Isabella, Catherine and Frederick the Greats, Napoleon and Victoria, Franz Josef and Tsar Nicholas; the diplomatic combinations of Richelieu, Talleyrand, Metternich, and Bismarck, of Castlereagh, Canning, and Disraeli; the nationalistic visions of Garibaldi and Mazzini; the poetic dreams of Dante and Milton; the drama of Chaucer and Cervantes, Proust, Mann, and Joyce, Shakespeare and Shaw, Tchekhov, Tolstoy, and Turgenev, Musil and Andrić; the philosophies of Plato and Aristotle, Erasmus, Descartes and Leibniz, Bentham and Rosseau, Hobbes and Locke, Hegel and Kant, Schopenhauer and Nietzsche, Kierkegaard and, yes, Heidegger; the artistic genius of Rembrandt and Rubens, Monet and Picasso; the music of Mozart, Chopin, Wagner, Tchaikovsky; the separatist hopes of Herzl and Jabotinsky and countless other public and private identities, narratives, and myths.

The myths, with their heroes and villains, connect political communities. Leaders and audiences, citizens and subjects, retell and reenact them as part of their everyday individual and collective lives. Thought, discourse, and behavior assume an identity within the overarching, culturally shared narrative. World War I, the interwar period, World War II, the Cold War, the post–Cold War period—these are part of the fabric and the material that the myths represent and form in the meaning that surrounds and incorporates war and peace.

Conclusion

Language and the Meaning of War and Peace

FRANCIS A. BEER

War and peace continue to matter greatly in our world, but they are difficult to understand, embedded as they are in complex webs of relationships. The meaning of war and peace lies in the patterns that emerge from that complexity. A multidimensional lattice of meaning includes patterns of behavior, patterns of cognition, patterns of language, and larger patterns of interaction between these and other smaller patterns. The patterns are like families of nested Russian dolls possessing individual identities and, at the same time, existing in larger sets of relationships. The networked relationships of thought, action, and behavior define the meaning of war and peace.

Words are critical mediators in representing and understanding the patterns, the meaning, of war and peace. The chapters in this book describe a number of different ways that language works in conveying and shaping meaning: These are grouped into somewhat arbitrary semantic, rhetorical, and audience sections. The core idea of the semantic section is that word strings help produce meanings as algebraic strings produce mathematical products. In the narrowest semantic sense, surrounding words subtly shade and modify the definitions of central terms and concepts like *war, reason,* and *validity.* The variable meanings that result have important scientific and political implications for war and peace. The rhetorical section extends this idea to broader clusters, constellations, and galaxies of words. It shows how rhetorical structures and stylistic devices of theory, argument, and metaphor reflect and construct the perception and interpretation of war and peace events. The section on audience carries the rhetorical concern forward and includes narrative as an important component. At the same time, it suggests the pragmatic interaction between political leaders and followers. Political actors speak strategically, shifting their language as they interact with their multiple internal and external audiences. At some point speakers and audiences merge into one as they jointly identify with powerful collective myths. In this moment thought, action, and language are joined collectively and individually in a unified structure of meaning.

The Language of Survival and Adaptation

The explorations of meaning in this book describe in detail some aspects of the relationship between war, peace, and language. These provide a platform for speculation about the future. Simple extrapolation suggests, first and most obviously, that language will continue to be important in reflecting and constructing the meaning of war and peace. Language will also articulate and form our understanding of survival and adaptation in the context of future war and peace.

We live in a time of accelerating change, and this change has an increasingly international dimension, dissolving national boundaries to an extent that could hardly have been imagined only a few generations ago. States have died and been reborn. Large empires, like dinosaurs, have moved toward extinction. The twentieth century has seen the collapse of the Russian state followed by its Soviet successor. The British, French, and Austro-Hungarian empires have joined their Turkish, Dutch, Spanish, and Portuguese predecessors. As the old empires have died, new smaller states, like tiny phoenixes, have been and continue to be born from their remains.

French statesman Georges Clemenceau stated at the end of the First World War that the key to victory was the stamina to remain standing fifteen minutes longer than one's opponents (Nicolson 1988). At the end of the twentieth century, the United States has indeed remained standing in the ring, the momentary national champion. In its hegemonic moment, the United States has used its position to promote its own values, ideology, and culture.

This American doctrine, which we shall call liberal internationalism, incorporates much from traditional realism.[1] For example, it carries forward the belief that states, particularly large ones, cannot simply withdraw into splendid isolation (Muravchik 1996; Nordlinger 1995). National governments have obligations to their citizens, themselves, and the wider international community. Liberal internationalism further shares with realism the belief that the world can be a dangerous place and that national governments need to use appropriate force, when necessary, to protect themselves and their citizens. National responsibility in a dangerous world implies continuing international political engagement, the imperatives of national military security, and vigilant self-defense.

Nevertheless, liberal internationalism suggests the incompleteness of realism and foreign policy based only on realism. Such defects have been as much political as military, resting on the inability of political leaders to connect fully with the values of the people they represented. Democratic governments have failed fully to represent popular preferences in a number of cases, for example, the policy of the French government of Pierre Mendès-France in Indochina, of the British government of Sir Anthony Eden on Suez, and U.S. policy in Vietnam under a succession of American presidents.

Unlike realism, liberal internationalism does not believe that the story ends with robust national military security in a permanent field of international power. Structural change, even progress, may be possible. At the end of the day, the collective state must reflect the collective mind. Thus, the American vision of the new world order includes political democratization. Such democratization is not necessarily (in Morgenthau's dismissive formulation of Woodrow Wilson) messianic. It does not have to happen all at once, in a single foundational event. It can come over the long term, bit by bit, through gradual, piecemeal, incremental evolution. Such democratization involves the standard institutional paraphernalia of free elections and a free press. It also includes a strong emphasis on the human rights of groups and individuals. Globalization is the name usually given to the economic dimension of this liberal international program for the new world order. The American vision of global liberalism includes economic democratization and the free operation of markets—free flows of capital, goods, services, labor, and information. The new world order will be a world that replicates and is safe for American democracy.

In the evolving environment of the early twenty-first century, war and peace achieve new meanings. Though specific forms may change, we are vividly reminded every day—as in the succession of actual, virtual, and potential Gulf Wars, the interminable Middle East peace process, and the chronic violence in the Balkans—that war continues. Rogue states, ethnic cleansing, narco-terrorism, and nuclear, chemical, and biological weapons of mass destruction continue to reinforce the realist argument that the world is a dangerous place requiring a continuing international security concern.

Liberal internationalist democracy and globalization are certainly consistent with the continuation of war in the twenty-first century. Access to important resources—oil, for example—and markets must be protected. Strong military means are sometimes necessary to safeguard physical security. At the same time, the Western powers are dramatically outnumbered by exponentially increasing non-Western populations.

Although democracies must sometimes fight, war is inconvenient and costly. It interferes with capital investment and consumer shopping; it unsettles profits. War interrupts voting, and when it does not, young men and women of draft age vote. They also have parents who vote and who do not like to lose their children. In this environment, peace becomes vastly preferable and war more and more dangerous, disruptive, and risky. Western political and military leaders have no desire to pay costs like those of the terrible trench warfare of World War I, the massed engagements of World War II, the hard winters of Korea, or the jungle warfare in French Indochina and later Vietnam. Moreover, their humanistic values make them unenthusiastic about repeating the human tragedies of conventional and atomic air bombardment. The Somme, Stalingrad, the Yalu, Dien Bien Phu, and Tet; Dresden and Hiroshima-Nagasaki are ghosts that rest uneasily. Modern military technology also demonstrates that weapons intended for others can have effects on one's own people as well. Agent Orange and nuclear winter convey somber lessons: backwash happens.

In the twenty-first century, international violence will continue, but the meaning of war will gradually evolve. It will become less physical in a directly human sense and more virtual. Doctrines of deterrence and containment developed in the second half of the twentieth century will continue to provide shields of virtual defense based on superior military technology. When combat is necessary, battle will become more automated as battlefield communications, computers, and robotics permeate national military establishments and doctrines. National security responses, like national security threats, will also become more multidimensional (Buzan, Waever, and de Wilde 1998). Violent military behavior will be translated into less direct economic, cultural, and scientific competition. Economic incentives and punishments will provide powerful and attractive alternatives to traditional forms of military engagement. Religious and economic doctrines will compete across traditional boundaries, as, in one formulation, Jihad versus McWorld (Barber 1996). International doctrine will recognize and develop the global mindscape and international mindshare as part of a world mind game. The meaning of war and peace in this virtual environment will evolve in both cooperative and competitive directions. Patterns and linkages will connect international actors more densely than before. At the same time, the struggle for control over emerging global networks will be an important strategic and tactical concern.

Language and communication will gain new importance for war and peace. Their significance has long been recognized as a cohesive force in international relations. Common language offers the possibility of complex communication and translation between different cultures. General international languages— Greek, Latin, French—bound together diverse states and formed the basis of the international community. Today, English is generally the global second language of choice where it is not the first. Modern communications and computers provide common global symbol systems that reach much deeper than previous elite international languages into popular culture: Disney and CNN, Microsoft and the Internet, are growing platforms for shared international understanding. More partial regional and local languages also unite people, but they simultaneously divide them. Such languages have historically served as cultural and ethnic markers, indexing different groupings with distinct identities and interests. Different languages point to multiple different possible worlds, following different purposes with different syntax and semantics, arrangements of order and signification (Lewis 1973). They point to different worlds of meaning.

Contemporary international diplomacy with its careful observation, reporting, and negotiation—its precise use of words—is in some ways the linguistic arm of the state, translating between sovereign languages. The diplomat stands beside the warrior in the arena of war and peace (cf. Kissinger 1995; Nicolson 1988; Kennan 1967; Murphy 1965). In the contemporary world, diplomacy remains central to international relations for its ability to encode, decode, and negotiate meaning. Nothing has yet replaced the human contact of personal conversation and ceremonies—the handshakes, toasts, and photo opportunities—between high-level leaders and officials. The nuances of international negotiation and agreement require skilled practitioners of the art. Yet some of the traditional functions of the closed world of diplomacy have been opened by modern technology. The media of mass global communication have proliferated and prospered in the contemporary world. For example, CNN is now the world's reporter and message center, the free press and storyteller for the global village. Its reports tell world leaders and ordinary citizens about military operations, financial events, and natural disasters. Reporting instantaneously, the media collapse time. Informing all equally, they collapse horizontal and vertical, geographical and social space. Through the modern media, war and peace occur continuously through the day and discontinuously in discrete stories and newsbreaks, globally across worldwide news channels and locally with on-the-spot reporters. Media diplomacy supplements traditional diplomacy as government officials spin war and peace issues in media-fed campaigns of propaganda and public relations. Media and the Web, in this guise, are channels of virtual war, actual and potential peace.

The emerging New World Order will thus include a strong linguistic and communications component. The liberal or the democratic peace rely on persuasive elites and practices to achieve their effects. Language in the twenty-first century will remain an important element of national power, survival, and adaptation—and of the meaning of war and peace.

The Language of Transformation and Transcendence

People of the twenty-first century will inherit from their forebears a mixed historical legacy of war and peace. As a part of this bequest, they will receive a closet full of terms and concepts; theories, arguments, and metaphors; narratives and myths; audiences and strategies—meanings—of war and peace. Our descendants will use their heritage as they simultaneously transform it into new patterns of meaning that will transcend our current understanding of war and peace.

Some of these new patterns will be political. A few theorists believe that it is now possible to imagine (very broadly and over a very long term) a possible great transition to a world with more peace and less war, as we understand these terms today (cf. Falk 1995; Rapoport 1992; J. R. Mueller 1989). As we noted earlier, long-term historical trends show that modern wars have been more damaging and costly than wars that occurred earlier in history. At the same time, modern war has tended to be shorter and less frequent than in the past. War and peace are indeed evolving and changing (Beer 1997) for many different and complex reasons.

As we have suggested, some of the evolution in war and peace will involve communication and language. Technology will drive transformation. Increasingly, virtual screen-to-screen contact will supplement face-to-face physical contact. The sounds and images of television, the icons of the World Wide Web, are accessible and gripping. They command our attention and help our understanding. They do not, however, replace our need for words. Verbal culture (the spoken and written word) will continue to develop (Ong 1991; Illich and Sanders 1988). In the end, there is no real choice. Even if we were to choose a world of no words, we should require the world of words to make and keep remaking that choice. Language will continue to be an important aspect of human evolution and the evolution of meaning, partly reflecting change, partly driving it.

Semantics are an important part of this process. War meant something very different in 1800 than in 1900 or 2000. And it will mean something very different again by the year 2100. Some things, of course, have remained the same—national governments aiming to impose control over others by using armed forces. Yet the global environment will be dramatically different, as will be weapons, logistics, strategy, and tactics. As we saw earlier, war, as a term or concept, may have a stable core, but context produces enormous variations in meaning. These variations are, from a general point of view, continuous and nonlinear. They are also specifically instantiated, bound locally into the network at particular points of space and time.

During the last half of the twentieth century we became used to the idea of "cold war." The crucial adjective here transformed war from a direct, physical, material activity fought with hard, sharp, and bloody weapons, and with shattering explosives, into something more extended, more multidimensional, more abstract. Technological modernization has created war as increasingly complex and indirect. In the first part of the twenty-first century we may well become used to the idea of "hot peace," "guerrilla peace," or other forms of "half peace." In this formulation, peace may be the name of the overarching framework of great-power relations within which smaller creatures may still fight and the elephants may occasionally trample the ants and the grass.

Different semantic networks will evolve with different meanings for war and peace. War, as Lewis Richardson suggested, is like weather: always present but infinitely changeable in different configurations. "Bad" or "good" weather comes and leaves. The configurations of war and peace fluctuate, and the language that we use to refer to them does likewise. What is true for war is also true for peace. In one sense, peace is the opposite of war, just as conflict appears to be the opposite of cooperation. Yet, from another point of view, peace and cooperation index arrays of attributes entirely separate from war and conflict (see Beer, Ringer, Healy, Sinclair, and Bourne 1992). As the meaning of war fluctuates over time, so will the meaning of peace.

Different rhetorics including theories, arguments, metaphors, and narratives will also evolve. International political realism has already gone through several transformations, again denoted by adjectives: classical realism (Thucydides), traditional realism (Hobbes, Machiavelli), modern realism (Kennan, Lippmann, Morgenthau, Herz), neorealism (Keohane), and structural realism (Waltz). The democratic aspirations of foreign policy, retrieved from Napoleonic revolutionary fervor, Wilsonian zeal, and Morgenthau's "idealist" marginalization, live and prosper today in the field of globalization and democratization. Incorporating many of the lessons of realism, contemporary global liberalism recalls Theodore Roosevelt's admonition to carry a big stick while walking softly.

The emergent theory of international relations for the twenty-first century clearly includes national interest, power, and military force. Yet there is a global dimension that goes beyond the international or the national. There is a concern for political ideas and forms; for values, ethics and morality; and for individual, human concerns to inform, energize, and support national and international policy. Security remains an important goal, but there are other aims—peace, freedom, welfare, and justice, to name a few. Foreign policy arguments must blend these different concerns. The doctrine of just war is only one ethical thread that runs through the rhetoric of war and peace. Concern for appropriate military tasks and effectiveness, human rights and casualties, environmental preservation and damage, are others. While the rhetoric of the power structure will continue to be important, so will people's higher aspirations to achieve better collective solutions to massive collective problems.

Metaphors will play a role in global evolution. The metaphors of body, gender, and family will continue to be important. Ordinary metaphors, ordinary language, connect the elite world of high policy with the normal lives that leaders share with ordinary people as part of the common human condition. As we have seen, bodily metaphors underlie many of the key concepts in realist theory. Bodily metaphors will continue to structure international theory. But they also support other theoretical forms. One of the primary human concerns is that of physical survival. Realist assumptions of war as the natural state and realist tendencies toward violent practices threaten the lives of at least some of the nation's citizens. Real bodies, real families—fathers, mothers, daughters, and sons—do not relish going into "harm's way." Within the program of global democratization, ordinary people can be expected increasingly to try to protect their lives as they also strive for security and community, liberty and happiness. Furthermore, the emergence of women from the shadows of the household into the networks of an increasingly wired society promises greater attention to feminine, if not feminist, concerns.

Women, as we have seen, have tended to speak politically in more family and maternalist terms. While the movement of women away from the home into the workplace may weaken this tendency, the biological fact of childbearing is too concrete to ignore. Until we move fully into the human hatcheries predicted in Aldous Huxley's *Brave New World,* women may be expected to try to protect the children they have physically borne from violence. At the same time, women will play the political roles that their careers and colleagues demand. The successors to Golda Meir, Indira Gandhi, and Margaret Thatcher will rise to political power and responsibility. Women will also participate on more equal terms in military careers and activities. In doing so, they will be faced with the imperatives of the international environment, which often are harsher than those for which the family has prepared them. Whatever the domestic situations of abuse, betrayal, or abandonment, few spouses have access to nuclear, biological, or chemical weapons. The imperatives of international environment and culture may narrow the gender gap in foreign policy. There are limits to the maternalist metaphor, and women's maternalist rhetoric may decline.

Women will retain a separate gender identity and will speak with at least something of a separate voice, different from men. Gender matters and will matter for the foreseeable future. Regardless of the socialization of women into world politics, the billions of women who do not aspire to political careers will continue to respond in ways that are consistent with their relations with their children, and their separate interests and identities. Global democratization suggests that women's voices—whatever the external professional influences—will speak differently than men's voices and more strongly in the world than they do today, giving war and peace different values and different meanings than they now carry.

The great narratives of good and evil—the myths that order our collective understanding of the world—rely on deep bodily metaphors. Yet they also have room for a broader myth, a wider identity, a larger self that can, in Walt Whitman's well-known phrase, contain multitudes. There are many narratives in the emergent metanarrative of war and peace—as many as there are actors, actresses, and actions; behaviors and events; observers and observations.

Growing concern for our natural environment will be a rich source of imagery. Visions of the apocalypse and the end of the world will vie with calls for global stewardship (cf. Kung 1998; Jonas 1996, 1984; Kaufman 1993; Clark 1977; Edwards 1973; Chardin 1965; Jaspers 1963). In a shrinking world, the challenge will be to use our knowledge—particularly our knowledge of language—to construct a more peaceful, less war-prone, less destructive environment to give war and peace meanings that are more compatible with broader human values.

Multiple audiences will participate in this great transition. Global democratization suggests much larger and more active audiences for a much broader politics. The worldwide expansion of television and the Internet promises much more political engagement in the twenty-first century. The emerging communications-linked world was simply unimaginable before the critical technical inventions that have made it possible. The global village implies global audiences. Political elites spring from these audiences and will respond to them. Political leaders will find the words to link different cognitions and emotions, different behaviors and actions, into the political coalitions and movements that will provide the future meaning of war and peace.

The Language of Connection

As we move through the twenty-first century, the international system will evolve and transform itself. Worlds, realities, and objective and subjective meanings will slowly shift of their own accord. Evolution implies learning, and the learning curve will help to carry us along. The actors in the global system will increasingly recognize its multiple, complex configurations of meaning—the multiple purposes and intentions, significations and truths, language and symbol systems. The recognition and appreciation of these concurrent, dynamic worlds of meaning will help us to become more conscious, active participants in the evolutionary process and allow us to participate in ways consistent with evolving world meanings.

Part of this process will involve using our language self-consciously to make new connections, new patterns, and new relationships—new, more complex, denser links of meaning—for war and peace (cf. Mulgan 1997). We observed at the beginning of the book that meaninglessness implied substantial disconnections, incomplete or partial patterns. For constructive evolution, it is particularly important that emerging patterns of meaning for war and peace include complex and strong links throughout the network. There are many such connections; we focus here on a few important ones.

These connections weave a web of interpretive time and space—in Bakhtin's (1981) term, the *chronotope*—of war and peace. An initial set of links strengthens connections in interpretive time—between past and present, present and future, and short- and long-term futures—of war and peace. The first connection is between the past and the present. The historical meaning of war and peace is embedded in their connection with the past in the theater of memory. As we move forward in time, these historical connections inevitably change. The old relations shift position and new ones emerge. It is important, in this process, to struggle against forgetting—against a creeping, collective Alzheimer's. Imagine an AIDS pandemic that left nobody alive past the age of twenty-five. Such an environment would destroy education as we know it and, with education, the knowledge that is the heritage of humankind. Our knowledge of historical war and peace is mostly in written form, composed of words. It allows us perspective, detail on bygone worlds of war and peace, an appreciation of their complexity. With the knowledge of these past worlds also comes a deeper understanding of future possible worlds of war and peace. It is important to retain this historical knowledge of past worlds of meaning, this present understanding of the meaning of war and peace, which we inherit from our parents, grandparents, and those before them.

The second set of important connections is the link between the present and the future of war and peace. One of the great contributions of psychologist Erik Erikson was the recognition of a discrete stage of life that centered on generativity. Rooted in the natural biology of our own aging process—the developmental transformations of our own bodies—generativity provides a model for our approach to the future. With the gradual graying of the global population comes at least the possibility of an increased global generativity. Global graying is, in some ways, the opposite of the global AIDS pandemic. Longer years with better health imply longer memories, longer retention of our knowledge of the past. Connection of the present with the future, together with other evolutionary tendencies, suggests that our knowledge of the human, material, and environmental costs of past wars will be balanced against what we want for our children and what they want for their children. Metaphors of the body, the family, and the environment lead directly to a narrative with a broader collective vision. The stakes of this game, the point of this story, are the lives of our children and grandchildren. Global graying raises our sights and also raises the stakes. Projections of accelerating increases in life expectancy also imply accelerating increases in war costs: Each life destroyed is potentially a longer, richer one. We must understand the present meaning of the future and the future meaning of the present in the deepest, most personal sense.

The third temporal connection is between the short-term and the long-term future of war and peace. Most decisions are based on short-term, immediate interests. Decision makers are often constrained by the logic of immediate necessity and the limits of hard choices. Without success in the short term, there is no long term, and long-term considerations are heavily discounted. Yet the evolution of global generativity, together with global wealth creation, suggests that interest needs to be defined in broader reaches of space and time. War's costs, war's frictions, put unnecessary burdens on the global system. Prudent people would prefer to reduce these costs if there were other more peaceful ways to achieve their goals. As in the economic sector, cost considerations may help to drive wider restructuring. The meaning of the long-term future for war and peace will help channel such choices.

Additional connections in the interpretive space of war and peace are also important. Some of these links go between the Self and Others, the objective and the subjective, power and values. The first of these is between Self and Others in the context of war and peace. The narrowest view of embodiment locks us into the Hobbesian world where man is a wolf to man—doomed to an eternal war of all against all in which life is solitary, poor, nasty, brutish, and short, and where the actors are selfish, egotistical, narrow-minded, myopic, competitive, and predatory. Yet even Hobbes had a denouement—the political Leviathan—for his narrative.

We have come a long way since Hobbes. His story of the world continues to guide some of our understanding, but we have seen other possibilities and constructed other worlds and meanings. Man is not always a wolf to man. There are also extensive zones of peace, and life need not be so relentlessly unpleasant as Hobbes described it. Life for many can be rich, generous, rewarding, and long. Some writers suggest the inevitability of the "clash of cultures," of worlds in collision. Our own analysis of the dynamics of multiple meaning and bodily metaphor is consistent with this projection. At the same time, it is also true that we are joined together on a shrinking planet with no immediately visible exit. Globalization, democracy, and the constraints of the environment all imply a possible gradual replacement of the narrow egotism, self-centeredness, and arrogance of the state-as-person Self with a more generous respect and appreciation for multiple different national and nonnational Others. A broader vision, a wider connectivity, suggests an increasing consciousness and appreciation of other worlds of meaning.

Another connection in interpretive space enhances the link between material, physical consciousness and psychological, interpretive consciousness of war and peace. It is abundantly clear that material connections are growing exponentially in physical space. The industrious robots of modern technology each day spin new strands of the global web. The evolutionary pattern of subjective space—the interconnections of multiple identities—is less obvious (Beer 1985).

A longstanding research program has explored the gradual emergence of a postmaterialist culture in Western societies (Inglehart 1997). Modern technology creates wealth. At the same time, it replaces smokestacks with information. Both of these tendencies rebalance our appreciation of the outer and inner dimensions of our lives. As this occurs, it can also help enhance our respect for others, less as objects for our own use and manipulation, and more as subjects with their own independent dignity and structures of meaning. It may even help us to discriminate between war as games, sports, or entertainment versus war as life or death. Just as we come to understand the meanings of other minds and hearts, we may also come to appreciate the meanings of other bodies.

The last connection in interpretive space is between power and values in war and peace. Some versions of realist theory have focused sharply on national power for its own sake, as a requisite for security and survival, or as the necessary condition for the realization of other values. There is much hard-earned, practically grounded wisdom in this narrative. At the same time, the meaning of war and peace is broader and deeper than standard realist theory would have us believe. Political power, as even these narrow formulations admit—and as we have already suggested—must be connected to other values, political prudence to other virtues on the world stage. Political prudence is concerned with power, survival and security. However, it also includes other attributes: intelligence, integrity, fairness, moderation, generosity, and charity (Hariman and Beer 1998). These broader values and virtues bind us with past and future, with our collective cultural inheritance and traditions, with our management of our resources, with the world that we create and pass on to our heirs. It is a truism that purpose without power is impotent and power without purpose is pointless and ultimately self-defeating. Each, without the other, is meaningless.

Just as meaning involves identifiable patterns of connections, meaninglessness involves isolation and disconnection. An absence of meaning emerges from discontinuities and inconsistencies, blind spots in the associative network. An example of this is the separation between the activities of our lives and the knowledge of our deaths. War and peace involve such activity and knowledge on the most massive and collective scale. The meaning of war and peace in the twenty-first century depends on the strength of these connections, and on many more. As we have tried to suggest, international relations is a struggle not just for power but also for other important values that help give that power a wider meaning: it is part of a more general struggle for meaning. Part myth, part reality, part experience, meaning ultimately is the schema, order, grammar, form that connects the chaos of the world in the developing New World Order.

Language and Meaning in War and Peace

In Tolstoy's *War and Peace*, the chronotope, the narrative space-time of the novel, includes the interaction of the characters' thoughts, words, and behavior. The author's interpretation, and that of the reader, creates a finely textured appreciation of Russian experience during the Napoleonic invasion of 1812. The larger chronotope of war and peace includes this segment of the Napoleonic wars, and many other instances of war and peace over a wide range of space and time. War and peace at their broadest comprehend a complex mosaic of experience—from the smallest to the greatest lives and worlds of meaning.

The meaning of any individual example of war or peace, for example the Napoleonic wars or the Cold War, the Long Peace or the Middle East peace process, is condensed in the name that identifies it. This name indexes the panoply of actions and interactions, events and processes, and thoughts and words that may be unpacked from it. Language is essential in all stages of this process. Language may be the most sophisticated technology of meaning that we have. It is a window on the outer world of war and peace, a medium for us to express our vision and understanding of them as external objective phenomena. It is also a mirror that shows the inner, subjective life-world—what we think and feel. It is a form of social behavior and a tool through which we act, influencing others and being influenced in ways that are sometimes intended and sometimes not. Language conveys the complexities and connections of warlike and peaceful intentions; it rationalizes, justifies, and manages international conflict and cooperation; it frames and expands our available choices.

Words speak and write the space and time of war and peace and also go well beyond them. The language of the characters, together with their thoughts and deeds, compose images of war and peace projected on the widest of wide screens: the surface of the globe. On the global monitor, within the context of war and peace, is also projected the emergent pattern of human identity, the enlarged image of who we are and who we want to be in planetary hyper-magnification. In this context, our words of war and peace provide clues to interpret major events and microbehaviors; they frame important actions and illuminate innermost thoughts. In the end, they also suggest the overlapping shapes and dense textures of the domain of war and peace, mapped in the number and variety, the relations and patterns, of local and global worlds of meaning.

NOTES

Introduction

1. The use of the term *dimensions* to characterize aspects of war and peace implies an objective reality independent of our own framing effects. I begin at this point because it is consistent with the dominant tendency of customary usage.

2. An enormous literature exists on this subject. Survey works include Geller and Singer (1998), Bremer and Cusack (1995), Barash (1991), Levy (1989, 1983), Blainey (1988), Dyer (1985), Waltz (1983), and Wright and Wright (1983).

3. See Axelrod (1997), Jervis (1997), Gilpin (1985), Keohane (1986), Waltz (1979), Bull (1977), and Morgenthau (1960).

4. See Ray (1998); Milner (1997); Maoz (1996); Keohane and Milner (1996); Downs and Rocke (1995); Kegley (1995); Risse-Kappen (1995); Russett (1995); Baldwin (1993); Evans, Jacobson, and Putnam (1993); and Rosecrance and Stein (1993).

5. See Green and Shapiro (1994); Levy (1994); Bueno de Mesquita and Lalman (1992); Sniderman, Brody, and Tetlock (1991); Cook and Levi (1990); Maoz (1990a, 1990b); Hogarth and Reder (1987); and Rapoport, Diekmann, and Miller (1986).

6. See, among others, M. Hermann (1998); Post (1997); Lifton (1996); Jervis (1993); Renshon (1993); Glad (1991); Sniderman, Brody, and Tetlock (1991); Tetlock (1991a, b, c); Kull (1988); Herrmann (1986); Lasswell (1986); Neustadt and May (1986); Janis and Mann (1985); Lebow (1984); Walker (1987); Fromm (1973); C. Hermann (1969); Frank (1967); George (1964); and Freud (1930).

7. In slightly more detail, the findings were as follows. (1) Individuals, identified with particular nation states, tended to reciprocate international conflict slowly and at a discount. They generally supported conflictual responses only up to the threshold of an opponent state's conflict actions even after several rounds of provocation. (2) Peace settlements did not necessarily have a significant cooperative effect when they were followed by continuing conflict. Gender made a difference. Women appeared more concerned with preserving relationships, men with retribution. In the presence of a prior peace settlement, women were more forgiving about an opponent's future conflictual actions. Men reacted in the opposite way: violations of a peace agreement provoked more extreme conflictual responses than if there had been no agreement. (3) Personality influenced international responses. Individuals with more dominant personalities tended to be more conflictual in international relations. As folk wisdom suggests, men were more dominant than women were, but the effect of personality on international conflict response was independent of gender. (4) Prior knowledge and textual materials interacted in complex and unpredictable ways to influence international behavior. For example, prior knowledge washed out the personality effect. (5) There is no psychological nuclear firebreak. Individuals perceived low level nuclear strikes as less conflictual than strong conventional military

actions (Bourne, Sinclair, Healy, and Beer 1996; Beer, Healy, Sinclair, and Bourne 1995; Beer, Ringer, Healy, Sinclair, and Bourne 1992; Beer, Healy, Sinclair, and Bourne 1987).

8. There is a vast library of books on meaning and its different facets. Psychological investigations of meaning include Power (1997), Bruner (1990), Overton and Palermo (1994), Piaget and Garcia (1991), Schwanenflugel (1991), Osgood and Tzeng (1990), Morgan (1988), Snider and Osgood (1969), Frankl (1962), and Gendlin (1962). Other work from different fields includes Dosse (1999), Jackson and Jackson (1997), Lance and O'Leary-Hawthorne (1997), Merrell (1997), Platts (1997), Stonier (1997), Dennett (1996), Frumkina and Mikhejev (1996), Gilroy (1996), Lerner (1996), Pessin and Goldberg (1996), Shore (1996), Larson and Segal (1995), Sauter and Bromiley (1995), Danesi (1994), Dupre (1994), Flower (1994), Holmberg (1994), Hacker (1993), Moore (1993), Munitz (1993), Solomon (1993), Wright (1993), Zito (1993), Singer (1992), Bordwell (1991), Cooper and Engel (1991), Garfield (1991), De Gramont (1990), Katz (1990), Blocker (1989), Ogden and Richards (1989), McGinn (1984), Schutz (1982), Ricoeur (1976), Blocker (1974), Boulding (1964), and Mouroux (1961). There is, interestingly, relatively little work on the specific topic of meaning in war and peace.

9. One formulation suggests that "meaning is *relational* in the sense that what an expression means is a function of its inferential/computational role in the person's internal *system* of representations" (Churchland 1986, 344). Cognitive meaning refers to the specific state of psychological schemata and the dynamic processes of schema activation and maintenance—including both substantive nodes and their connecting links in the internal network.

Part I: Semantics

1. See, for example, Hauser (1999); Nelson (1998); Schmidt (1998); Fairclough (1997); Riker (1996); Van Dijk (1997); Hariman (1995); Dolan and Dumm (1993); Fischer and Forester (1993); Campbell (1992); Campbell and Jamieson (1990); Lakoff (1990); Baumgartner (1989); Mailloux (1989); Pocock (1989); Edelman (1988); Lewis (1988); Gamson (1992); Nelson, Megill, and McCloskey (1987); Parek and Pantham (1987); Johnston (1986); Dallmayr (1984); Shapiro (1984); Graber (1976); Lasswell, Lerner, and Pool (1952); Lasswell and Leites (1949).

Chapter 1. Words of War

1. Peace may be defined simply as the absence of war, but there are many other possibilities. See for example Johnson (1976).

2. The constant is a base that may also include cognitive, behavioral, and linguistic dimensions. The asterisk indicates an indeterminate mathematical operator.

3. "Anterior meaning shifter" is my own term and not a part of contemporary linguistics usage. Posterior meaning shifters can also be important, as in Thomas Hobbes's war of all against all or a host of other possibilities, e.g., war damage, war hero, war game, war room. For structural linguistic discussions of complex, compound word formation and morphology see, among others, Lieber (1992); Ritchie, Russell, Black, and Pulman (1992); Bauer (1988, 1983); Levi (1978); Meys (1975); Matthews (1974); Adams (1973); Marchand (1969).

4. Crockett (1994) elucidates the frame problem in artificial intelligence. Hudson (1991) includes discussions of artificial intelligence applications in international relations.

5. The dictionary is a prime example of the illusion of context-free meaning. Willinsky (1994) analyzes the political, economic, social, and cultural context of the *Oxford English Dictionary*.

Chapter 2. Words of Reason

1. An earlier version of this chapter appeared as Beer (1994).

Chapter 3. Validities

1. An earlier version of this chapter appeared as Beer (1993).
2. Austin and Searle, in some readings, also lend themselves to this interpretation (Fish 1989; Norris 1987, Ch.7). See also Quine (1960).
3. For an interesting parallel in international-domestic politics, see Hoffmann (1987).
4. This formulation is similar to that of Rorty (1982, 92). There . . . are two ways of thinking about various things. . . . The first . . . thinks of truth as a vertical relationship between representations and what is represented. The second . . . thinks of truth horizontally—as the culminating reinterpretation of our predecessors' reinterpretation. . . . It is the difference between regarding truth, goodness, and beauty as eternal objects which we try to locate and reveal, and regarding them as artifacts whose fundamental design we often have to alter.
5. Harry Collins, "The Core Set and the Public Experiment," typescript, cited in MacKenzie (1990, 371).

Chapter 4. Postrealism, Just War, and the Gulf War Debate

1. An earlier version of this chapter appeared as Beer and Hariman (1998).
2. Textual references are to line numbers in the electronic text of the congressional debate.

Chapter 5. Body, Mind, and Soul in the Gulf War Debate

1. An earlier version of this chapter appeared as Beer and Balleck (1996).
2. Quotations are from U.S. Congress, 1991, referred to as CR. H and S refer to House and Senate debates.

Chapter 6. Women's Words

1. Connections between gender, embodiment, and epistemology have been explored and developed by many feminist theorists and political scientists. Feminist theorists have asserted that "not just opinions but also a culture's best beliefs—what it calls knowledge—are socially situated" (Harding 1991, 119). They argue that all experiences are mediated by physical bodies and the historical and social meanings we have attached to them. Therefore, our understandings of the world are filtered and shaped by the components of our social "situations" such as our genders, ethnicities, or classes. "[T]he assertion is that human activity, or 'material life,' not only structures but sets limits on human understanding: what we do shapes and constrains what we can know" (Harding 1991, 120). Thus, in a gender-stratified society, women and men are likely to develop distinct epistemologies because they experience and

participate in life in different ways. This is not to say that all women (or all men) share a common experience or epistemology. In standpoint theory, the subject is multiple and contradictory (Harding 1991, 285). Thus, standpoint theory calls attention to the many tensions among our identities and the practices that these multiple identities lead us to pursue.

Men and women may have substantially different value systems (Gilligan et. al. 1988; Gluck 1987; Gilligan 1982; Chodorow 1978; Dinnerstein 1976; Miller 1976) as well as gender differences in orientations to rules and relationships, freedom and obligation, and a host of other traditional normative tropes relevant to cooperation and conflict (e.g., Hirschmann 1989; Kittay and Meyers 1987). In the area of legislative process, Kathlene (1991) found evidence of gendered approaches to legislative policy-making behavior and Thomas and Welch (1991) found that women may rank legislative priorities differently than men. Furthermore, Clarke and Kathlene (1992) found that women and men legislators characterize the "gender-neutral" policy problem of criminal justice in different terms. See also Kahn (1996).

2. A growing corpus of writing has applied gender-related perspectives to international relations (Cooke 1996; Alonso 1993; Enloe 1993; McGlen and Sarkees 1993; Peterson and Runyan 1993; Reardon 1993; Silver and Giordano 1993; Sylvester 1994; Peterson 1992; Tickner 1992; Grant and Newland 1991; Elshtain and Tobias 1990; Harris and King 1989; Jeffords 1989; Millennium 1988). Psychological work investigates multiple additional aspects of the relationship between gender, cooperation, and conflict. It includes, for example, studies by Johnson and Newcomb (1992); Kroon, van Kreveld and Rabbie (1992); DeVoe (1990); Jaggar and Bordo (1989); Stockard, Van de Kragt, and Dodge (1988); Hamilton, Knox, Keilin, and Chavez (1987).

3. See particularly Sylvan and Voss (1998); Hybel (1993); Snow and Benford (1992); Mefford (1991); Lakoff (1987); Johnson (1987); Lakoff and Johnson (1980).

4. Although Ruddick uses the words *mother* and *maternal,* she does not exclude men from maternal practice or thinking. She defines a mother as "a person who takes on responsibility for children's lives and for whom providing child care is a significant part of her or his working life" (1989, 40). Ruddick explains that she chose to retain the terms *mothering* and *maternal* because "[a]t the simplest level, I want to recognize and honor the fact that even now, and certainly through most of history, women have been mothers. To speak of 'parenting' obscures that historical fact, while to speak even-handedly of mothers and fathers suggests that women's history has no importance. Moreover, I want to protest the myth and practice of Fatherhood and at the same time underline the importance of men undertaking maternal work. The linguistically startling premise that men can be mothers makes these points while the plethora of literature celebrating fathers only obscures them" (1989, 44).

5. Quotations are from the electronic text of the Congressional debate. There are no page numbers.

6. Because of the nature of our data we have used Ward's method of clustering and the S-Euclid measure of distance, in which the distance between cases is the sum of the squared differences in values for each variable.

Chapter 7. Talking about Dying

1. Transcripts of the hearings were obtained from Legi-Slate, an electronic service, which facilitated the analysis. The quotations in each section were taken from the transcript of that hearing, but there are no page numbers for more precise reference.

2. The criteria were very quickly tested. Events in Rwanda, resulting in a catastrophe as great or greater than that which occurred in Somalia, followed hard on its heels. Seven months after this hearing, in May 1994, UN Secretary General Boutros Boutros-Ghali asked the Security Council to expand the small peacekeeping force in Rwanda. The United States was against immediately expanding the peacekeeping force, using arguments much like these criteria (Rowe 1994). Secretary General Boutros-Ghali was never able to find nations willing to commit sufficient troops for the peacekeeping operation (Preston 1994; Preston and Williams 1994). France eventually sent troops, with the United Nations' blessing, and established a safe haven in Rwanda. But France's efforts were not enough to stop the killing or the mass exodus to Zaire.

Chapter 8. Beer and Quiche in the Fast Lane

1. See the introduction above for a discussion of the democratic peace hypothesis. See also Beer (1981a, 282–84) for a review of earlier literature on the reciprocal relationships between peace and democracy and war and military regimes; Balleck (1992) for a discussion of the cognitive dynamics of democratic war debate; and Lichbach (1996, 1995) for a discussion of collective-action dilemmas.
2. Metaphors and models, of course, are much simpler than the complex realities they aspire to represent. Thus the model includes two unitary actors; the realities of international and domestic actors are much more pluralistic and fragmented. The model avoids the esoterica of extended multilayered deterrence and the subtle relationships between capabilities and intentions, strength and resolve. Space does not permit the full treatment of dichotomous distortion, mixed signals, the relationship between structure and culture, or the tension between positivism and phenomenology. Occam's razor shaves clean—and close.

Chapter 9. Between Maastricht and Sarajevo

1. See, among others, Braun (2000); Dinan (1998); Moravcsik (1998a, 1998b); Whitman (1998); Cafruny and Lankowski (1997); Newhouse (1997); Hama (1996); Ross (1995); Laurent (1994); Joffe (1993); Kurth (1993); Gati (1992); Goldstein (1992); Jackson (1992); Sbraggia (1992); Treverton (1992); Keohane and Hoffmann (1991); Wistrich (1991); Mearsheimer (1990); Hoffmann, Keohane, and Mearsheimer (1990).
2. See Lapid and Kratochwil (1996); Shapiro and Alker (1995); Saxonhouse (1992); Bauman (1991); Connolly (1991); Giddens (1991); Jacques (1991); Safran (1991); Bloom (1990); Glass (1989); Taylor (1989); Braudel (1988); Norton (1988); Tugendhat (1986).

Conclusion

1. The package has been variously labeled as liberal internationalism, international liberalism, global liberalism, or liberal globalism. See Ruggie (1998, 1996); Kegley (1995); Baldwin (1993).

REFERENCES

Abramson, P., B. Silver, and B. Anderson. 1987. The effects of question order in attitude surveys: The case of the SRC/CPS citizen duty items. *American Journal of Political Science* 31:900–908.

Adams, L. 1973. *An Introduction to Modern English Word Formation.* London: Longman.

Albrecht-Carrié, R. 1965. *The Meaning of the First World War.* Englewood Cliffs: Prentice-Hall.

Alker, H. 1988. The dialectical logic of Thucydides' melian dialogue. *American Political Science Review,* 82:805–20.

Allen, J. L. 1998. *Student Atlas of World Politics.* 3rd ed. Guilford: Dushkin/McGraw-Hill.

Alonso, H. H. 1993. *Peace as a Women's Issue: A History of the Women's Movement for World Peace and Women's Rights.* Syracuse, N.Y.: Syracuse University Press.

Alperovitz, G. 1985. *Atomic Diplomacy: Hiroshima and Potsdam: The Use of the Atomic Bomb and the American Confrontation With Soviet Power.* New York: Penguin.

Andrews, F. M. 1984. Construct validity and error components of survey measures: A structural modeling approach. *Public Opinion Quarterly* 48:409–42.

Apter, D. 1994. *Revolutionary Discourse in Mao's Republic.* Cambridge, Mass.: Harvard University Press.

———. 1997. *The Legitimization of Violence.* Basingstoke: Macmillan.

Arendt, H. 1971. *The Life of the Mind.* New York: Harcourt, Brace, Jovanovich.

Arlin, P. K. 1982. A multitrait-multimethod validity study of a test of formal reasoning. *Educational and Psychological Measurement* 42:1077–88.

Aron, R. 1966. *Peace and War: A Theory of Peace and War.* Garden City, N.Y.: Doubleday.

Arrow, K. J. 1988. Workshop on the economy as an evolving complex system: Summary. In *The Economy as an Evolving Complex System,* ed. P. W. Anderson, K. J. Arrow, and D. Pines. Redwood City: Addison Wesley.

Attali, J. 1991. *Millennium: Winners and Losers in the Coming World Order.* Trans. L. Conners and N. Gardels. New York: Times Books.

Axelrod, R. 1997. *The Complexity of Cooperation: Agent-Based Models of Competition and Collaboration.* Princeton, N.J.: Princeton University Press.

Bakhtin, M. M. 1981. Frames of time and of the chronotope in the novel. In *The Dialogic Imagination: Four Essays,* ed. M. Holquist. Trans. C. Emerson and M. Holquist. Austin: University of Texas Press.

Baldwin, D. 1985. *Economic Statecraft.* Princeton, N.J.: Princeton University Press.

———, ed. 1993. *Neorealism and Neoliberalism: The Contemporary Debate.* New York: Columbia University Press.

Balleck, B. 1992. Integrative complexity in the Gulf War debate. Paper presented at the annual meeting of the American Political Science Association, Chicago.

———. 1994. Talking war and peace: Realist and idealist rhetoric in the Persian Gulf debate. Ph.D. diss., University of Colorado.

Bangio, O. 1992. *Saddam Speaks on the Gulf Crisis: A Collection of Documents.* Tel Aviv: Shiloah Institute.

Banks, J. S. 1991. *Signaling Games in Political Science.* Chur, Switzerland: Harwood.

Barash, D. P. 1991. *Introduction to Peace Studies.* Belmont: Wadsworth.

Barber, B. R. 1996. *Jihad vs. McWorld: How Globalism and Tribalism are Reshaping the World.* New York: Ballantine.

Barthes, R. 1972. *Mythologies.* Trans A. Lavers. New York: Hill and Wang.

Baudrillard, J. 1983. *Simulations.* Trans. P. Foss, P. Patton, and P. Beitchman. New York: Semiotext(e).

Bauer, L. 1983. *English Word Formation.* Cambridge: Cambridge University Press.

———. 1988. *Introducing Linguistic Morphology.* Edinburgh: Edinburgh University Press.

Bauman, Z. 1991. *Modernity and Ambivalence.* Ithaca, N.Y.: Cornell University Press.

Baumgartner, F. R. 1989. *Conflict and Rhetoric in French Policymaking.* Pittsburgh: University of Pittsburgh Press.

Beer, F. A. 1969. *Integration and Disintegration in NATO: Processes of Alliance Cohesion and Prospects for Atlantic Community.* Columbus: Ohio State University Press.

———. 1974. *How Much War in History: Definitions, Estimates, Extrapolations, and Trends.* Beverly Hills: Sage.

———. 1979. The epidemiology of peace and war. *International Studies Quarterly* 23:45–86.

———. 1981a. *Peace Against War: The Ecology of International Violence.* San Francisco: W. H. Freeman.

———. 1981b. War and disease. *Notes,* Center for Biopolitical Research, Northern Illinois University, April/July, 1981.

———. 1983a. Peace, war, and American presidents. *Journal of Political and Military Sociology* 11:1–10.

———. 1983b. Trends in American major war and peace. *Journal of Conflict Resolution* 27:661–86.

———. 1984. American major peace, war, and presidential elections. *Peace and Change* 10:23–40.

———. 1985. Multiple loyalties and alienation. In *Theories, Models and Simulations in International Relations,* ed. M. D. Ward. Boulder, Colo.: Westview Press.

———. 1986. Games and metaphors. *Journal of Conflict Resolution* 30:171–91.

———. 1987. Just war. In *World Encyclopedia of Peace.* Vol. 1, ed. L. Pauling, E. Lasso, and J. Y. Yaw. Oxford: Pergamon Press.

———. 1992. Reflections on collective consciousness: The Persian Gulf debate. *Normal Science and Vedic Science* 5:7–13.

———. 1993. Validities: A political science perspective. *Social Epistemology: A Journal of Knowledge, Culture, and Policy* (Special issue: The social epistemology of politics) 7:85–105.

———. 1994. Words of reason. *Political Communication* 11:185–201.

———. 1997. International Studies Quarterly: Special issue, evolutionary paradigms in the social sciences, *Journal of Memetics* (electronic) 1 (http://www.fmb.mmu.ac.uk/jom-emit/1997/vol1/beer_fa.html).

Beer, F. A., A. F. Healy, G. P. Sinclair, and L. E. Bourne, Jr. 1987. War cues and foreign policy acts. *American Political Science Review* 81:701–16

Beer, F. A., and B. Balleck. 1994. Realist/idealist texts: Psychometry and semantics. *Peace Psychology Review* 1:38–44.

———. 1996. Body, mind, and soul in the Gulf War debate. In *The Theory and Practice of Political Communication Research,* ed. M. Stuckey. Buffalo: State University of New York Press.

Beer, F. A., and C. de Landtsheer. 1999. Metaphorical politics: Mobilization or tranquilization?

In *Proceedings of the Fourth International Conference of the International Society for the Study of Argumentation,* ed. F. H. van Eemeren, R. Grootendorst, J. A. Blair, and C. A. Willard. Amsterdam: SIC STAT.

Beer, F. A., and G. R. Boynton. 1991. Paths through a conversation: A senate foreign relations committee talks about Cambodia (Forthcoming).

———. 1996. Realistic rhetoric but not realism: A senatorial conversation on Cambodia. In *Post-Realism: The Rhetorical Turn in International Relations,* ed. F. A. Beer and R. Hariman. East Lansing: Michigan State University Press.

Beer, F. A., and R. Hariman. 1998. Post-realism, just war, and the Gulf War debate. In *Politically Speaking: A Worldwide Examination of Language Use in the Public Sphere,* ed. O. Feldman and C. de Landtsheer. Westport: Praeger.

Beer, F. A., and T. F. Mayer. 1986. Why wars end: Some hypotheses. *Review of International Studies* 12:95–106.

Beer, F. A., G. P. Sinclair, A. F. Healy, and L. E. Bourne, Jr. 1995. Peace agreement, intransigent conflict, escalation trajectory: A psychological laboratory experiment. *International Studies Quarterly* 39:297–312.

Beer, F. A., J. F. Ringer, A. F. Healy, G. P. Sinclair, and L. Bourne, Jr. 1992. Ranking international cooperation and conflict. *International Interactions* 17:321–48.

Beer, F. A., and R. Hariman, eds. 1996. *Post-Realism: The Rhetorical Turn in International Relations.* East Lansing: Michigan State University Press.

Bell, J. S. 1987. *Speakable and Unspeakable in Quantum Mechanics.* Cambridge: Cambridge University Press.

Benveniste, E. 1971. *Problems in General Linguistics.* Trans M. E. Meek. Miami Linguistic Series no. 8. Coral Gables, Fla.: University of Miami Press.

Berman, M. 1989. *Coming to Our Senses: Body and Spirit in the Hidden History of the West.* New York: Bantam.

Bernstein, R. J. 1985. *Beyond Objectivism and Relativism: Science, Hermeneutics, and Praxis.* Philadelphia: University of Pennsylvania Press.

Bishop, G. F., R. W. Oldendick, and A. J. Tuchfarber. 1982. Political information processing: question order and context effects. *Political Behavior* 4:177–200.

———. 1984. What must my interest in politics be if I just told you I don't know? *Public Opinion Quarterly* 48:510–19.

Black, M. 1962. *Models and Metaphors.* Ithaca, N.Y.: Cornell University Press.

Blainey, G. 1988. *The Causes of War.* 3rd ed. New York: Free Press.

Blocker, H. G. 1974. *The Meaning of Meaninglessness.* The Hague: Martinus Nijhoff.

Bloom, W. 1990. *Personal Identity, National Identity, and International Relations.* Cambridge: Cambridge University Press.

Blume, S. S. 1974. *Toward a Political Sociology of Science.* New York: Free Press.

Boorstin, D. J. 1975. *The Image: A Guide to Pseudo-Events in America.* New York: Atheneum.

Booth, W. C. 1988. *The Company We Keep: An Ethics of Fiction.* Berkeley: University of California Press.

Bordwell, D. 1991. *Making Meaning: Inference and Rhetoric in the Interpretation of Cinema.* Harvard Film Studies. Cambridge, Mass.: Harvard University Press.

Bostdorff, D. M. 1994. *The Presidency and the Rhetoric of Foreign Crisis.* Columbia: University of South Carolina Press.

Boulding, K. 1964. *The Meaning of the Twentieth Century: The Great Transition.* New York: Harper and Row.

Bourdieu, P. 1993. *Field of Cultural Production: Essays on Schizophrenia and Multiple Personality.* Cambridge: Polity Press.

Bourne, L. E., Jr., F. A. Beer, G. P. Sinclair, A. F. Healy. 1996. Peace and gender: differential reactions to international treaty violations. *Peace and Conflict: Journal of Peace Psychology* 2:143–49.

Boynton, G. R. 1990. Practical reasoning: politics in action. Unpublished paper. Iowa City, Iowa.

Boynton, G. R., and M. Lodge. 1993. Voters' images of candidates. In *Presidential Campaigning and America's Self-Images*, ed. B. Gronbeck and A. Miller. Boulder, Colo.: Westview.

Boynton, G. R., and P. Dozark. 1993. Looking forward by looking back: Deliberation in the senate foreign relations committee. Paper presented at the 1993 meeting of the International Studies Association.

Bradham, N. H., and W. H. Mason. 1964. The effect of question order on responses. *Journal of Marketing Research* 1:57-61.

Bratman, M. E. 1987. *Intention, Plans, and Practical Reason.* Cambridge, Mass.: Harvard University Press.

Braudel, F. 1988. *The Identity of France.* Vol. 1, *History and Environment.* Trans. S. Reynolds. New York: Harper and Row.

Braun, M. J. 2000. *A Wider Europe: The Process and Politics of European Union Enlargement.* London: Rowman and Littlefield.

Bremer, S., and T. Cusack. 1995. *The Process of War: Advancing the Scientific Study of War.* Luxembourg: Gordon and Breach.

Brinkley, D. 1992. *Dean Acheson: The Cold War Years, 1953–1971.* New Haven, Conn.: Yale University Press.

Brody, C. J. 1986. Things are rarely black and white: Admitting gray into the converse model of attitude stability. *American Journal of Sociology* 92:657–77.

Brooks, P. 1993. *Body Work.* Cambridge, Mass.: Harvard University Press.

Brown, J. R. 1984. *Scientific Rationality: The Sociological Turn.* Dordrecht: D. Reidel.

Brown, N. O. 1966. *Love's Body.* Berkeley: University of California Press.

Brown, R. H. 1987. Reason as rhetorical: on relations among epistemology, discourse, and practice. In *The Rhetoric of the Human Sciences: Language and Argument in Scholarship and Public Affairs*, ed. J. S. Nelson, A. Megill, and D. S. McCloskey. Madison: University of Wisconsin Press.

Bruner, J. S. 1986. *Actual Minds, Possible Worlds.* Cambridge, Mass.: Harvard University Press.

———. 1990. *Acts of Meaning.* Cambridge, Mass.: Harvard University Press.

Brzezinski, Z. 1993. *Out of Control: Global Turmoil on the Eve of the 21st Century.* New York: Charles Scribner's Sons.

Bueno de Mesquita, B., and D. Lalman. 1986. Reason and war. *American Political Science Review* 80:1113–29.

———. 1992. *War and Reason: Domestic and International Imperatives.* New Haven, Conn.: Yale University Press.

Bueno de Mesquita, B., and R. Siverson. 1995. War and the survival of political leaders: a comparative study of regime types and political accountability. *American Political Science Review* 89:841–55.

———. 1997. Nasty or nice? Political systems, endogenous norms, and the treatment of adversaries. *Journal of Conflict Resolution* 41:175–99.

Bull, H. 1977. *The Anarchic Society: A Study of Order in World Politics.* New York: Columbia University Press.

Bundy, M. 1988. *Danger and Survival: Choices about the Bomb in the First Fifty Years.* New York: Random House.

———. 1994. *Reducing Nuclear Danger: The Road Away from the Brink.* New York: Council on Foreign Affairs, Brookings Institution Press.

Burch, K. 1997. *Property and the Making of the International System.* Boulder, Colo.: Lynne Rienner.

Burke, K. 1966. The thinking of the body (Comments on the imagery of catharsis in literature). In *Language as Symbolic Action: Essays on Life, Literature, and Method.* Berkeley: University of California Press.

Buzan, B., O. Weaver, and J. de Wilde. 1998. *Security: A New Framework for Analysis.* Boulder, Colo.: Lynne Rienner.

Cafruny, A. A., and C. Lankowski, eds. 1997. *Europe's Ambiguous Unity: Conflict and Consensus in the Post-Maastricht Era.* Boulder, Colo.: Lynne Rienner.

Calder, B. J., and L. W. Phillips. 1983. Beyond external validity. *Journal of Consumer Research* 10:112–14.

Calder, B. J., L. W. Phillips, and A. M. Tybout. 1982. The concept of external validity. *Journal of Consumer Research* 9:240–44.

Campbell, D. 1992. *Writing Security: United States Foreign Policy and the Politics of Identity.* Minneapolis: University of Minnesota Press.

Campbell, D. T. 1987. Evolutionary epistemology. In *Evolutionary Epistemology, Rationality, and the Sociology of Knowledge.* Vol. 3, ed. G. Radnitzky and W. W. Bartley. La Salle, Ill.: Open Court.

Campbell, K. K., and K. H. Jamieson. 1990. *Deeds Done in Words: Presidential Rhetoric and the Genres of Governance.* Chicago: University of Chicago Press.

Carmines, E. G., and R. A. Zeller. 1979. *Reliability and Validity Assessment.* Beverly Hills: Sage.

Carrocci, N. M. 1988. Trust and gender ten years later: the more things change. *Women's Studies in Communication* 11:63–89.

Casti, J. L. 1989. *Alternate Realities: Mathematical Models of Nature and Man.* New York: John Wiley.

Chambers, S. 1996. *Reasonable Democracy: Jurgen Habermas and the Politics of Discourse.* Ithaca, N.Y.: Cornell University Press.

Chardin, P. T. de. 1965. *Building the Earth.* New York: Avon.

Chilton, P. 1996. *Security Metaphors: Cold War Discourse from Containment to Common House.* New York: Peter Lang.

Cho, I. K., and D. M. Kreps, 1987. Signaling games and stable equilibria. *Quarterly Journal of Economics* 102:179–221.

Chodorow, N. 1978. *The Reproduction of Mothering: Psychoanalysis and the Sociology of Gender.* Berkeley: University of California Press.

Churchland, P. S. 1986. *Neurophilosophy: Toward a Unified Science of the Mind-Brain.* Cambridge: Massachusetts Institute of Technology Press.

Clark, J. R. 1977. *The Great Living System: Religion Emerging from the Sciences.* Pacific Grove, Calif.: Boxwood.

Clark, T. 1997. *Art and Propaganda in the Twentieth Century: The Political Image in the Age of Mass Culture.* London: Weidenfeld and Nicolson.

Clarke, S. E., and L. Kathlene. 1992. Women as political actors and policy analysts. Paper delivered at the Association for Public Policy Analysis and Management Annual Meeting, Denver, October 29–31.

Collier, D., and J. D. Mahon, Jr. 1993. Conceptual 'stretching' revisited: Adapting categories in comparative analysis. *American Political Science Review* 87:845–55.

Collier, D., and S. Levitsky. 1997. Democracy with adjectives: Conceptual innovation in comparative research. *World Politics* 49:430–51.

Connolly, W. E. 1991. *Identity/Difference: Democratic Negotiations of Political Paradox.* Ithaca, N.Y.: Cornell University Press.

Cook, K. S., and M. Levi, eds. 1990. *The Limits of Rationality.* Chicago: University of Chicago Press.

Cook, T. D. 1985. Postpositivist critical multiplism. In *Social Science and Social Policy,* ed. R. L. Shotland and R. R. Mark. Beverly Hills: Sage.

Cook, T. D., and D. T. Campbell. 1979. *Quasi-Experimentation: Design and Analysis Issues for Field Settings.* Chicago: Rand McNally.

Cooke, M. 1996. *Women and the War Story.* Berkeley: University of California Press.

Cooper, N., and P. Engel, eds. 1991. *New Inquiries into Meaning and Truth.* New York: St. Martin's Press.

Crockett, L. J. 1994. *The Turning Test and the Frame Problem: A Mistaken Understanding of Intelligence.* Norwood, N.J.: Ablex.

Crow, S. M., L. Y. Fok, S. J. Hartman, and D. M. Payne. 1991. Gender and values: what is the impact on decision making? *Sex Roles* 25:255–68.

Dallmayr, F. R. 1984. *Language and Politics: Why Does Language Matter to Political Philosophy?* Notre Dame: University of Notre Dame Press.

Danesi, M. 1994. *Messages and Meanings: An Introduction to Semiotics.* Toronto: Canadian Scholars' Press.

Davis, P. K., and J. Arquilla. 1991. *Deterring or Coercing Opponents in Crisis: Lessons from the War with Saddam Hussein.* Santa Monica, Calif.: RAND.

De Gramont, P. 1990. *Languages and the Distortion of Meaning.* New York: New York University Press.

Deleuze, G., and F. Guattari. 1986. *Nomadology: The War Machine.* New York: Semiotext(e).

Dennett, D. 1996. *Darwin's Dangerous Idea: Evolution and the Meaning of Life.* London: Penguin.

Der Derian, J., and M. J. Shapiro, eds. 1989. *International / Intertextual Relations.* Lexington, Mass.: Lexington Books.

Derrida, J. 1992. *The Other Heading: Reflections on Today's Europe.* Trans. P. A. Brault and M. B. Naas. Bloomington: Indiana University Press.

Desjardins, R. 1990. *The Rational Enterprise: Logos in Plato's Theaetetus.* Albany: State University of New York Press.

Deutsch, K., et al. 1957. *Political Community and the North Atlantic Area: International Organization in the Light of Historical Experience.* Princeton, N.J.: Princeton University Press.

De Voe, D. E. 1990. The influence of teacher gender and student grade level on teachers' beliefs concerning student decision-making. *Journal of Instructional Psychology* 17:197–201.

Diesing, P. 1976. *Reason in Society: Five Types of Decisions and their Social Conditions.* Westport, Conn.: Greenwood Press.

Digeser, P. 1995. *Our Politics, Our Selves? Liberalism, Identity, and Harm.* Princeton, N.J.: Princeton University Press.

Dinan, D., ed. 1998. *Encyclopedia of the European Union.* Boulder, Colo.: Lynne Rienner.

Dinnerstein, D. 1976. *The Mermaid and the Minotaur.* New York: Harper Colophon Books.

Dobbs, D. 1987. Reckless rationalism and heroic reverence in Homer's *Odyssey. American Political Science Review* 81:491–508.

Dolan, F. M., and T. L. Dumm, eds. 1993. *Rhetorical Republic: Governing Representations in American Politics.* Amherst: University of Massachusetts Press.

Dosse, F. *Empire of Meaning: The Humanization of the Social Sciences.* Trans. H. Melehy. Minneapolis: University of Minnesota Press.

Doty, R. L. H. 1996. *Imperial Encounters: The Politics of Representation in North-South Relations.* Minneapolis: University of Minnesota Press.

Downs, A. 1972. Up and down with ecology—the "issue-attention cycle." *The Public Interest* 25:38–50.

Downs, G. W., and D. M. Rocke. 1995. *Optimal Imperfection: Domestic Uncertainty and Institutions in International Relations.* Princeton, N.J.: Princeton University Press.

Duncan, O. D., and M. Stenbeck. 1988. No opinion or not sure. *Public Opinion Quarterly* 52:513–25.

Dupre, W. 1994. *Patterns in Meaning: Reflections on Meaning and Truth in Cultural Reality, Religious Traditions, and Dialogical Encounters.* Kampen: Kok Pharos.

Dyer, G. 1985. *War.* Toronto: Stoddart Press.

Eco, U., and T. A. Sebeok. 1988. *The Sign of Three: Dupin, Holmes, and Peirce.* Bloomington: Indiana University Press.

Edel, L. 1984. *Writing Lives: Principia Biographica.* New York: W. W. Norton.

Edelman, M. 1988a. *Constructing the Political Spectacle.* Chicago: University of Chicago Press.

———. 1988b. Skeptical studies of language, the media, and mass culture. *American Political Science Review* 82:1333–39.

Edwards, D. V. 1973. *Creating A New World Politics.* New York: David McKay.

Elshtain, J. B., and S. Tobias, eds. 1990. *Women, Militarism, and War: Essays in History, Politics, and Social Theory.* Savage, Md.: Rowman and Littlefield.

Enloe, C. 1990. *Bananas, Beaches, and Bases: Making Feminist Sense of International Politics.* Berkeley: University of California Press.

———. 1993. *The Morning After: Sexual Politics at the End of the Cold War.* Berkeley: University of California Press.

Evans, P. B., H. K. Jacobson, and R. D. Putnam, eds. 1993. *Double-Edged Diplomacy: International Bargaining and Domestic Politics.* Berkeley: University of California Press.

Fairclough, N. 1997. *Critical Discourse Analysis: The Critical Study of Language.* Redwood City, Calif.: Addison Wesley.

Falk, R. 1995. *On Humane Governance: Toward a New Global Politics: The World Order Project Report of the Global Civilization Initiative.* Cambridge, Mass.: Polity Press.

Fauconnier, G. 1985. *Mental Spaces: Aspects of Meaning Construction in Natural Language.* Cambridge, Mass.: Bradford.

———. 1997. *Mappings in Thought and Language.* Cambridge: Cambridge University Press.

Fearon, J. D. 1993. Domestic political audiences and the escalation of international disputes. *American Political Science Review* 88:577–92.

———. 1997. Signaling foreign policy interests: tying hands versus sinking costs. *Journal of Conflict Resolution* 41:68–90.

Feyerabend, P. 1987. *Farewell to Reason.* London: Verso.

Fienberg, S. E. 1989. *The Evolving Role of Statistical Assessments as Evidence in the Courts.* New York: Springer-Verlag.

Fischer, F., and J. Forester, eds. 1993. *The Argumentative Turn in Policy Analysis and Planning.* Durham, N.C.: Duke University Press.

Fish, S. 1989. *Doing What Comes Naturally: Change, Rhetoric, and the Practice of Theory in Literary and Legal Studies.* Durham, N.C.: Duke University Press.

Flathman, R. E. 1987. *The Philosophy and Politics of Freedom.* Chicago: University of Chicago Press.

Fleishman, J. A. 1988. The effect of decision framing and others' behavior on cooperation in a social dilemma. *Journal of Conflict Resolution* 32:162–80.

Flower, L. 1994. *The Construction of Negotiated Meaning: A Social Cognitive Theory of Writing.* Carbondale: Southern Illinois University Press.

Fodor, J. A. 1975. *The Language of Thought.* Cambridge, Mass.: Harvard University Press.

Folse, H. J. 1985. *The Philosophy of Niels Bohr: The Framework of Complementarity.* Amsterdam: North-Holland.

Foucault, M. 1961. *Folie et déraison: Histoire de la folie à l'âge classique.* Paris: Plon.

Frank, J. 1967. *Sanity and Survival: Psychological Aspects of War and Peace.* New York: Random House.

Frankl, V. E. 1962. *Man's Search for Meaning: An Introduction to Logotherapy.* Boston: Beacon Press.

Freedman, L., and V. Gamba Stonehouse. 1991. *Signals of War: The Falklands Conflict of 1982.* Princeton, N.J.: Princeton University Press.

Freud, S. 1930. *Civilization and Its Discontents.* London: Hogarth Press and the Institute of Psychoanalysis.

Freund, T., A. W. Kruglanski, and A. Shpitzajzen. 1985. The freezing and unfreezing of impressional primacy: Effects of the need for structure and the fear of invalidity. *Personality and Social Psychology Bulletin* 11:479–87.

Friedrich, C. J. 1957. *Constitutional Reason of State: The Survival of the Constitutional Order.* Providence, R.I.: Brown University Press.

Fromm, E. 1973. *The Anatomy of Destruction.* New York: Holt, Rinehart, and Winston.

Frumkina, R. M., and A. V. Mikhejev. 1996. *Meaning and Categorization.* Horizon Psychology.

Fukuyama, F. 1992. *The End of History and the Last Man.* New York: Free Press.

Fuller, S., W. Shadish, and D. Myers. 1995. The social psychology of science. *Contemporary Psychology* 40:1180.

Gaddis, J. L. 1989. *The Long Peace: Inquiries into the History of the Cold War.* Oxford: Oxford University Press.

———. 1997. *We Now Know: Rethinking Cold War History.* Oxford: Oxford University Press.

Gamson, W. A. 1992. *Talking Politics.* Cambridge: Cambridge University Press.

Garfield, J. L. 1991. *Meaning and Truth: Essential Readings in Modern Semantics.* New York: Paragon House.

Gati, C. 1992. From Sarajevo to Sarajevo. *Foreign Affairs* 71:64–78.

Gaubatz, K. T. 1991. Election Cycles and War. *Journal of Conflict Resolution* 35:212–44.

———. 1996. Democratic states and commitment in international relations. *International Organization* 50:109–39.

Geller, D., and D. Singer. 1998. *Nation's at War: A Scientific Study of International Conflict.* Cambridge: Cambridge University Press.

Gendlin, E. T. 1962. *Experiencing and the Creation of Meaning: A Philosophical and Psychological Approach to the Subjective.* New York: Free Press.

George, A. 1964. *Woodrow Wilson and Colonel House a Personality Study.* New York: Dover.

Gerhart, M., and A. Russell. 1984. *Metaphoric Process: The Creation of Scientific and Religious Understanding.* Fort Worth: Texas Christian University Press.

Gerstein, D. R., R. D. Luce, N. I. Smelser, and S. Sperlich, eds. 1988. *The Behavioral and Social Sciences: Achievements and Opportunities.* Washington DC: National Academy Press.

Giddens, A. 1991. *Modernity and Self Identity.* London: Polity Press.

Gilligan, C. 1982. *In a Different Voice: Psychological Theory and Women's Development.* Cambridge, Mass.: Harvard University Press.

Gilligan, C., J. V. Ward, J. McLean Taylor, B. Bardige. 1988. *Mapping the Moral Domain.* Cambridge, Mass.: Harvard University Press.

Gilman, S. 1991. *The Jew's Body.* New York: Routledge.

Gilpin, R. 1985. *War and Change in World Politics.* Cambridge: Cambridge University Press.

Gilroy, P. 1996. *Meaning Without Words: Philosophy and Non-Verbal Communication.* Aldershot, U.K.: Avebury.

Glad, B., ed. 1991. *Psychological Dimensions of War.* Newbury Park, Calif.: Sage.

Glass, J. M. 1989. *Private Terror in Public Life: Psychosis and the Politics of Community.* Ithaca, N.Y.: Cornell University Press.

Glenn, N. 1989. What we know, what we say we know: discrepancies between warranted and stated conclusions. In *Crossroads of Social Science: The ICPSR 25th Anniversary Volume,* ed. H. Eulau. New York: Agathon Press.

Gluck, H. F. 1987. The difference. *State Government* 60:223–26.

Goatly, A. 1997. *The Language of Metaphors.* London: Routledge.

Goldstein, J., and R. O. Keohane, eds. 1993. *Ideas and Foreign Policy: Beliefs, Institutions, and Political Change.* Ithaca, N.Y.: Cornell University Press.

Goldstein, W. 1992. Europe after Maastricht. *Foreign Affairs* 71:117–32.

Gordon, M. E., L. A. Slade, and N. Schmitt. 1986. The 'science of the sophomore' revisited: From conjecture to empiricism. *Academy of Management Review* 1:191–207.

———. 1987. Student guinea pigs: Porcine predictors and particularistic phenomena. *Academy of Management Review* 12:160–63.

Graber, D. 1976. *Verbal Behavior and Politics.* Urbana: University of Illinois Press.

Grant, R., and K. Newland, eds. 1991. *Gender and International Relations.* Bloomington: Indiana University Press.

Green, D. P., and I. Shapiro. 1994. *Pathologies of Rational Choice Theory: A Critique of Applications in Political Science.* New Haven, Conn.: Yale University Press.

Greenberg, J. 1987. The college sophomore as guinea pig: setting the record straight. *Academy of Management Review* 12:157–59.

Greenfield, L. 1992. *Nationalism: Five Roads to Modernity.* Cambridge, Mass.: Harvard University Press.

Greiner, R. 1988. Learning by understanding analogies. *Artificial Intelligence* 35:81–125.

Grice, P. 1989. *Studies in the Way of Words.* Cambridge, Mass.: Harvard University Press.

Haas, E. B. 1958. *The Uniting of Europe: Political, Social, and Economic Forces, 1950–1957.* Stanford: Stanford University Press.

———. 1990. *When Knowledge is Power: Three Models of Change in International Organizations.* Berkeley: University of California Press.

Habermas, J. 1970. *Towards a Rational Society.* Trans. J. J. Shapiro. London: Heinemann.

Hacker, P. M. 1993. *Wittgenstein, Meaning and Mind.* Oxford: Blackwell.

Hallett, G. L. 1988. *Language and Truth.* New Haven, Conn.: Yale University Press.

Hama, N. 1996. *Disintegrating Europe: The Twilight of the European Construction.* New York: Praeger.

Hamilton, S. B., T. A. Knox, W. G. Keilin, and E. L. Chavez. 1987. In the eye of the beholder: Accounting for variability in attitudes and cognitive/affective reactions. *Journal of Applied Social Psychology* 17:927–52.

Harding, S. 1991. *Whose Science? Whose Knowledge?* Ithaca, N.Y.: Cornell University Press.

Hariman, R. 1995. *Political Style: The Artistry of Power (New Practices of Inquiry).* Chicago: University of Chicago Press.

Hariman, R., and F. A. Beer. 1998. What would be prudent? *Rhetoric and Public Affairs* 1:299–330.

Harris, A., and Y. King. 1989. *Rocking the Ship of State: Toward a Feminist Peace Politics.* Boulder, Colo.: Westview.

Harris, F. C., and B. B. Lahey. 1982. Subject reactivity in direct observational assessment: A review and critical analysis. *Clinical Psychology Review* 2:523–38.

Hauser, G. 1999. *Vernacular Voices: The Rhetoric of Publics and Public Spheres.* Columbia: University of South Carolina Press.

Haynes, S. N., and W. F. Horn. 1982. Reactivity in behavioral observation: A review. *Behavioral Assessment* 4:369–85.

Hearing. 1987. U.S. policy in the Persian Gulf, hearings before the Committee on Foreign Relations, United States Senate May 29, June 16, October 23 and 28. Washington DC: U.S. Government Printing Office, 1988.

Hearing. 1992a. Crisis and chaos in Somalia: Hearing of the Subcommittee on Africa of the House Foreign Affairs Committee, September 16, 1992, Legi-Slate.

Hearing. 1992b. The situation in Somalia: Hearing of the House Foreign Affairs Committee, December 17, 1992, Legi-Slate.

Hearing. 1993a. U.S. policy in Somalia: Hearing of the Senate Foreign Relations Committee, July 29, 1993, Legi-Slate.

Hearing. 1993b. UN peacekeeping in Somalia: Hearing of the Senate Foreign Relations Committee, October 20, 1993, Legi-Slate.

Held, D. 1989. *Political Theory and the Modern State: Essays on State, Power, and Democracy.* Stanford: Stanford University Press.

Hermann, C. 1969. International crisis as a situational variable. In *International Politics and Foreign Policy*, ed. J. Rosenau. New York: Free Press.

Hermann, M. 1998. International decision making: Leadership matters. *Foreign Policy* 110:124.

Herring, P. F. 1987. *Joyce's Uncertainty Principle.* Princeton, N.J.: Princeton University Press.

Herrmann, R. 1986. *Perceptions and Behavior in Soviet Foreign Policy.* Pittsburgh: University of Pittsburgh Press.

Herzog, A. R., and J. G. Bachman. 1981. Effects of questionnaire-length on response quality. *Public Opinion Quarterly* 45:549–59.

Hinds, L. B., and T. O. Windt. 1991. *The Cold War as Rhetoric: The Beginnings, 1945–1950.* New York: Praeger.

Hirschmann, N. J. 1989. Freedom, recognition, and obligation: A feminist approach to political theory. *American Political Science Review* 83:1227–44.

Hobbes, T. 1958. *Leviathan.* Indianapolis: Bobbs Merrill.

————. 1986. *Leviathan.* Ed. C. B. Macpherson. Harmondsworth: Penguin.

Hobsbawm, E. J. 1990. *Nations and Nationalism Since 1780: Programme, Myth, Reality.* Cambridge: Cambridge University Press.

Hoffmann, S., R. O. Keohane, and J. J. Mearsheimer. 1990. Back to the future, part ii: International relations theory and post–Cold War Europe. *International Security* 15:191–99.

Hoffmann, S., ed. 1987. *Janus and Minerva: Essays in the Theory and Practice of International Politics.* Boulder, Colo.: Westview.

Hogarth, R. M., and M. W. Reder, eds. 1987. *Rational Choice: The Contrast between Economics and Psychology.* Chicago: University of Chicago Press.

Hollis, M. 1987. *The Cunning of Reason.* Cambridge: Cambridge University Press.

Holmberg, M. 1994. *Narrative, Transcendence, and Meaning: An Essay on the Question about the Meaning of Life.* Uppsala, Sweden: Almquist and Wiksell International.

Hudson, V. M., ed. 1991. *Artificial Intelligence and International Politics.* Boulder, Colo.: Westview.

Hunt, L., ed. 1991. *Eroticism and the Body Politic.* Baltimore: Johns Hopkins University Press.

Hussein, S. 1991. Saddam Hussein's message to President Bush, 16 January 1991. In *Excerpts from Ofra Bengio, 1992, Saddam Speaks on the Gulf Crisis: A Collection of Documents.* Tel Aviv: Shiloah Institute.

Huxley, J. 1979. *UNESCO: Its Purpose and Its Philosophy.* Washington D.C.: Public Affairs Press.

Hybel, A. R. 1986. *Logic of Surprise in International Conflict.* Lexington, Mass.: Lexington Press.

———. 1993. *Power over Rationality: The Bush Administration and the Gulf Crisis.* Albany: State University of New York Press.

Illich, I., and B. Sanders. 1988. *ABC: The Alphabetization of the Popular Mind.* San Francisco: North Point Press.

Inglehart, R. 1997. *Modernization and Postmodernization: Culture, Economic, and Political Change in 43 Societies.* Princeton, N.J.: Princeton University Press.

Isaacson, W., and E. Thomas. 1986. *The Wise Men: Six Friends and the World They Made.* New York: Simon and Schuster.

Jackson, L., and S. B. Jackson. William Harmon, ed. 1997. *Rational Meaning: A New Foundation for the Definition of Words and Supplementary Essays.* Charlottesville: University Press of Virginia.

Jackson, R. J., ed. 1992. *Europe in Transition: The Management of Security after the Cold War.* New York: Praeger.

Jackson, S., and S. Jacobs. 1983. Generalizing about messages: Suggestions for design and analysis of experiments. *Human Communication Research* 9:169–81.

Jacobson, H., and W. Zimmerman. 1993. *Behavior, Culture, and Conflict in World Politics.* Ann Arbor: University of Michigan Press.

Jacques, F. 1991. *Difference and Subjectivity: Dialogue and Personal Identity.* Trans. A. Rothwell. New Haven, Conn.: Yale University Press.

Jaggar, A., and S. R. Bordo, eds. 1989. *Gender, Body, Knowledge: Feminist Reconstructions of Being and Knowing.* New Brunswick, N.J.: Rutgers University Press.

Jagtenberg, T. 1983. *The Social Construction of Science: A Comparative Study of Goal Direction, Research Evaluation and Legitimation.* Dordrecht, Netherlands: D. Reidel.

James, W. A., ed. *Singular Europe: Economy and Polity of the European Community After 1992.* Ann Arbor: University of Michigan Press.

Janis, I. 1983. *Groupthink: Psychological Studies of Policy Decisions and Fiascos.* Boston: Houghton Mifflin.

Janis, I., and L. Mann. 1985. *Decision Making: A Psychological Analysis of Conflict, Choice, and Commitment.* New York: Free Press.

Jaspers, K. 1958. *The Future of Mankind.* Trans. E. B. Ashton. Chicago: University of Chicago Press.

Jaspers, K. 1963. *The Atom Bomb and the Future of Man.* Chicago: University of Chicago Press.

Jeffords, S. 1989. *The Remasculinization of America: Gender and the Vietnam War.* Bloomington: Indiana University Press.

Jensen, K., ed. 1991. *Origins of the Cold War: the Novikov, and Roberts 'Long Telegrams' of 1946.* Washington D.C.: United States Institute of Peace.

Jensen, K., and D. Wurmser. 1990. *The Meaning of Munich Fifty Years Later.* Washington D.C.: United States Institute of Peace.

Jervis, R. 1976. *Perception and Misperception in International Politics.* Princeton, N.J.: Princeton University Press.

————. 1989. *The Meaning of the Nuclear Revolution: Statecraft and the Prospect of Armageddon.* New York: Cornell University Press.

————. 1993. *Hypotheses on Misperception.* Irvington, N.Y.: Irvington Publishers.

————. 1997. *System Effects: Complexity in Political Life and Social Life.* Princeton, N.J.: Princeton University Press.

Joffe, J. 1993. The new Europe: Yesterday's ghosts. *Foreign Affairs* 72:29–43.

Johnson, J. G. 1975. *Ideology, Reason and Limitation of War: Secular and Religious Concepts.* Princeton, N.J.: Princeton University Press.

Johnson, L. G. 1976. *Conflicting Concepts of Peace in Contemporary Peace Studies.* London: Sage.

Johnson, M. 1987. *The Body in the Mind: The Bodily Basis of Meaning, Imagination, and Reason.* Chicago: University of Chicago Press.

Johnson, M. J., and M. D. Newcomb. 1992. Gender, war, and peace: Rethinking what we know. *Journal of Humanistic Psychology* 32:108–37.

Johnston, D. 1986. *The Rhetoric of Leviathan: Thomas Hobbes and the Politics of Cultural Transformation.* Princeton, N.J.: Princeton University Press.

Jonas, H. 1984. *The Imperative of Responsibility: In Search of an Ethics for the Technological Age.* Chicago: University of Chicago Press.

————. 1996. *Mortality and Morality: A Search for the Good after Auschwitz.* Evanston, Ill.: Northwestern University Press.

Kahn, H. 1960. *On Thermonuclear War.* Princeton, N. J. Princeton University Press.

Kahn, K. 1996. *The Political Consequences of Being a Woman.* New York: Columbia University Press.

Kahneman, D., P. Slovic, and A. Tversky, eds. 1982. *Judgment under Uncertainty: Heuristics and Biases.* Cambridge: Cambridge University Press.

Kathlene, L. 1991. Gender, public policy, and the legislative process: Delineating the gendered perspectives and outcomes of policymaking in the 1989 Colorado state house. Ph.D. diss. University of Colorado.

Katz, J. J. 1990. *The Metaphysics of Meaning.* Cambridge: Massachusetts Institute of Technology Press.

Katzenstein, P. J., R. O. Keohane, and S. D. Krasner, eds. 1999. *Exploration and Contestation in the Study of World Politics.* Cambridge: Massachusetts Institute of Technology Press.

Kaufman, G. D. 1993. *In Face of Mystery: A Constructive Theology.* Cambridge, Mass.: Harvard University Press.

Kegley, C. W., Jr. 1991. *The Long Postwar Peace: Contending Explanations and Projections.* New York: Harper Collins.

————. 1995. *Controversies in International Relations Theory: Realism and the Neoliberal Challenge.* New York: St. Martin's Press.

Kennan, G. F. 1967. *Memoirs, 1925–1950.* Boston: Little, Brown, Atlantic Monthly Press.

————. 1996. *At Century's End: Reflections, 1982–1995.* New York: W. W. Norton.

Keohane, R. O., ed. 1986. *Neorealism and Its Critics.* New York: Columbia University Press.

Keohane, R. O., and H. Milner. 1996. *Internationalization and Domestic Politics.* Cambridge: Cambridge University Press.

Keohane, R. O., and S. Hoffmann, eds. 1991. *The New European Community: Decisonmaking and Institutional Change.* Boulder, Colo.: Westview.

Keohane, R. O., J. S. Nye, and S. Hoffmann, eds. 1993. *After the Cold War: International Institutions and State Strategies in Europe, 1989–1991.* Cambridge, Mass.: Harvard University Press.

Kerby, A. P. 1991. *Narrative and the Self.* Bloomington: Indiana University Press.

King, G. 1989. Event count models for international relations: Generalizations and applications. *International Studies Quarterly* 33:123–48.

Kissinger, H. 1995. *Diplomacy.* New York: Simon and Schuster.

Kittay, E. F., and D. T. Meyers. 1987. *Women and Moral Theory.* Totowa, N.J.: Rowman and Littlefield.

Kopstein, J., and K. O. Richter. 1992. Communist social structure and post-communist elections: Voting for reunification in East Germany. *Studies in Comparative Communism* 25:363–80.

Korzybski, A. 1980. *Science and Sanity: An Introduction to Non-Aristotelian Systems and General Semantics.* Lakeville, Conn.: International Non-Aristotelian Library.

Kratochwil, F. 1989. *Rules, Norms, and Decisions on the Conditions of Practical and Legal Reasoning in International Relations and Domestic Affairs.* Cambridge: Cambridge University Press.

Kroon, M. B. R., D. van Kreveld, and J. M. Rabbie. 1992. Group versus individual decision making: Effects of accountability and gender on groupthink. *Small Group Research* 23:427–58.

Krosnick, J. A., and D. F. Alwin. 1988. A test of the form resistant correlation hypothesis. *Public Opinion Quarterly* 52:526–38.

Kubalkova, V., N. G. Onuf, and P. Kowert, eds. 1998. *International Relations in a Constructed World.* Armonk, N.Y.: M. E. Sharpe.

Kull, S. 1988. *Minds at War: Nuclear Reality and the Inner Conflicts of Defense Policymakers.* New York: Basic Books.

———. 1992. *Burying Lenin: The Revolution in Soviet Ideology and Foreign Policy.* Boulder, Colo.: Westview.

Kung, H. 1998. *A Global Ethic for Global Politics and Economics.* Oxford: Oxford University Press.

Kurth, J. 1993. Mitteleuropa and East Asia: The return of history and the redefinition of security. In *Past as Prelude: History in the Making of a New World Order,* ed. M. Woo-Cumings and M. Loriaux. Boulder, Colo.: Westview.

Lake, D. A. 1992. Powerful pacifists: Democratic states and war. *American Political Science Review* 86:24–37.

Lakoff, G. 1987. *Women, Fire, and Dangerous Things: What Categories Reveal about the Mind.* Chicago: University of Chicago Press.

———. 1991. Metaphor and war: The metaphor system used to justify war in the Gulf. *Peace Research* 23:25–32.

———. 1997. *Moral Politics: What Conservatives Know that Liberals Don't.* Chicago: University of Chicago Press.

Lakoff, G., and M. Johnson. 1980. *Metaphors We Live By.* Chicago: University of Chicago Press.

Lakoff, R. T. 1990. *Talking Power: the Politics of Language.* New York: Basic Books.

Lambeth, B. 1992. *Desert Storm and Its Meaning: The View from Moscow.* Santa Monica, Calif.: Rand.

Lance, M. N., and J. O'Leary-Hawthorne. 1997. *The Grammar of Meaning: An Exploration of the Normative Character of Semantic Discourse.* Cambridge: Cambridge University Press.

Lapid, Y., and F. Kratochwil, eds. 1996. *The Return of Culture and Identity in IR Theory.* Boulder, Colo.: Lynne Rienner.

Larson, R., and G. Segal. 1995. *The Knowledge of Meaning.* Cambridge: Massachusets Institute of Technology Press.

Lasswell, H. D. 1962. The garrison-state hypothesis today. In *Changing Patterns of Military Politics*, ed. S. P. Huntington. New York: Free Press.

———. 1986. *Psychopathology and Politics*. Chicago: University of Chicago Press.

Lasswell, H. D., D. Lerner, and I. D. S. Pool. 1952. *The Comparative Study of Symbols*. Stanford: Stanford University Press.

Lasswell, H. D., N. Leites et al. 1949. *The Language of Politics: Studies of Quantitative Semantics*. Cambridge: Massachusetts Institute of Technology Press.

Latour, B. 1987. *Science in Action: How to Follow Scientists and Engineers through Society*. Cambridge, Mass.: Harvard University Press.

Laurent, P. H. 1994. *The European Community: To Maastricht and Beyond, Analysis of the American Academy of Political and Social Science*. Beverly Hills: Sage.

Lebow, R. N. 1984. *Between Peace and War: The Nature of International Crisis*. Baltimore: Johns Hopkins University Press.

Lee, J. A., K. E. Moreno, and J. B. Sympson. 1986. The effects of test administration on test performance. *Educational and Psychological Measurement* 46:467–74.

Lehrer, A., and E. Kittay, eds. 1992. *Frames, Fields, and Contrasts: New Essays in Semantic and Lexical Organization*. Hillsdale, N.J.: L. Erlbaum Associates.

Leichsenring, F. 1985. Die probleme der 'externen' validity in der psychotherapieforschung: Zeitschrift für Klinische Psychologie. *Forschung und Praxis* 14:214–27.

Lerner, M. 1996. *The Politics of Meaning: Restoring Hope and Possibility in an Age of Cynicism*. Reading, Pa.: Addison Wesley.

Levi, N. J. 1978. *The Syntax and Semantics of Complex Nominals*. New York: Academic Press.

Levine, R. A. 1992. *Transition and Turmoil in the Atlantic Alliance*. New York: Crane Russak.

Levy, J. 1983. *War in the Modern Great Power System, 1495–1975*. Lexington: University Press of Kentucky.

———. 1989. The causes of war: a review of theories and evidence. In *Behavior, Society, and Nuclear War*. Vol. 1, ed. P. Tetlock. Oxford: Oxford University Press.

———. 1994. Prospect theory and international relations: theoretical implications. In *Avoiding Losses/Taking Risks: Prospect Theory and International Conflict*, ed. B. Farnham. Ann Arbor: University of Michigan Press.

Lewis, B. 1988. *The Political Language of Islam*. Chicago: University of Chicago Press.

Lewis, D. 1973. *Counterfactuals*. Cambridge, Mass.: Harvard University Press.

Lewis, W. 1989. *Political History in Theory and Practice*. Research Triangle Park, N.C.: National Humanities Center.

Lichbach, M. 1995. *The Rebel's Dilemma*. Ann Arbor: University of Michigan Press.

———. 1996. *The Cooperator's Dilemma*. Ann Arbor: University of Michigan Press.

Lieber, R. 1992. *Deconstructing Morphology: Word Formation in Syntactic Theory*. Chicago: University of Chicago Press.

Lifton, R. 1996. *Hiroshima in America: A Half Century of Denial*. New York: Avon Books.

Lifton, R., and E. Markusen. 1991. *The Genocidal Mentality: Nazi Holocaust and Nuclear Threat*. London: Macmillan.

Lindberg, L., and S. A. Scheingold. 1970. *Europe's Would-Be Polity: Patterns of Change in the European Community*. Englewood Cliffs, N.J.: Prentice-Hall.

Litfin, K. 1994. *Ozone Discourses: Science and Politics in Global Environmental Cooperation*. New York: Columbia University Press.

Lodge, M., K. M. McGraw, and P. Stroh. 1989. An impression-driven model of candidate evaluation. *American Political Science Review* 83:399–420.

Lohmann, S. 1993. A signaling model of informative and manipulative political action. *American Political Science Review* 87:319–33.

Luttwak, E. 1995. Toward post-heroic warfare. *Foreign Affairs* 74,3:109–22.

Maaz, H. J. 1990. *Der Geftihlsstau: Ein Psychogramm der DDR.* Berlin: Argon.

McCloskey, D. 1998. *The Rhetoric of Economics (Rhetoric of the Human Sciences).* Madison: University of Wisconsin Press.

McCullough, D. 1992. *Truman.* New York: Simon and Schuster.

McGinn, C. 1984. *Wittgenstein on Meaning: An Interpretation and Evaluation.* Oxford: Basil Blackwell.

McGlen, N. E., and M. R. Sarkees. 1993. *Women in Foreign Policy: The Insiders.* New York: Routledge.

Macintyre, A. 1999. *Dependent Rational Animals: Why Human Beings Need the Virtues.* La Salle, Ill.: Open Court.

McKechnie, J. L. 1979. *Webster's New Twentieth Century Dictionary of the English Language Unabridged.* 2nd ed. N.p.: William Collins.

MacKenzie, D. 1990. *Inventing Accuracy: A Historical Sociology of Missile Guidance.* Cambridge: Massachusetts Institute of Technology Press.

Mailloux, S. 1989. *Rhetorical Power.* Ithaca, N.Y.: Cornell University Press.

Mali, J. 1992. *The Rehabilitation of Myth: Vico's 'New Science'.* Cambridge: Cambridge University Press.

Malmkjaer, K. 1991. *The Linguistics Encyclopedia.* London: Routledge.

Manchester, W. 1978. *American Caesar: Douglas MacArthur, 1880–1964.* New York: Dell.

Mansbridge, J. J., ed. 1990. *Beyond Self-Interest.* Chicago: University of Chicago Press.

Maoz, Z. 1990a. *National Choices and International Processes.* Cambridge: Cambridge University Press.

———. 1990b. *Paradoxes of War: On the Art of National Self-Entrapment.* Boston: Unwin Hyman Press.

———. 1996. *Domestic Sources of Global Change.* Ann Arbor: University of Michigan Press.

Marchand, H. 1969. *The Categories and Types of Present-Day English Word-Formation: A Synchronic-Diachronic Approach.* Munich: C. H. Bek'sche.

Matthews, P. H. 1974. *Morphology: An Introduction to the Theory of Word-Structure.* Cambridge: Cambridge University Press.

May, E. R., ed. 1993. *American Cold War Strategy: Interpreting NSC 68.* New York: St. Martin's.

Mearsheimer, J. J. 1990. Back to the future: Instability in Europe after the Cold War. *International Security* 15:5–56.

Medhurst, M. J. 1994. *Eisenhower's War of Words: Rhetoric and Leadership.* East Lansing: Michigan State University Press.

Medhurst, M. J., R. L. Ivie, P. Wander, and R. L. Scott. 1990. *Cold War Rhetoric: Strategy, Metaphor, and Ideology.* New York: Greenwood.

Mefford, D. 1991. Steps toward artificial intelligence: Rule-based, case-based, and explanation-based models of politics. In *Artificial Intelligence and International Politics,* ed. V. M. Hudson. Boulder, Colo.: Westview.

Merrell, F. 1997. *Peirce, Signs, and Meaning.* Toronto: University of Toronto Press.

Meys, W. J. 1975. *Compound Adjectives in English and the Ideal Speaker-Listener: A Study of Compounding in a Transformational-Generative Framework.* Amsterdam: North-Holland.

Millennium: Journal of International Studies. 1988. Special issue: Women and international relations. 18.

Miller, J. B. 1976. *Toward a New Psychology of Women.* Boston: Beacon Press.

Miller, J. G. 1978. *Living Systems.* New York: McGraw-Hill.

Miller, J. H. 1990. Narrative. In *Critical Terms for Literary Study,* ed. F. Lentricchia and T. McLaughlin. Chicago: University of Chicago Press.

Milner, H. V. 1997. *Interests, Institutions, and Information: Domestic Politics and International Relations.* Princeton, N.J.: Princeton University Press.

Minsky, M. 1994. *The Society of Mind.* Irvington, N.Y.: Voyager.

Mio, J. S., and A. N. Katz, eds. 1996. *Metaphor: Implications and Applications.* Mahwah, N.J.: Lawrence Erlbaum Associates.

Mook, D. G. 1983. In defense of external invalidity. *American Psychologist* 38:379–87.

Moore, A. W., ed. 1993. *Meaning and Reference.* Oxford: Oxford University Press.

Moravcsik, A., ed. 1998a. *Centralization or Fragmentation: Europe before the Challenges of Deepening, Diversity, and Democracy.* New York: Council on Foreign Relations.

———. 1998b. *The Choice for Europe: Social Purpose and State Power from Messina to Maastricht.* Ithaca, N.Y.: Cornell University Press.

Morey, L. C., R. K. Blashfield, W. W. Webb, and J. Jewell. 1988. MMPI scales for DSM-III personality disorders: A preliminary validation study. *Journal of Clinical Psychology* 44:47–50.

Morgan, J. H. 1988. *From Freud to Frankl: Our Modern Search for Personal Meaning.* Bristol, U.K.: Wyndham Hall Press.

Morgenthau, H. J. 1960. *Politics among Nations: The Struggle for Power and Peace.* New York: Knopf.

Mouroux, J. 1961. *The Meaning of Man.* Trans. A. H. G. Downes. Garden City, N.Y.: Doubleday.

Moynihan, D. 1993. *Pandemonium: Ethnicity in International Politics.* Oxford: Oxford University Press.

Mueller, D. C. 1989. Democracy: The public choice approach. In *Politics and Process: New Essays in Democratic Thought,* ed. G. Brennan and L. E. Lomasky. Cambridge: Cambridge University Press.

Mueller, J. R. 1989. *Retreat from Doomsday: The Obsolescence of Major War.* New York: Basic Books.

Mukerji, C. 1990. *A Fragile Power: Scientists and the State.* Princeton, N.J.: Princeton University Press.

Mulgan, G. 1997. *Connexity: How to Live in a Connected World.* Boston: Harvard Business School Press.

Munitz, M. K. 1993. *Does Life Have A Meaning?* Buffalo, N.Y.: Prometheus Books.

Muravchik, J. 1996. *The Imperative of American Leadership: A Challenge to Neo-Isolationism.* Washington D.C.: American Enterprise Institute.

Murphy, R. D. 1965. *Diplomat among Warriors.* New York: Pyramid Books.

Neisser, U. 1976. *Cognition and Reality: Principles and Implications of Cognitive Psychology.* New York: W. H. Freeman.

Nelson, J., and G. R. Boynton. 1997. *Video Rhetorics: Televised Advertising in American Politics.* Urbana: University of Illinois Press.

Nelson, J. S. 1987. Seven rhetorics of inquiry: A provocation. In *The Rhetoric of the Human Sciences: Language and Argument in Scholarship and Public Affairs,* ed. J. S. Nelson, A. Megill, and D. S. McCloskey. Madison: University of Wisconsin Press.

———. 1998. *Tropes of Politics: Science, Theory, Rhetoric, Action.* Madison: University of Wisconsin Press.

Nelson, J. S., A. Megill, and D. S. McCloskey, eds. 1987. *The Rhetoric of the Human Sciences: Language and Argument in Scholarship and Public Affairs.* Madison: University of Wisconsin Press.

Neustadt, R., and E. May. 1986. *Thinking in Time: The Uses of History for Decision-Makers.* New York: Free Press and Collier Macmillan.

Newhouse, J. 1997. *Europe Adrift.* New York: Pantheon.

Nicolson, H. G. 1988. *Diplomacy*. Washington, D.C.: Georgetown University Press.

Niebuhr, R. 1987. *Moral Man and Immoral Society: A Study in Ethics and Politics*. New York: Charles Scribner's Sons.

Nordlinger, E. A. 1995. *Isolationism Reconfigured: American Foreign Policy for a New Century*. Princeton, N.J.: Princeton University Press.

Norpoth, H., and M. Lodge, 1985. The difference between attitudes and nonattitudes in mass publics: Just measurement? *American Journal of Political Science* 29:291–307.

Norris, C. 1987. *Derrida*. Cambridge, Mass.: Harvard University Press.

Norton, A. 1988. *Reflections on Political Identity*. Baltimore: Johns Hopkins University Press.

Nye, J. S. 1990. *Bound to Lead & the Changing Nature of American Power*. New York: Basic Books.

Oakeshott, M. 1991. *Rationalism in Politics and Other Essays*. Indianapolis: Liberty Press.

Ogden, C. K., and I. A. Richards. 1989. *The Meaning of Meaning: A Study of the Influence of Language upon Thought and of the Science of Symbolism*. San Diego: Harcourt Brace Jovanovich.

Ong, W. 1991. *Orality and Literacy: The Technologizing of the Word*. New York: Routledge.

Onuf, N. 1989. *World of Our Making: Rules and Rule in Social Theory and International Relations*. Columbia: University of South Carolina Press.

Ortony, A., ed. 1993. *Metaphor and Thought*. Cambridge: Cambridge University Press.

Osgood, C. E., and O. C. S. Tzeng, eds. 1990. *Language, Meaning, and Culture: The Selected Papers of C. E. Osgood and Oliver C. S. Tzeng*. New York: Praeger.

Overton, W. F., and D. S. Palermo, eds. 1994. *The Nature and Ontogenesis of Meaning*. Jean Piaget Symposium Series. Hillsdale: Lawrence Erlbaum Associates.

Parek, B., and T. Pantham. 1987. *Political Discourse: Explorations in Indian and Western Political Thought*. New Delhi: Sage.

Park, A. 1988. War cues and foreign policy acts in South Korea. Master's thesis, University of Colorado.

Pessin, A., and S. Goldberg, eds. 1996. *The Twin Earth Chronicles: Twenty Years of Reflection on Hilary Putnam's "The Meaning of Meaning."* Armonk, N.Y.: M. E. Sharpe.

Peterson, S. 1992. *Gendered States: Feminist Revisions of International Relations Theory*. Boulder, Colo.: Lynne Rienner.

Peterson, S., and A. S. Runyan, eds. 1993. *Global Gender Issues*. Boulder, Colo.: Westview.

Piaget, J. and R. Garcia. 1991. *Toward a Logic of Meanings*. Hillsdale, N.J.: Lawrence Erlbaum.

Platts, M. 1997. *Ways of Meaning: An Introduction to Philosophy of Language*. Cambridge: Massachusetts Institute of Technology Press.

Pocock, J. G. A. 1989. *Politics, Language, and Time*. Chicago: University of Chicago Press.

Pollock, J. C. 1981. *The Politics of Crisis Reporting*. New York: Praeger.

Post, J. 1997. *Political Paranoia: The Psychopolitics of Hatred*. New Haven, Conn.: Yale University Press.

Power, M. J. 1997. *The Transformation of Meaning in Psychological Therapies: Integrating Theory and Practice*. New York: John Wiley and Sons.

Preston, J. 1994. UN chief denounces response to Rwanda: 'Failure' laid to UN, leading countries. *Washington Post*, May 26, 1994.

Preston, J., and D. Williams. 1994. Tepid response from U.S., world contributed to crisis, UN says. *Washington Post*, July 23, 1994.

Priewe, J., and R. Hickel, 1991. *Der Preis der Einheit: Bilanz und Perspektiven der deutschen Vereinigung*. Frankfurt: Fischer.

Puchala, D. J. 1984. *Fiscal Harmonization in the European Communities: National Politics and International Cooperation*. London: F. Pinter.

Putnam, H. 1996. The meaning of meaning. In *The Twin Earth Chronicles: Twenty Years of Reflection on Hilary Putnam's "The Meaning of 'Meaning,'"* ed. A. Pessin and S. Goldberg. Armonk, N.Y.: M. E. Sharpe.

Quine, W. v. O. 1960. *Word and Object.* Cambridge: Massachusetts Institute of Technology Press.

———. 1987. *Quiddities.* Cambridge, Mass.: Belknap Press.

———. 1992. *Pursuit of Truth.* Cambridge, Mass.: Harvard University Press.

Rapoport, A. 1992. *Peace: An Idea Whose Time Has Come.* Ann Arbor: University of Michigan Press.

Rapoport, A., and A. Chammah. 1965. *Prisoner's Dilemma.* Ann Arbor: University of Michigan Press.

Rapoport, A., A. Diekmann, and P. Miller. 1986. *Paradoxical Effects of Social Behavior: Essays in Honor of Anatol Rapoport.* Heidelberg: Physica-Verlag.

Rasmussen, E. 1987. *Complementarity and Political Science: An Essay on Fundamentals of Political Science Theory and Research Strategy.* Aarhus, Denmark: Odense University Press.

Ray, J. L. 1998. *Democracy and International Conflict: An Evaluation of the Democratic Peace Proposition.* Columbia: University of South Carolina Press.

Raz, J. 1990. *Practical Reason and Norms.* Princeton, N.J.: Princeton University Press.

Reardon, B. A. 1993. *Women and Peace: Feminist Visions of Global Security.* Albany: State University of New York Press.

Redner, H. 1987. *The Ends of Science: An Essay in Scientific Authority.* Boulder, Colo.: Westview.

Renshon, S. A., ed. 1993. *The Political Psychology of the Gulf War: Leaders, Publics, and the Process of Conflict.* Pittsburgh: University of Pittsburgh Press.

Ricoeur, P. 1976. *Interpretation Theory: Discourse and the Surplus of Meaning.* Fort Worth: Texas Christian University Press.

———. 1977. *The Rule of Metaphor: Multi-disciplinary Studies of the Creation of Meaning in Language.* Trans. R. Czerny, K. McLaughlin and J. Costello. Toronto: University of Toronto Press.

———. 1988. *Time and Narrative.* Vol. 3. Trans. K. Balmey. Chicago: University of Chicago Press.

Riker, W. H. 1986. *The Art of Political Manipulation.* New Haven, Conn.: Yale University Press.

———. 1996. *The Strategy of Rhetoric: Campaigning for the American Constitution.* New Haven, Conn.: Yale University Press.

Risse-Kappen, T. 1995. *Cooperation among Democracies: The European Influence on U.S. Foreign Policy.* Princeton, N.J.: Princeton University Press.

Ritchie, G. D., G. J. Russell, A. W. Black, and S. G. Pulman. 1992. *Computational Morphology: Practical Mechanisms for the English Lexicon.* Cambridge, Mass.: Bradford Press.

Robinson, R. 1954. *Definition.* Oxford: Clarendon Press.

Roe, E. 1994. *Narrative Policy Analysis: Theory and Practice.* Durham, N.C.: Duke University Press.

Rorty, R. 1979. *Philosophy and the Mirror of Nature.* Princeton, N.J.: Princeton University Press.

———. 1982. *The Consequences of Pragmatism.* Minneapolis: University of Minnesota Press.

———. 1991. *Objectivity, Relativism, and Truth.* Cambridge: Cambridge University Press.

Rosecrance, R., and A. A. Stein, eds. 1993. *The Domestic Bases of Grand Strategy.* Ithaca, N.Y.: Cornell University Press.

Rosnow, R. L., and M. Georgoudi, eds. 1986. *Contextualism and Understanding in Behavioral Science: Implications for Research and Theory.* New York: Praeger.

Ross, D. 1991. *The Origins of American Social Science.* Cambridge: Cambridge University Press.

Ross, G. 1995. *Jacques Delors and European Integration.* Oxford: Oxford University Press.

Rowe, T. 1994. U.S. opts to limit force for Rwanda. *Washington Post,* May 17.

Ruddick, S. 1989. *Maternal Thinking: Toward a Politics of Peace.* New York: Ballantine.

Ruggie, J. 1996. *Winning the Peace: America and World Order in the New Era.* New York: Columbia University Press.

―――. 1998. *Constructing the World Polity: Essays on International Institutionalization (The New International Relations).* London: Routledge.

Ruhl, C. 1989. *On Monosemy: A Study in Linguistic Semantics.* Albany: State University of New York Press.

Russett, B. 1995. *Grasping the Democratic Peace: Principles for a Post-Cold War World.* Princeton, N.J.: Princeton University Press.

Safran, W. 1991. State, nation, national identity, and citizenship: France as a test case. *International Political Science Review* 12:219–38.

Sauter, G., and G. W. Bromiley. 1995. *The Question of Meaning: A Theological and Philosophical Orientation.* Grand Rapids, Mich.: William B. Eerdmans.

Saxonhouse, A. 1992. *Fear of Diversity: The Birth of Political Science in Ancient Greek Thought.* Chicago: University of Chicago Press.

Sbraggia, A. M., ed. 1992. *Euro-Politics: Institutions and Policymaking in the "New" European Community.* Washington D.C.: Brookings Institution.

Scarry, E. 1985. *The Body in Pain: The Making and Unmaking of the World.* Oxford: Oxford University Press.

Schank, R. C. 1990. *Tell Me A Story: A New Look at Real and Artificial Memory.* New York: Charles Scribner's Sons.

Scheffler, I. 1979. *Beyond the Letter: A Philosophical Inquiry into Ambiguity, Vagueness, and Metaphor in Language.* London: Routledge and Kegan Paul.

Schelling, T. C. 1963. *The Strategy of Conflict.* New York: Oxford University Press.

Schleifer, R., R. C. Davis, and N. Mergler. 1992. *Culture and Cognition: The Boundaries of Literary and Scientific Inquiry.* Ithaca, N.Y.: Cornell University Press.

Schmidt, B. C. 1998. *The Political Discourse of Anarchy: A Disciplinary History of International Relations.* Albany: State University of New York Press.

Schnur, R. 1975. *Staatsräson: Studien zur Geschichte eines politischen Begriffs.* Berlin: Duncker and Humblot.

Schuman, H. 1986. Ordinary questions, survey questions, and policy questions. *Public Opinion Quarterly* 50:432–42.

Schuman, H., and J. Ludwig. 1983. The norm of even-handedness in surveys as in life. *American Sociological Review* 48:112–20.

Schuman, H., and J. Scott. 1987. Problems in the use of survey questions to measure public opinion. *Science* 236:957–59.

Schuman, H., and S. Presser. 1981. *Questions and Answers in Attitude Surveys: Experiments in Question Form, Wording, Context.* New York: Academic Press.

Schuman, H., J. Ludwig, and J. A. Krosnick. 1986. The perceived threat of nuclear war, salience, and open questions. *Public Opinion Quarterly* 50:519–36.

Schutz, A. 1982. *Life Forms and Meaning Structure.* London: Routledge.

Schwanenflugel, P. J., ed. 1991. *The Psychology of Word Meanings.* Hillsdale, N.J.: Lawrence Erlbaum Associates.

Searle, J. R. 1998. *Mind, Language, and Society: Philosophy in the Real World.* New York: Basic Books.

Sears, D. O. 1986. College sophomores in the laboratory: Influences of a narrow data base on social psychology's view of human nature. *Journal of Personality and Social Psychology* 51:515–30.

Shafer, G., and J. Pearl, eds. 1990. *Readings in Uncertain Reasoning.* San Mateo, Calif.: Morgan Kaufmann.

Shapiro, M. J. 1981. *Language and Political Understanding: The Politics of Discursive Practices.* New Haven, Conn.: Yale University Press.

———. 1997. *Violent Cartographies: Mapping Cultures of War.* Minneapolis: University of Minnesota Press.

———, ed. 1984. *Language and Politics.* New York: New York University Press.

Shapiro, M., and H. Alker, eds. 1995. *Challenging Boundaries: Global Flows, Territorial Identities.* Minneapolis: University of Minnesota Press.

Shore, B. 1996. *Culture and Mind: Cognition, Culture, and the Problem of Meaning.* Oxford: Oxford University Press.

Sifry, M. L., and C. Cerf, eds. 1991. *The Gulf War Reader: History, Documents, and Opinions.* New York: Random House.

Sigelman, L. 1981. Question order effects on presidential popularity. *Public Opinion Quarterly* 45:199–207.

Silver, K., and E. Giordano, eds. 1993. Gender in international relations. *The Fletcher Forum on World Affairs* 17:1–116.

Simon, H. 1983. *Reason in Human Affairs.* Stanford: Stanford University Press.

Singer, E. 1988. Pushing back the limits to surveys. *Public Opinion Quarterly* 52:416–26.

Singer, I. 1992. *Meaning in Life: The Creation of Value.* New York: Free Press.

Small, S., G. W. Cottrell, and M. K. Tanenhaus, 1988. *Lexical Ambiguity Resolution.* San Mateo, Calif.: Morgan Kaufmann.

Snider, J. G., and C. E. Osgood. 1969. *Semantic Differential Technique: A Sourcebook.* Chicago: Aldine.

Sniderman, P. M., R. A. Brody, and P. E. Tetlock, eds. 1991. *Reasoning and Choice: Explorations in Political Psychology.* Cambridge: Cambridge University Press.

Snow, D. A., and R. D. Benford. 1992. Master frames and cycles of protest. In *Frontiers in Social Movement Theory,* ed. A. D. Morris and C. M. Mueller. New Haven, Conn.: Yale University Press.

Snyder, J. 1984. Averting anarchy in the new Europe. *International Security* 14:5–41.

———. 1989. *The Ideology of the Offensive: Military Decision Making and the Disasters of 1914.* Ithaca, N.Y.: Cornell University Press.

Solomon, R. C. 1993. *The Passions: Emotions and the Meaning of Life.* 3rd ed. Garden City, N.Y.: Anchor Press/Doubleday.

Spence, D. P. 1982. *Narrative Truth and Historical Truth: Meaning and Interpretation in Psychoanalysis.* New York: Norton.

Steen, G. 1994. *Understanding Metaphor in Literature.* Harlow: Longman.

Stich, S. 1990. *The Fragmentation of Reason.* Cambridge: Bradford/Massachusetts Institute of Technology.

Stockard, J., A. J. Van de Kragt, and P. J. Dodge. 1988. Gender roles and behavior in social dilemmas: Are there sex differences in cooperation and in its justification? *Social Psychology Quarterly* 51:154–63.

Stonier, T. 1997. *Information and Meaning: An Evolutionary Perspective.* Berlin: Springer.

Sudman, S., and N. M. Bradburn. 1974. *Response Effects in Surveys.* Chicago: Aldine.

Sussmann, M., and D. U. Robertson. 1986. The validity of validity: An analysis of validation study designs. *Journal of Applied Psychology* 71:461–68.

Sylvan, D., and J. Voss. 1998. *Problem Representation in Foreign Policy Decision Making.* Cambridge: Cambridge University Press.

Sylvester, C. 1994. *Feminist Theory and International Relations Theory in a Postmodern Era.* Cambridge: Cambridge University Press.

Taylor, C. 1989. *Sources of the Self: The Making of the Modern Identity.* Cambridge, Mass.: Harvard University Press.

Taylor, M. C. 1983. The black-and-white model of attitude stability: A latent class examination of opinion and nonopinion in the American public. *American Journal of Sociology* 89:373–401.

Tetlock, P. 1991a. *Behavior, Society, and Nuclear War.* Vol. 1. Oxford: Oxford University Press.

———. 1991b. *Behavior, Society, and Nuclear War.* Vol. 2. Oxford: Oxford University Press.

———. 1991c. *Behavior, Society, and International Conflict.* Vol. 3. Oxford: Oxford University Press.

Thomas, S., and S. Welch. 1991. The impact of gender on activities and priorities of state legislators. Paper presented at the Annual Meeting of the Midwestern Political Science Association, Chicago.

Tickner, A. 1992. *Gender in International Relations: Feminist Perspectives on Achieving Global Security.* New York: Columbia University Press.

Toulmin, S. E. 1958. *The Uses of Argument.* Cambridge: Cambridge University Press.

———. 1986. *The Place of Reason in Ethics.* Chicago: University of Chicago Press.

Treverton, G. F. 1992. The new Europe. *Foreign Affairs* 71:194–212.

Tugendhat, E. 1986. *Self-Consciousness and Self-Determination.* Trans. P. Stern. Cambridge: Massachusetts Institute of Technology Press.

Turner, C. F., and E. Martin, eds. 1984. *Surveying Subjective Phenomena.* New York: Russell Sage.

United Nations. 1996. *The United Nations and Somalia, 1992–1996.* New York: United Nations, Department of Public Information.

U.S. Congress. 1991 (CR). *Congressional Records and Proceedings and Debates of the 102nd Congress,* 1st sess., vol. 37, nos. 7, 8 (January 11–12). Washington D.C.: U.S. Government Printing Office.

U.S. Senate. 1990. *Hearing before the Subcommittee on East Asia and Pacific Affairs of the Committee on Foreign Relations: Prospects for Peace in Cambodia.* Washington D.C.: Government Printing Office.

Van Dijk, T. A. 1984. *Structures of International News: A Case Study of the World's Press.* Amsterdam: Department of General Literary Studies, University of Amsterdam.

———, ed. 1997a. *Discourse Studies: A Multidisciplinary Introduction.* Vol. 1, *Discourse as Structure and Process.* London: Sage.

———. 1997b. *Discourse Studies: A Multidisciplinary Introduction.* Vol. 2, *Discourse as Social Interaction.* London: Sage.

Van Noppen, J. P., and Hols, E. 1990. *Metaphor II: A Classified Bibliography of Publications 1985 to 1990.* Philadelphia: John Benjamins.

Vaux, K. L. 1992. *Ethics and the Gulf War: Religion, Rhetoric, and Righteousness.* Boulder, Colo.: Westview.

Voss, J. F., J. Kennet, J. Wiley, and T. Engstler-Schooler. 1998. Experts at debate: The use of metaphor in the U.S. Senate debate on the Gulf crisis. *Metaphor and Symbolic Activity* 7:197–214.

Walker, R. B. J. 1993. *Inside/Outside: International Relations as Political Theory.* Cambridge: Cambridge University Press.

Walker, S. 1987. *Role Theory and Foreign Policy.* Durham, N.C.: Duke University Press.

Waltz, K. 1979. *Theory of International Politics.* New York: McGraw-Hill.

———. 1983. *Man, the State, and War: a Theoretical Analysis.* New York: Columbia University Press.

Walzer, M. 1977. *Just and Unjust Wars: A Moral Argument with Historical Illustrations.* New York: Basic Books.

Washington, E. D., and V. C. McLoyd. 1982. The external validity of research involving American minorities. *Human Development* 25:324–39.

Wavell, B. 1986. *Language and Reason.* Berlin: Mouton de Gruyter.

Weizenbaum, J. 1976. *Computer Power and Human Reason.* New York: W. H. Freeman.

Welch, D. 1993. *Justice and the Genesis of War.* Cambridge: Cambridge University Press.

Wendt, A. 1999. *Social Theory of International Politics.* Cambridge: Cambridge University Press.

West, S. G. 1986. Methodological developments in personality research: An introduction. *Journal of Personality* 54:1–17.

Whitman, R. G. 1998. *From Civilian Power to Superpower: The International Identity of Europe.* New York: St. Martin's Press.

Willinsky, J. 1994. *The Empire of Words: The Reign of the OED.* Princeton, N.J.: Princeton University Press.

Wistrich, E. 1991. *After 1992: The United States of Europe.* London: Routledge.

Wohlstetter, R. 1962. *Pearl Harbor: Warning and Decision.* Stanford, Calif.: Stanford University Press.

Wolf, F. A. 1988. *Parallel Universes: The Search for Other Worlds.* New York: Simon and Schuster.

Woodward, B. 1991. *The Commanders.* New York: Simon and Schuster.

Wright, C. 1993. *Realism, Meaning and Truth.* 2nd ed. Oxford: Basil Blackwell.

Wright, Q., and L. L. Wright. 1983. *Study of War.* Chicago: University of Chicago Press.

Yergin, D. 1977. *Shattered Peace.* Boston: Houghton Mifflin.

Zito, G. V. 1993. *The Death of Meaning.* Westport: Praeger.

INDEX

causal explanation, 4, 69
"cause of freedom," 117–18
center-periphery metaphors, 99–100
Central and Eastern Europe and European identity, 159–60
change and language adjustments, 165
Cheney, Richard, 144
chronology of debates and historical narrative, 128
chronotype, 173–76
Churchill, Winston S., 155
Cicero, 95
circularity of meaning, 43–45, 73–74
Clausewitz, Carl von, 85–86
Clemenceau, Georges, 165
Clinton administration and Somalia conflict, 134–35
cognition: in continuous variable approach to meaning, 31; hot cognition, 12, 95, 119; and metaphorical thinking, 94–95; and normative view of strategic thinking, 87; rational-psychological models, 6–8; reason's influence on, 54
cognitive meaning: and associative networks, 9, 13; role of, 10–12; and schema theory, 8–9; subjectivity of, 37
Cohen, Herman, 120, 123, 124, 127
Cohen, William, 97
Cold War, 117–18, 151–56
collection as metaphor (collective), 100
collective consciousness on peace and war, 93–94
collective construction of meaning: Cold War myth, 151–56; expansion of, 174; and reason, 50–51; and validity, 61–62, 71–75
collective responsibility, 101
Collier, D., 30
communication, signaling game, 139–49. *See also* audiences
Communist enemy and European identity, 152–56, 157
competition for power, 83, 85
complexity: behavioral aspects of war and peace discourse, 4–6; in consciousness of peace and war, 94; of language in war and peace, 164, 170, 173; of validity in political science, 70–78

compulsion as metaphor, 101
Congress, U.S.: debate over Gulf War debate, 144–45; foreign policy debates and rationality, 42–43; gender-based differences in Gulf War debate, 107–10; rhetorics of Gulf War debate, 88–92; Somalia debate, 118, 120–37
connection, language of, 173–76
Conrad, Kent, 90
consciousness of war and peace, 93–94, 104, 175
constant, semantic, 31
Constitution, U.S., and just war, 89
construction of meaning, 84. *See also* collective construction of meaning
contact, personal, 101, 143, 168
containment, metaphor of, 102, 153–54, 167
content analysis, 65–66
context: and body metaphor, 174–75; in continuous variable approach to meaning, 31; experiments vs. life, 59–60; and multiple meanings, 46, 47–49, 76; and political validity, 71; and reason, 49, 55–57; and text in political science research, 60–63; textual modifier components, 31–37; and transformation of war and peace, 170
continuous variation of meaning, 30–31, 38–40, 75–78
control in postrealist view, 85
Cook, T. D., 71, 75
cooperative-conflictual behavior, 39–40
core text in research, 60–62
correspondence theory of reality vs. meaning as continuously variable, 40
cost-benefit analysis of war, 6–7, 43, 104
Coverdell, Paul, 130, 131
critical reason, 54, 85–86
critical reflection in death and dying language, 127–31, 132, 137

data, and terms and concepts, 38–40
death and dying language: critical reflection, 127–31, 132, 137; elements, 119; mobilizing attention and support, 120–23; and policy making, 131–38; rhetorical evolution, 117–18; self-congratulation, 124–27

debate: effect on strength projection, 140–42, 143–49; embodiment metaphor in, 93–105; rationality assumptions in, 42; rhetorics of Gulf War, 88–92; Somalia conflict, 118, 120–37

decision makers in postrealist world, 84

deconstruction and reconstruction, 84

democracies: and Cold War, 153–56; influence on war and peace, 5; and Kuwait/Iraq social structures, 90; and multiple meanings of reason, 56; preference for peace, 167; spread of, 166; strength vs. weakness of U.S., 140–48

democratic defeat, 141

democratic escape, 141

democratic peace hypothesis, 5, 140, 141, 157

democratic victory, 141

democratization and audiences for politics, 172–73

Democrats in Congress: body metaphors, 96; gender-based rhetorical differences, 107

denotative meaning vs. meaning as continuously variable, 40

Derrida, Jacques, 98

deterrence, 142, 146, 167

dictionary definitions: reason, 43–44; validity, 61

dimensions of war and peace, 179n 1

diplomacy: future development of, 168–69; price of ambiguity in, 143

discrete variables, meaning as, 27–30, 39

Dodd, Christopher, 130

Dole, Robert, 90

domestic politics/regime: as important characters in postrealism, 84; increased linkage to war and peace, 5

duality of mind and body, 104

Dulles, John Foster, 152

dying. See death and dying language

Dymally, Mervyn, 120, 122–23

Eastern and Central Europe and European identity, 159–60

economic issues: benefits of war, 7; and containment, 102; and continuation of war, 167; economics as alternative to war, 14; and European identity, 154–55, 158; and future of war and peace, 174; globalization, 166; global poverty, 4; oil as motivator in Persian Gulf, 90, 143

ECSC (European Coal and Steel Community), 155–56

Edelman, M., 62

Eisenhower, Gen. Dwight D., 154

electoral cycles and war and peace tendencies, 5

Eliade, Mircea, 151

elite consensus and reality definition, 72–73

embargo, 98

embodiment metaphor. *See* body metaphor

emotional meaning: and death and dying language, 119; and postrealistic view, 84; and reason, 57; role of, 12; and Sarajevo mentality, 160

Enemy, the, and Cold War meaning of war and peace, 152–56

English language as currency of international communication, 168

environmental issues, 3–4, 171, 172

Erikson, Erik, 174

ethics and morality: and future transformation of war and peace, 175–76; humanistic values and contemporary meaning of war, 167; in postrealist view, 86–87; and reason, 52, 53

euphemisms for death and dying, 117–18, 128

Europe, identity issues, 150–63

European Coal and Steel Community (ECSC), 155–56

European Monetary Union, 158, 159

events data analysis, 65–66

executive defeat, 141

executive escape, 141

executive peace, 141, 142

executive victory, 141

experimental validities, 59–64

explanation and behavioral meaning, 4–6, 10

facts in objective world: and behavioral meaning, 9; and terms and concepts, 38–40 faith and reason, 57

Falklands/Malvinas War, 143

family. *See* maternal thinking

Fasbinder, Rainer Werner, 160

Fauconnier, Gilles, 10–11

feelings. *See* emotional meaning

feminism and gender-based rhetorical differences, 106, 181–82*n* 1. *See also* gender-based rhetorical differences

foreign policy: debates and rationality, 42–43; domestic political effects on, 5. *See also* debate

freedom: in embodied metaphor, 98; Kuwaiti lack of, 90; postrealist view, 84

Gaddis, John Lewis, 153

gain-loss analysis of war, 6–7, 43

Galtung, Johan, 157

game theory in signaling game, 139–49

gender-based rhetorical differences: and feminism, 181–82*n* 1; and future of meaning in war and peace, 171–72; in Gulf War debate, 106–14; and signaler's dilemma, 140

Gephardt, Dick, 112

Germany, role in new Europe, 159, 160

Glaspie, April, 143

globalization, 166–67, 171

good and evil, archetypal struggle between, 152–55, 172

Goodling, William, 124

Grass, Gunther, 160

Gulf War debate: body metaphors in, 96–103; gender-based rhetorical differences, 106–14; postrealism and just war, 88–92; rationality role in, 42–43; signaling game, 142–48

Hariman, Robert, 84, 85

Hatch, Orrin, 99

Helms, Jesse R., 89–90, 134, 135

Hempstone, Smith, 123

hierarchical order of meaning, narrow scope of, 30

historical roots of meaning: and connections in language of war and peace, 173–74; and European identity evolution, 151–56, 160, 161–63; reason, 46–47; and Somalia debate, 128; and

transformation of war and peace, 169–70

Hobbes, Thomas, 47, 95, 175

hot cognition, 12, 95, 119

Houghton, Amo, 123

humanistic values and contemporary meaning of war, 167

human rights, 4, 171

Hussein, Saddam, 89–90, 99, 101, 143, 145–46, 147

hypothetical critical realism, 71

idealism vs. realism in gender-based rhetorical differences, 107–10, 112, 113–14

ideas as motivators in world politics, 9

identity, European, 150–63

imagined worlds, behavioral meaning, 9

implicit roots of meaning, 46–47

individuals: effects on war and peace, 5–6, 84; and multiple definitions, 48–49, 67; private lexicon of, 62

"in harm's way," 117

instrumental rationality, 158, 160

intentional meaning, 11, 51–52

intercoder reliability, 66

interest as motivator in world politics, 9, 52, 83, 100

internal variables, meaning as, 30–31

international communication and audiences, 139–49

international law as definer of just war, 88

international organizations as important characters in postrealism, 84

international relations: diplomacy's future role in, 168; and duality of mind and body, 104; future trends in meaning, 171; ideas and interests as motivators, 9; nation-states as agents of, 83, 104; personality in, 179*n* 7; power and realism in, 4–5; reason of state concept, 42, 52; rhetoric development in, 80; and signaling model, 148–49; uses of power in, 56

Internet, the, 172

interpersonal interaction, 101, 143, 168

interpretation: and chronotype of war and peace, 173–76; and strategic thinking in postrealist view, 86–87;

meaning (*cont.*)

values and contemporary meaning of war, 167; imagined worlds, behavioral meaning, 9; implicit roots of meaning, 46–47; intentional meaning, 11, 51–52; as internal variables, 30–31; linguistic meaning, 10–12; linguistic modifiers and multiple meanings for validity, 76; microtext and meaning, 34–35; modes of, 8–14; myth of absolute meaning, 40; and narrative, 151; as nominal variables, 27–30; opponent and Cold War meaning of war and peace, 152–56; pattern recognition and continuous variation in meaning, 39; possible real worlds and behavioral meaning, 9; relational nature of, 180*n* 9; role of linguistic meaning, 10–12; role of scientific meaning, 12–13, 38; temporal factors in, 38–39; worlds of, 12, 52. *See also* cognitive meaning; collective construction of meaning; emotional meaning; historical roots of meaning; multiple meanings; normative approach to meaning; semantics

measurement, scientific, and variations in meaning, 63–64, 69

media: and death and dying language, 123, 127; diplomatic role of, 168–69; and Somalia conflict, 133–34, 136; and virtual warfare, 161

Merriam, Charles E., 70

metaphor: alliance as metaphor, 97; attraction as metaphor, 97; balance as metaphor, 97–98; body, 93–105, 108–109, 110, 171–72, 174–75; body metaphor and spatio-temporal referents, 96; body metaphor in politics, 95, 96; breakfast, 140; center-periphery metaphors, 99–100; collection as metaphor (collective), 100; compulsion as metaphor, 101; containment in Cold War, 102, 153–54, 167; context and body metaphor, 174–75; freedom in embodied metaphor, 98; future uses in war and peace language, 171–72; Iron Curtain, 155; over-simplicity of, 183*n* 2. *See also* body metaphor

methodology: gender-based rhetorical differences, 111; for Somalia debate analysis, 119

microtext and meaning, 34–35

military force: and liberal internationalism, 166; male predilection for, 110; and post-Cold War Europe, 157–63; trends in use of, 14; U.S. role in Somalia, 130, 132–37

Mink, Patsy, 110

Mitchell, George, 89

mobilizing attention and support, death and dying language, 120–23, 137

modifiers, linguistic, and multiple meanings for validity, 76

Moltke, Helmuth von, 101

morality. *See* ethics and morality

Moynihan, Daniel Patrick, 89, 101, 145

multiple causality, 69

multiple meanings: and objectivity in experiments, 61; and reason, 46–49, 50. *See also* complexity

multiple validities, 75–78

Muskie, Edmund S., 42

myth: of absolute meaning, 40; and embodied understanding, 103; importance in European identity, 150–63

naive verification, 69

narrative: importance in European identity, 150–63; in postrealistic view, 84–85; reason as embedded in, 49; semantic importance of, 35–37

nation-states, 83, 104, 158

NATO (North Atlantic Treaty Organization), 102, 154

Natsios, Andrew, 120, 122, 123, 125

Nelson, John, 46

neorealism, 83

New World Order: and death and dying language, 118; and European identity, 161; linguistic component, 169; and Somalia conflict, 127

nominal referents: reason, 47–49; war, 32, 34

nominal variables, meaning as, 27–30

nonexperimental validities, 64–70

nonrational models of cognition, 8

nonrealism and just-war argument, 87–88

normative approach to meaning, 52, 53, 86–87. *See also* ethics and morality

North Atlantic Treaty Organization (NATO), 102, 154

nuclear weapons, 154

Nunn, Sam, 147

Oberstar, James, 124–25

observation, invasive nature of, 59–60

OECD (Organization for Economic Cooperation and Development), 154

OEEC (Organization for European Economic Cooperation), 154

opponent: and Cold War meaning of war and peace, 152–56; as non-democratic, 141–42. *See also* Other, essential

Organization for Economic Cooperation and Development (OECD), 154

Organization for European Economic Cooperation (OEEC), 154

Other, essential: as enslaved, 101; and evolving meanings of war and peace, 152–53, 160; and war and peace context, 174–75

Pascal, Blaise, 57

path, 96–97

pattern recognition and continuous variation in meaning, 39

Patton, Gen. George S., 154

Payne, Donald, 118, 124

peace: definition, 180*n* 1; democracies' preference for, 167; democratic peace hypothesis, 5, 140, 141, 157; multiple effects of, 4; transformation of, 170; women's focus on, 106

peaceful coexistence, 161

peaceful end, 88, 90

Pell, Claiborne, 129, 131

penetration, 98

peripheral text in research, 62–63

Persian Gulf War. *See* Gulf War debate

personality in international relations, 179*n* 7

Plato, 95

pluralistic environment. *See* democracies

pluralistic reason, 55–57

poetic form of narrative, 35

Poisson-regression models, 68

policy making: death and dying language, 131–38; domestic political effects on, 5; and just war argument, 88

political agency and rational choice theory, 41–42

political science: and complexities of validity, 70–78; role of reason in, 50–52; validity, 58–64

politics: body metaphor in, 95, 96; democratization as evolutionary, 166; electoral cycles and war and peace tendencies, 5; of identity in Europe, 150–63; importance of debate in, 148–49; role of reason in, 47–52. *See also* debate; rhetorics

polity (political community): and reason as collectively constructed, 50–51; and validity in political science, 71–75, 78

polysemy and reason, 46–49

positivism, 58, 83–84

possible real worlds: behavioral meaning, 9; and semantic analysis of reason, 50, 51; and validity, 69, 75

postpositivist critical multiplism, 75

postrealism and rhetorics of war and peace, 83–92

poverty, global, 4

Powell, Gen. Colin, 144

power: balance of, 147; collective nature of, 100; competition for, 83, 85; international relations as struggle for, 4, 52; post-realist view of, 84; reason as, 56; and transformation of war and peace, 175–76

pragmatism and political science research, 71

presidents, U.S.: Bush, George, 123, 125, 128, 143, 144; Clinton administration and Somalia conflict, 134–35; domestic political effects on foreign policy, 5

Pressler, Larry, 130, 131

psychology and cognitive models, 6–8

public opinion as important character in postrealism, 84

Putnam, Hilary, 11

ratio, 46

rational choice theory, 7–8, 41–42, 50

statistical methods, biases in, 64

strategic rhetoric: and political reason, 49–52; in postrealist view, 85–87; as rationalization for behavior, 40

strong democracy: and debate effects, 143–46; United States as, 142–43

strong reason of state, 52–54, 56

structured approach to meaning, scientific basis for, 39

subjectivity of meaning, 36–37, 40, 50–51, 85, 103

subjects, research: predispositions, 60; relationship with researchers, 74; textual semantic variations, 62

suffering, talk about, 120–23, 125, 131

survey research and validity, 62, 63, 64–65

survival and adaptation language, 165–69

Symms, Steven, 99, 102

syntax: and meaning shifts, 34–35; and research subjects' interpretations of text, 62

Tarnoff, Peter, 128, 131

technological developments, 168, 169, 172, 175

television. *See* media

temporal factors in meaning, 38–39

terms and concepts, approaches to meaning, 27–40

terrorism, 99

text: in continuous variation of meaning, 31, 39; and reason in narrative, 49; role in determining meaning, 36; and validity issues in experimentation, 60–62. *See also* context

textual modifiers, components of, 31–37

theory development: and just war argument, 88; and rhetorics, 80

thoughts. *See* cognition

Thucydides, 142

Thurmond, Strom, 144–45

Tolstoy, Leo, 22, 176

totalitarianism, 157

Toulmin, Stephan E., 50

transformation and transcendence language, 169–73

truth: circularity of meaning in, 73–74; nature of, 181*n* 4; vs. validity, 71

Unified Task Force (UNITAF), 118, 128

United Nations: authority and just war, 89; peacekeeping force and Somalia conflict, 127–28, 132–35, 137

United Nations Operations in Somalia (UNOSOM I/II), 118, 128

United States: post-Cold War position of, 157, 165; and Somalia conflict, 132–35, 137; status of troops in Somalia, 130; strong vs. weak democracy projection, 142–48

UNOSOM I/II (United Nations Operations in Somalia), 118, 128

U.S. Congress. *See* Congress, U.S.

utilitarian meaning, 11

validities: experimental, 59–64; introduction, 58–59; multiple, 75–78; nonexperimental, 64–70; scientific and political, 70–75

values, and future transformation of war and peace, 175–76. *See also* ethics and morality

variables, meanings as, approaches, 27–31

Vietnam War, 142

virtual war, 167

vital interests, 100

Voss, J. F., 96

war: continuation in globalized community, 166–67; fuzzy semantic boundaries of, 67–68; and reason, 52–55; semantic analysis of term, 27–40; trends in, 3, 4

War and Peace (Tolstoy), 176

Warner, John, 117

weak democracy, United States as, 142–43, 146–48

weak reason of state, 54–55, 56

Weiss, Ted, 123

Whitman, Walt, 172

Wirth, Tim, 90–91

Wittgenstein, Ludwig, 47

women. *See* gender-based rhetorical differences

Woods, James, 124

words. *See* language; meaning

worlds of meaning, and reason, 52, 54–55

World Trade Organization (WTO), 158